Raspberry Pi Zero Cookbook

Delve into the practical world of the Raspberry Pi Zero

Edward Snajder

BIRMINGHAM - MUMBAI

Raspberry Pi Zero Cookbook

First published: March 2017

Production reference: 2230317

Published by Packt Publishing Ltd.
Livery Place
35 Livery Street
Birmingham
B3 2PB, UK.
ISBN 978-1-78646-385-2

www.packtpub.com

Credits

Author

Edward Snajder

Reviewer

Ed Venaglia

Commissioning Editor

Pratik Shah

Acquisition Editor

Vijin Boricha

Content Development Editor

Amedh Pohad

Technical Editor

Mohit Hassija

Copy Editor

Madhusudan Uchil

Project Coordinator

Judie Jose

Proofreader

Safis Editing

Indexer

Pratik Shirodkar

Graphics

Kirk D'Penha

Production Coordinator

Nilesh Mohite

About the Author

Edward Snajder takes on the challenges of performance, optimization, scalability, and portability for PostgreSQL, Oracle, SQL Server, and MySQL DB engines for the databases behind the Jive platform. He's got hands-on experience with system design, HA, virtualization, and distributed systems, and has had the opportunity to interface with quality engineering, support, technical operations, and professional services when not building things in engineering. In his spare time, he is an Internet of Things enthusiast and has spoken on the wonders of the Raspberry Pi at conferences and user groups. He loves his Raspberry Pis. He has also built his own 3D printer and has several 75%-complete Arduino projects.

First, I would like to thank Packt Publishing for giving me my first chance to write a book. It has always been one of those things I've thought about, but until someone asks you to do it, you can put it off indefinitely. I'd also like to thank the author of Raspberry Pi Sensors, Rushi Gajjar, for putting together a fantastic outline. It covers such a broad scope of popular and applicable projects, I don't think I would have put together such a comprehensive list together myself.

This book also wouldn't have been possible without the Raspberry Pi Foundation and community, which has grown so much over the years. Without the docs, forums, and discussions, I would find myself still trying to figure out some of these recipes.

To my parents, who always enabled and encouraged me to play with technology and take things apart. My brothers continue to be a source of inspiration.

Finally, to Lindsay, and our Shih-Tzus, Gizmo and Obi-wan, for giving me the love, time, space, and encouragement to take this on, while taking occasional walk breaks.

About the Reviewer

Ed Venaglia was born to be an engineer. He's been tinkering with electronics and mechanical things since he could see over the counter at Radio Shack, back when you could actually buy radio parts there. Professionally, Ed is a software engineer, but after hours, he can be found engaged in machining, making, robotics, chemistry, and all manner of mad science in his workshop.

I'd like to thank my friend Ed Snajder, this book's author, for the opportunity to help with recipes in this book. I'd also like to thank my loving wife for supporting me and giving me the time to make this happen.

www.PacktPub.com

For support files and downloads related to your book, please visit `www.PacktPub.com`.

Did you know that Packt offers eBook versions of every book published, with PDF and ePub files available? You can upgrade to the eBook version at `www.PacktPub.com` and as a print book customer, you are entitled to a discount on the eBook copy. Get in touch with us at `service@packtpub.com` for more details.

At `www.PacktPub.com`, you can also read a collection of free technical articles, sign up for a range of free newsletters and receive exclusive discounts and offers on Packt books and eBooks.

`https://www.packtpub.com/mapt`

Get the most in-demand software skills with Mapt. Mapt gives you full access to all Packt books and video courses, as well as industry-leading tools to help you plan your personal development and advance your career.

Why subscribe?

- Fully searchable across every book published by Packt
- Copy and paste, print, and bookmark content
- On demand and accessible via a web browser

Customer Feedback

Thanks for purchasing this Packt book. At Packt, quality is at the heart of our editorial process. To help us improve, please leave us an honest review on this book's Amazon page at https://www.amazon.com/dp/1786463857.

If you'd like to join our team of regular reviewers, you can e-mail us at customerreviews@packtpub.com. We award our regular reviewers with free eBooks and videos in exchange for their valuable feedback. Help us be relentless in improving our products!

Table of Contents

Preface

Thank you for picking the Raspberry Pi Zero Cookbook! In this book, we explore the awesome potential of what this $5 computer can deliver. With a Raspberry Pi Zero and a few accessories, you have your hands on a miniature computer that has the same functionality, applications, and connectivity that you would get with a system costing hundreds or thousands of dollars.

The cookbook starts with introducing the Raspberry Pi Zero and its operating system and shows ways that make the Raspberry Pi Zero unique in the Raspberry Pi family, aside from being the only one that will fit in a mint tin. From there, we move right into operating system control and simple programming, predominantly in Python. For many, this will be a revisit, though I did make every recipe as useful as possible, and almost everything in the first few chapters will be possible with just a Raspberry Pi Zero and typical accessories you would need for a computer. I've truly made every attempt not to Hello World you to death, with a few scripts you can sink your teeth into.

Once we get through installation, configuration, and some basic programming, we will begin to learn the Raspberry Pi Zero's GPIO Interface and how you would get it to interact with the physical world. Here is where you'll play with sensors, motors, and controllers so you can ultimately monitor or alert anything to anyone, wherever they are.

As a cookbook, it is intended to have each recipe possible to create without anything else. There are some recipes that are helpful or provide prerequisites to later recipes, but for the most part, with the ingredients listed, you can get right to creating whatever interests you the most. If you are more of a beginner, the recipes should be iterative, in that each recipe is similar but a bit more challenging that the last. In the end, you'll see that there are some very common patterns, and even the more seemingly complex solutions use the same simple concepts consistently with respect to the GPIO Interface.

Electronics, sensors, and motors can add up in cost rather quickly. Some of the recipes do have specific boards I've used for the recipe, but in the hardware and software section, I've also found some kits with most of what the cookbook uses, and only for the cost of about maybe 10 Raspberry Pi Zeroes.

I hope you enjoy the book and have enough fun that you end up with Raspberry Pi Zeroes to share; for friends and kids, just starting with computers is the most inspiring part of the $5 computer. If every kid can get their hands on one, we will soon see the days of flying cars and Star Trek replicators. I hope this book introduces enough concepts to open the doors to immensely more creative and interesting ideas than any recipe in this book.

What this book covers

Chapter 1, *Kick-Start Your Raspberry Pi Zero*, starts right out of the box and covers what you'll need to get your Raspberry Pi running. Then we install and configure the operating system.

Chapter 2, *Setting Up Physical and Wireless Connections*, covers the many ways you can communicate with your Raspberry Pi Zero, how to get it on your home network, and USB configurations that make the Raspberry Pi Zero unique to its siblings.

Chapter 3, *Programming with Linux*, goes over some of the useful things to know when using a Linux operating system. From basic filesystem operation to application installation and upgrades, this will provide a set of tools you will find necessary for using your Raspberry Pi Zero.

Chapter 4, *Programming with Python*, begins with a brief introduction of Python and its major versions, and must-have libraries when using Python and a Raspberry Pi. From there, we move on to creating a solution that monitors, graphs, and notifies Raspberry Pi Zero board temperatures over time.

Chapter 5, *Getting Your Hands Dirty Using the GPIO Header*, gets into some basic hardware and usage of the versatile General Purpose Input Output (GPIO) interface. We'll explore the different GPIO modes and methods of communication, using a variety of languages and tools.

Chapter 6, *Controlling the LEDs and Displays*, starts with more advanced LED exercises and moves on to the control and operation of LED matrices, LCD displays, and controllers for operating several LEDs individually.

Chapter 7, *Controlling the Hardware*, shows how easy it is to control motors, relays, and buzzers. It also touches on more advanced circuitry to control high-voltage systems from your Raspberry Pi. More advanced electrical experience is needed for some of these recipes.

Chapter 8, *Taking Digital Inputs to the RPZ*, moves into receiving inputs from external devices for the Raspberry Pi Zero to detect. We also cover receiving triggers and data from devices: RFID scanners, GPS boards, and more!

Chapter 9, *Interfacing Sensors with RPZ*, dives deeper into the options for receiving sensor data on the Raspberry Pi Zero. At this point, there shouldn't be a device available that you can't have your Raspberry Pi Zero talk to.

Chapter 10, *Cooking Up Projects to Amaze the World!*, wraps up with bringing home automation and monitoring to your Raspberry Pi Zero to centralize all of the sensor inputs and monitors to one place.

If you go through the chapters completely, my hope is that you will have ideas for dozens of projects where these recipes are only a component of your larger solution. I also hope that it will get you more involved in the Raspberry Pi community and its immense wealth of shared ideas and that you'll be telling your friends about how they need to get their hands on one (and an extra for your birthday!).

What you need for this book

The operating system used in this book is the open source Raspbian, designed specifically for the Raspberry Pi family of computers.

Pretty much any part in this book, outside of common components such as resistors and capacitors, is available through Adafruit. Adafruit sells high-quality components and boards that are great for all kinds of Internet of Things and maker projects. Purchasing each piece individually can add up fast; fortunately, sites such as Amazon offer some great kits that are perfect for beginners. The Elegoo Most Complete Ultimate Starter Kit is the one I used. It costs around $60 US and includes most of the sensors, displays, and motors used in this cookbook as well as common components, such as a breadboard, jumper wires, power supplies, LEDs, resistors, and capacitors. It is a great way to get started! Everything marked with an asterisk (*) is something that is included in the Elegoo kit. In the specific recipes, I will reference the equivalent Adafruit part if available.

Hardware requirements

- Raspberry Pi Zero
- 5V/1.2 A micro USB power supply
- Micro USB–OTG adapter
- 4-port powered USB hub
- Micro HDMI to standard HDMI adapter and a standard HDMI cable; alternatively, a standard HDMI to micro HDMI cable
- Micro SD card, 4 GB or greater (8 GB recommended)
- USB keyboard and mouse: I used the Logitech MK270, a wireless keyboard/mouse combo that uses a single USB port.
- HDMI-compatible monitor
- Another computer and slot or adapter to write SD card images

- Raspberry Pi Cobbler and a breadboard: Adafruit has a great one, though there are a few alternatives
- Jumper cables
- USB-to-serial port adapter
- USB Wi-Fi adapter
- Standard-to-micro USB cable
- Standard LEDs, various colors*
- RGB 4-lead LED*
- Two 4xAA battery packs and batteries
- Adafruit SI4713 FM radio transmitter
- Adafruit ESP8266 Wi-Fi module
- Seven-segment LED display*
- 8X8 LED matrix display*
- 16x2 LCD display*
- 74HC595N shift register*
- Various resistors*
- Various electrolytic and ceramic capacitors*
- P222N transistors*
- 5V mechanical ("sugar cube") relay*
- Stepper motor*
- DC motor*
- Piezo buzzer*
- Adafruit bidirectional level shifter
- PiFace Digital Revision 2 shield
- Push switches*
- Toggle switches
- Sixteen-digit keypad*
- Real-time clock board with battery*
- RFID scanner board*
- Adafruit Ultimate GPS breakout board
- Photoresistor*
- Ultrasonic sensor*
- Adafruit MCP3008 8-channel 10-bit analog-to-digital convertor
- Infrared receiver and remote*
- Motion sensor*

- Temperature and humidity sensor*
- Gyroscope/accelerometer*
- Heart rate/pulse sensor (via Adafruit or `www.pulsesensor.com`, which I used)

Who this book is for

This book is for programmers and hobbyists who are eager to dive deep into the Raspberry Pi Zero. If you have basic or zero knowledge of the Raspberry Pi Zero or if you're looking for examples of ways to utilize the Raspberry Pi's GPIO interface, then this book is ideal for you. Basic knowledge of Python will be beneficial, and experience with circuitry and electronics will be needed for the later chapters in the book.

Sections

In this book, you will find several headings that appear frequently (Getting ready, How to do it, How it works, There's more, and See also).

To give clear instructions on how to complete a recipe, we use these sections as follows:

Getting ready

This section tells you what to expect in the recipe, and describes how to set up any software or any preliminary settings required for the recipe.

How to do it...

This section contains the steps required to follow the recipe.

How it works...

This section usually consists of a detailed explanation of what happened in the previous section.

There's more...

This section consists of additional information about the recipe in order to make the reader more knowledgeable about the recipe.

See also

This section provides helpful links to other useful information for the recipe.

Conventions

In this book, you will find a number of text styles that distinguish between different kinds of information. Here are some examples of these styles and an explanation of their meaning.

Code words in text, database table names, folder names, filenames, file extensions, pathnames, dummy URLs, user input, and Twitter handles are shown as follows: "As you can see, `/dev/disk2s6` and `/dev/disk2s1` were added. This creates two partitions on `disk2` -- most SD cards will only have one, but however many there are mounted, you need to `unmount` them with `diskutil`."

A block of code is set as follows:

```
@app.route('/update_pin', methods=['POST'])
def update_pin():
        #Read in form entry. Since they are all buttons, you should only
get
```

Any command-line input or output is written as follows:

```
$ sudo diskutil eject /dev/rdisk2
Disk /dev/rdisk2 ejected
```

New terms and **important words** are shown in bold. Words that you see on the screen, for example, in menus or dialog boxes, appear in the text like this: "Just click on **Download ZIP** from a browser, and it will automatically begin."

Warnings or important notes appear in a box like this.

Tips and tricks appear like this.

Reader feedback

Feedback from our readers is always welcome. Let us know what you think about this book-what you liked or disliked. Reader feedback is important for us as it helps us develop titles that you will really get the most out of.

To send us general feedback, simply e-mail `feedback@packtpub.com`, and mention the book's title in the subject of your message.

If there is a topic that you have expertise in and you are interested in either writing or contributing to a book, see our author guide at `www.packtpub.com/authors`.

Customer support

Now that you are the proud owner of a Packt book, we have a number of things to help you to get the most from your purchase.

Downloading the example code

You can download the example code files for this book from your account at `http://www.packtpub.com`. If you purchased this book elsewhere, you can visit `http://www.packtpub.com/support` and register to have the files e-mailed directly to you.

You can download the code files by following these steps:

1. Log in or register to our website using your e-mail address and password.
2. Hover the mouse pointer on the **SUPPORT** tab at the top.
3. Click on **Code Downloads & Errata**.
4. Enter the name of the book in the **Search** box.
5. Select the book for which you're looking to download the code files.
6. Choose from the drop-down menu where you purchased this book from.
7. Click on **Code Download**.

You can also download the code files by clicking on the **Code Files** button on the book's webpage at the Packt Publishing website. This page can be accessed by entering the book's name in the **Search** box. Please note that you need to be logged in to your Packt account.

Once the file is downloaded, please make sure that you unzip or extract the folder using the latest version of:

- WinRAR / 7-Zip for Windows
- Zipeg / iZip / UnRarX for Mac
- 7-Zip / PeaZip for Linux

The code bundle for the book is also hosted on GitHub at `https://github.com/PacktPublishing/Raspberry-Pi-Zero-Cookbook`. We also have other code bundles from our rich catalog of books and videos available at `https://github.com/PacktPublishing/`. Check them out!

Downloading the color images of this book

We also provide you with a PDF file that has color images of the screenshots/diagrams used in this book. The color images will help you better understand the changes in the output. You can download this file from `https://www.packtpub.com/sites/default/files/downloads/RaspberryPiZeroCookbook_ColorImages.pdf`.

Errata

Although we have taken every care to ensure the accuracy of our content, mistakes do happen. If you find a mistake in one of our books-maybe a mistake in the text or the code-we would be grateful if you could report this to us. By doing so, you can save other readers from frustration and help us improve subsequent versions of this book. If you find any errata, please report them by visiting `http://www.packtpub.com/submit-errata`, selecting your book, clicking on the **Errata Submission Form** link, and entering the details of your errata. Once your errata are verified, your submission will be accepted and the errata will be uploaded to our website or added to any list of existing errata under the Errata section of that title.

To view the previously submitted errata, go to `https://www.packtpub.com/books/content/support` and enter the name of the book in the search field. The required information will appear under the **Errata** section.

Piracy

Piracy of copyrighted material on the Internet is an ongoing problem across all media. At Packt, we take the protection of our copyright and licenses very seriously. If you come across any illegal copies of our works in any form on the Internet, please provide us with the location address or website name immediately so that we can pursue a remedy.

Please contact us at copyright@packtpub.com with a link to the suspected pirated material.

We appreciate your help in protecting our authors and our ability to bring you valuable content.

Questions

If you have a problem with any aspect of this book, you can contact us at questions@packtpub.com, and we will do our best to address the problem.

1
Kick-Start Your Raspberry Pi Zero

In this chapter, we will cover the following recipes:

- Understanding the standard connectors and test points
- Reviewing power supply requirements
- Choosing an operating system to install
- Writing to an SD card with NOOBS
- Using Windows to write a Raspbian image to an SD card
- Using OS X to validate a Raspbian image and write it to an SD card
- Using Ubuntu 16.04 to validate a Raspbian image and write it to an SD card
- Identifying RCA solder points for analog video connections
- Adding a USB extension over a USB OTG connector
- Connecting to displays and changing the configuration settings
- Logging in to the RPZ desktop for the first time, creating users, and rebooting

Introduction

The smallest, most inexpensive member of the Raspberry Pi family, the Zero, has once again improved upon its promise of computer accessibility to everyone in the world. At 40 percent of the size of the larger Raspberry Pis and a fraction of the cost (around 5 US dollars), the Raspberry Pi Zero opens more doors to portability, data collection, and experimentation while being affordable so that anyone can get started, anywhere, on learning about computers, Linux, and the Internet of Things.

With such a small form factor, there are some sacrifices made compared to the full-size Raspberry Pi. It uses the same single-core chip as the original Pi, so it is a bit slower than today's quad-core models. It also has limited physical connections, at least by default, compared to the larger Pi models. This chapter will explore some of the differences and how to work around them and get your Raspberry Pi Zero set up for more interesting recipes. The recipes here will focus on getting familiar with the Raspberry Pi Zero board, deciding on an operating system and methods for creating your first SD card, and getting enough things connected so you can start using your Zero.

Understanding the standard connectors and test points

If you've worked with a Raspberry Pi 1, 2, or 3 before, you will find the Raspberry Pi Zero to be similar, but quite a bit smaller. To accommodate such a small size, several connectors had to be miniaturized or reduced. Taking a close look, you will find that the same potential is contained in this small board. Throughout the following recipes, we will look at the Raspberry Pi Zero, its functional components, and how it compares to the larger Raspberry Pi boards. By the end of this chapter, you will have a running Raspberry Pi Zero!

Getting ready

To get your Raspberry Pi Zero online on HDMI, the following equipment will be needed:

- A Raspberry Pi Zero
- A micro-USB power adapter, 5 V/1.2 A out

 The Raspberry Pi documentation allows up to 2.5 A for the Pi's power supply, in case you don't want to use a powered USB hub. For this cookbook, we will start with a powered USB hub but work toward low-power and low-profile solutions.

- A micro-USB OTG (On-The-Go) adapter
- A 4-port powered USB hub
- A micro-HDMI to standard HDMI adapter and HDMI cable or a micro-HDMI to standard HDMI cable
- A micro SD card (4 GB minimum, 8 GB recommended)
- A USB keyboard and mouse

- A monitor that takes HDMI, or DVI with a DVI-HDMI adapter
- A computer with an SD card interface running Mac OS X, Windows, or Linux

 A great resource for checking device compatibility are the Raspberry Pi pages in the Embedded Linux wiki (www.elinux.org). This has a rather large list of known compatible devices as well as known problematic ones and ones that will likely require a powered USB hub to operate.

How to do it...

Take a look at your Raspberry Pi Zero and examine each of the connections. They really fit a lot into a small space:

Raspberry Pi components

The numbers in the figure denote the following components:

1. The **GPIO header** is the same one you will find on the Raspberry Pi B and later versions. The big difference here is that a header hasn't been soldered on. If you project requires your Raspberry Pi to be very thin, then you can solder your connections directly to the board. If you are using your Zero for prototyping, you can attach whichever header makes your life easiest. For this book, we will have the female 90-degree header soldered on for easy interfacing to the Adafruit Pi Cobbler.

2. The **Micro SD card slot** is very much the same as previous versions, with the big difference being that it is push-in/pull-out instead of other boards' push-in/push-out slot.

3. The **mini-HDMI port** works just like a regular-sized port, though it requires an HDMI mini-to-regular adapter or cable to connect to LCD monitors.

4. The first **USB port** is **micro-USB**, and the only USB port available for data use on the Raspberry Pi Zero. For use with standard USB components such as mice and keyboards, you will need a micro-USB OTG adapter and a powered USB hub. As we move forward in the book, we will discover ways to run "headless" so that not all the connections are required, but to get started, you will want an adapter and a hub.

5. The second **USB port** is the Raspberry Pi's **power connection**, which we will take a closer look at in the next recipe.

6. This **bus** is to attach the Raspberry Pi's camera cable.

7. While RCA video is no longer available on the Raspberry Pi Zero, we will hack it later to understand how to use the older, non-HDMI way to see video.

8. Finally, on this side of the board, the connectors marked **RUN** are for resetting the Raspberry Pi. Shorting these connections will reset your Raspberry Pi.

The back side of the board contains test connector points:

Raspberry Pi Zero test pads

Not all the test points are documented for the Raspberry Pi Zero, but several are known:

Label	Function	Label	Function
PP1	5-V-micro USB	**PP18**	SD_DAT2
PP3	GND	**PP19**	SD_DAT3
PP4	GND	**PP20**	
PP5	GND	**PP22**	
PP6	GND	**PP23**	
PP8	3.3 V	**PP35**	GND
PP9		**PP36**	
PP14	SD_CLK	**PP37**	CAM_GPIO0
PP15	SD_CMD	**PP38**	CAM_GPIO1
PP16	SD_DAT0	**PP39**	SCL0
PP17	SD_DAT1	**PP40**	SDA0

Test points are great for validating that your Raspberry Pi is seeing the right voltage and/or frequencies. Many of the test points require an oscilloscope to observe and are thus beyond the scope of this book, but testing and troubleshooting prototypes is as easy on a Raspberry Pi Zero as it is on one of the larger boards.

Reviewing power supply requirements

One of the outstanding things about the Raspberry Pi Zero is its low power requirement, even compared to its siblings. The power is received through the second micro-USB slot on the board, and it should never need greater than a 5-V/1 A power supply. A well-configured Raspberry Pi in idle state can draw as little as 30 mA, and even under stress, it has not been shown to use more than 350 mA! Your Raspberry Pi Zero could run for free with a small solar panel and rechargeable battery pack. The Raspberry Pi 2 and 3, while more powerful, generally use from two to five times as much power to run.

How to do it...

You can also power your Raspberry Pi Zero over the GPIO ports, though it is important to be careful to have consistent and predictable power so you don't fry your board. The easiest method is certainly to find steady 5V source that works over micro-USB, but with careful design, you can run your board from any power supply with consistent 5 V and current up to 1 A. We will run our Raspberry Pi Zero on batteries later in this cookbook.

Of course, as you add peripherals, there will be a need to draw more current. If on USB, using a powered USB port will help a lot. When working with devices you have connected directly to GPIO, you just need to make sure your Raspberry Pi Zero power source can provide enough current to run the board and what's attached to it.

Until you have an SD card ready, you won't really be able to test the power completely – you can plug the adapter into the Raspberry Pi, but keep it unplugged from the power for now.

Choosing an operating system to install

Because the Raspberry Pi Zero uses the same ARMv6 chip offered in the original Raspberry Pi, it won't be ideal for the latest of all varieties of Linux that the newer generation of models can support. The clear choice right now for the RPZ is Raspbian Jessy. Adafruit Industries has a great set of instructions for installing Fedora Pi on the RPZ, and you can install pretty much any OS that runs on the ARMv6 chip, but the Raspbian Jessie release on the Raspberry Pi website is the most stable and easy-to-use distribution available for the RPZ. For this cookbook, we will use Raspbian Jessie.

How to do it...

On the Raspberry Pi website, the **Downloads** page offers both a full version (offline install) and a "Lite" (network install) version of the images. Select the full version when setting up the Raspberry Pi Zero, as you will not have network connectivity right away to download the parts missing from the Lite version. Once you have the full version installed, it is easy to get networking configured and everything updated, which we will cover later in the book. Download the latest full version of NOOBS from the Raspberry Pi website, and unzip it to a new directory. After the extraction is complete, you are ready to move on to the next recipe to install NOOBS on your SD card.

Just click on **Download ZIP** from a browser, and it will automatically begin:

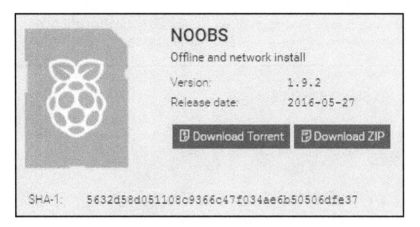

The NOOBS download and SHA-1 signature

Writing to an SD card with NOOBS

New Out Of Box Software (**NOOBS**) is the easiest way to get started with any Raspberry Pi. All you need is a formatted SD card, ideally 4 GB or larger. The SD Association website has a formatter tool for Windows and Mac users to clean the card. Always ensure you are formatting the right card.

Getting ready

This is where you'll need your SD card. A 4-GB card is the minimum, but as card prices have dropped a lot over the years, I'd recommend an 8-GB or 16-GB card. I also always recommend hackers to get a couple of cards (for example, get two 8-GB cards instead of one 16-GB card), so you can always have a spare card to write a test operating system to while you have the other SD card in use. If you really get into Raspberry Pi development, you will find having spare SD cards a must.

If you are a Linux user, you should just skip ahead to the Raspbian installation on Ubuntu.

How to do it...

If you are an OS X or Windows user, you can use the SDFormatter utility from the SD Association (`https://www.sdcard.org/downloads/formatter_4/`) to format your SD card:

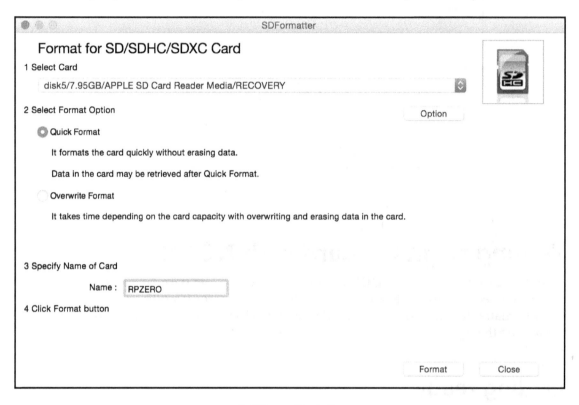

The SDFormatter SD card utility

Once your card is formatted, copy the files from your extracted NOOBS download from the last recipe to the newly formatted SD card. Once this is done, you will be ready to finish building your Raspberry Pi Zero.

Once you've downloaded the file, unzip it and copy it to your SD card:

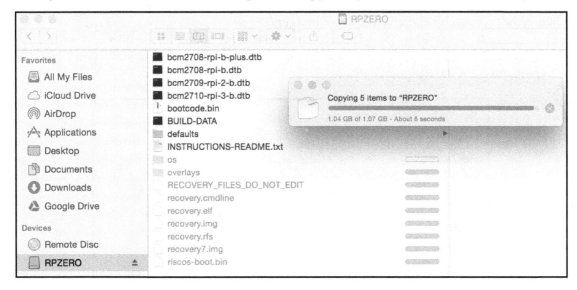

Installing NOOBS is as simple as copying files to a formatted SD card

There's more...

Writing a Raspbian SD card without NOOBS: If you want to skip the NOOBS setup and jump right into Raspbian or if you want to try out a different distribution to see how it works on your Raspberry Pi Zero, there are some great tools available to make this easy to do. First, you need to download the Raspbian image file from the Raspberry Pi website (https://www.raspberrypi.org/downloads/raspbian/). Unzipping the file creates a single, larger file, called the image file. Be sure to download the full file, not the Lite version, as you will be starting without a network connection.

Using Windows to write a Raspbian image to an SD card

In this recipe, you will take a Raspbian image file (.img) and write it directly to an SD card using the free and easy Win32 Disk Imager utility.

How to do it...

On a Windows machine, the Win32 Disk Imager (`https://sourceforge.net/projects/wi
n32diskimager/`) is an easy-to-use open source project for taking image files and writing
them to your SD card. Insert your SD card, and select the unzipped image file you
downloaded from the Raspberry Pi site:

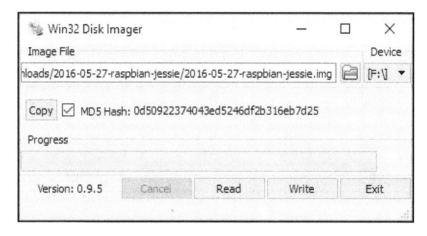

Win32 Disk Imager for Windows

Once you have verified that you've selected the right `.img` file and the correct drive letter
associated with your SD card, click on **Write** and wait for the process to finish. Once it
completes successfully, eject the card and it will be ready to start your Raspberry Pi Zero.

Using OS X to validate a Raspbian image and write it to an SD card

If you are a Mac user, the process will be a little different from the Windows recipe, but still
not too difficult. To do it, we'll leverage OS X's built-in *nix system tools.

Mac OS X used to have a lot of options for easy GUI image writers, but
many of them were not updated over time. After Yosemite 10.10.5, the
Raspberry Pi community recommends using command-line tools.
Fortunately, it is a pretty easy process.

How to do it...

The process for validating and copying a NOOBs installation on OS X is fairly straightforward:

1. Open a Terminal window in OS X.
2. Next, run `shasum` against the downloaded ZIP file to validate the signature:

```
$ shasum ~/Downloads/2016-05-27-raspbian-jessie.zip
64c7ed611929ea5178fbb69b5a5f29cc9cc7c157
/Users/ed/Downloads/2016-05-27-raspbian-jessie.zip
```

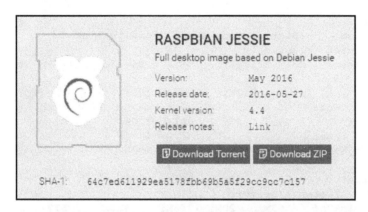

The Raspbian Jessie download and SHA-1 signature

3. If the return value matches the SHA-1 signature provided on the Raspberry Pi downloads page, your file is good and can be unzipped:

 As the downloads change, the SHA-1 will change too, so you'll likely be comparing a different number to your shasum output.

```
$ unzip ~/Downloads/2016-05-27-raspbian-jessie.zip
Archive:  /Users/ed.snajder/Downloads/2016-05-27-
raspbian-jessie.zip
  inflating: 2016-05-27-raspbian-jessie.img
```

4. Next, look at the filesystem before inserting the SD card:

```
$ df -h
Filesystem      Size   Used  Avail Capacity  iused
ifree %iused  Mounted on
```

```
/dev/disk1      232Gi   216Gi    16Gi    94% 56751574
4163032    93%    /
devfs           205Ki   205Ki     0Bi   100%      710
0   100%    /dev
map -hosts        0Bi     0Bi     0Bi   100%        0
0   100%    /net
map auto_home     0Bi     0Bi     0Bi   100%        0
0   100%    /home
map -fstab        0Bi     0Bi     0Bi   100%        0
0   100%    /Network/Servers
```

5. Then, insert the SD card and run the command again:

```
$ df -h
Filesystem      Size    Used   Avail Capacity   iused
ifree %iused   Mounted on
/dev/disk1      232Gi   216Gi    16Gi    94% 56751576
4163030    93%    /
devfs           211Ki   211Ki     0Bi   100%      730
0   100%    /dev
map -hosts        0Bi     0Bi     0Bi   100%        0
0   100%    /net
map auto_home     0Bi     0Bi     0Bi   100%        0
0   100%    /home
map -fstab        0Bi     0Bi     0Bi   100%        0
0   100%    /Network/Servers
    /dev/disk2s6    63Mi    20Mi    43Mi    32%      512
    0   100%    /Volumes/boot
    /dev/disk2s1   1.1Gi   1.0Gi    92Mi    92%        0
    0   100%    /Volumes/RECOVERY
```

6. As you can see, /dev/disk2s6 and /dev/disk2s1 were added. This creates two partitions on disk2 - most SD cards will only have one, but however many there are mounted, you need to unmount them with diskutil:

```
$ sudo diskutil unmount /dev/disk2s1
Password:
Volume RECOVERY on disk2s1 unmounted
$ sudo diskutil unmount /dev/disk2s6
Volume boot on disk2s6 unmounted
```

 Very important: Running dd on the wrong device will be disastrous – use with extreme caution!

7. There is a critical difference now from typical Linux drives and dd use. Let's say you had the aforementioned configuration and see that the SD card disk is disk2. For the dd command, you will change this to rdisk2:

```
$ sudo dd bs=1m if=./2016-05-27-raspbian-jessie.img
of=/dev/rdisk2
3833+0 records in
3833+0 records out
4019191808 bytes transferred in 377.097088 secs (10658241 bytes/sec)
```

 The dd command can take a while to run, and doesn't provide any output while it is, so you can get that feeling it might be stuck. Be patient, depending on the speed of your SD Card it could take several minutes to copy. Newer versions of dd (on Ubuntu 16.04 and newer) include the status=progress flag, which will indicate copying progress.

8. Finally, eject the disk, and you are ready to go!

```
$ sudo diskutil eject /dev/rdisk2
Disk /dev/rdisk2 ejected
```

Using Ubuntu 16.04 to validate a Raspbian image and write it to an SD card

If you are using Ubuntu 12.04 or earlier, the Ubuntu ImageWriter is a GUI tool that makes the installation very easy. If you are using a newer version, usb-imagewriter is not available, but SD cards can still be created from the command line. This will generally work on most flavors of Linux; check with your project's documentation to see the recommended method.

How to do it...

1. I find the easiest method is to look at what is mounted. If the SD card is inserted, it should be automatically recognized:

```
$ mount -l
```

2. Another way to find the mount(s) on the SD card is looking using the `dmseg` command. Ubuntu's documentation recommends using `dmesg` to find out which device the SD card is. Insert the SD card and run this:

```
$ dmesg | tail -20
```

3. You'll get a response similar to this:

```
[ 4577.380445] usb-storage 1-2:1.0: USB Mass Storage device detected
[ 4577.382857] scsi host3: usb-storage 1-2:1.0
[ 4577.383080] usbcore: registered new interface driver usb-storage
[ 4577.386719] usbcore: registered new interface driver uas
[ 4578.409298] scsi 3:0:0:0: Direct-Access     Generic- Compact Flash  1.00 PQ: 0 ANSI: 0 CCS
[ 4578.420769] scsi 3:0:0:1: Direct-Access     Generic- SM/xD-Picture  1.00 PQ: 0 ANSI: 0 CCS
[ 4578.430684] scsi 3:0:0:2: Direct-Access     Generic- SD/MMC         1.00 PQ: 0 ANSI: 0 CCS
[ 4578.441072] scsi 3:0:0:3: Direct-Access     Generic- M.S./M.S.Pro/HG 1.00 PQ: 0 ANSI: 0 CCS
[ 4578.444676] sd 3:0:0:0: Attached scsi generic sg2 type 0
[ 4578.444808] sd 3:0:0:1: Attached scsi generic sg3 type 0
[ 4578.444909] sd 3:0:0:2: Attached scsi generic sg4 type 0
[ 4578.445844] sd 3:0:0:3: Attached scsi generic sg5 type 0
[ 4579.347921] sd 3:0:0:2: [sdd] 15644672 512-byte logical blocks: (8.01 GB/7.46 GiB)
[ 4579.409471] sd 3:0:0:2: [sdd] Write Protect is off
[ 4579.409477] sd 3:0:0:2: [sdd] Mode Sense: 03 00 00 00
[ 4579.474834] sd 3:0:0:2: [sdd] No Caching mode page found
[ 4579.474838] sd 3:0:0:2: [sdd] Assuming drive cache: write through
[ 4579.893360] sd 3:0:0:0: [sdb] Attached SCSI removable disk
[ 4579.918830]  sdd: sdd1 sdd2
```

dmesg output after SD card insertion

4. Before overwriting, you need to detach the disks that are mounted. In this case, `sdd1` and `sdd2` are the mounted partitions for device `sdd`, as shown in the last line of the image above.

5. In Linux, your disk devices are usually identified by looking in the `/dev/` folder for devices starting with sd (for example sda, sdb, sdc). A partition is a division of the physical volume so it can be treated as different devices, and they can be identified by having incremental numbers (for example sdd has partitions sdd1 and sdd2):

```
$ sudo umount /dev/sdd1
$ sudo umount /dev/sdd2
```

6. After downloading the latest ZIP file of the Raspbian image from the Raspberry Pi website, you can validate it using the `sha1sum` tool:

```
$ sudo sha1sum ~/Downloads/2016-05-27-raspbian-
jessie.zip
64c7ed611929ea5178fbb69b5a5f29cc9cc7c157
/media/sf_Downloads/2016-05-27-raspbian-jessie.zip
```

7. If your return value matches the SHA-1 value on the Raspberry Pi **Downloads** page, unzip the file, and run the `dd` command to write your image to the SD card. Make sure you are using the correct device!

> The dd command is for entire disks, so we reference sdd instead of the partitions `sdd1` or `sdd2`. We don't want to duplicate things to partitions, we want to duplicate the entire disk, and whatever partitions your source has will be applied to the destination, our SD card.
> ```
> $ sudo dd bs=1M if=/path/to/raspbian-jessie.img
> of=/dev/sdd
> ```

 The dd command can take a while to run, and doesn't provide any output while it is, so you can get that feeling it might be stuck. Be patient, depending on the speed of your SD Card it could take several minutes to copy.

The output will be similar to this:

```
sudo dd bs=1M if=/opt/vbsh/2016-05-27-raspbian-jessie/2016-05-27-raspbian-jessie
.img of=/dev/sdd
3833+0 records in
3833+0 records out
4019191808 bytes (4.0 GB, 3.7 GiB) copied, 598.751 s, 6.7 MB/s
```

dd command input and output

After several minutes, your card will be ready to go!

Whichever way you decided to set up your SD card, you are just a few connections away from getting your Raspberry Pi Zero online!

Identifying RCA solder points for analog video connections

Let's say you don't have HDMI or need to output video to a device that only accepts the older RCA video connections. With a little bit of soldering, this is very easy! On the Raspberry Pi, you will see two pins marked **RCA**. By attaching this to a standard RCA plug, you can output your video through this instead of (or even in addition to) the HDMI output.

Getting ready

If you just want to get started with HDMI, this is not a required recipe, and you can skip ahead. You will need:

- A soldering iron
- An RCA video connector
- Connections that can be soldered from the cable to the connector
- The board itself

How to do it…

1. The **TV** pins in the figure are the connections you can use to connect RCA video to the Raspberry Pi:

Raspberry Pi Zero RCA video

"RCA Video" is technically referred to as Composite Video, and the connectors are typically yellow.

2. Solder wires or connectors here that will connect to the RCA video plug.

Adding a USB extension over a USB OTG connector

OTG is an adapter connection that allows some devices' USB connections to work as hosts. On the Raspberry Pi Zero, we can use a USB OTG adapter to connect any USB device, whether it's a webcam, keyboard, or printer.

Getting ready

You will need a micro-USB OTG adapter. One end is the *male* micro-USB to connect to the Raspberry Pi Zero, and the other end is the *female* standard USB to connect devices (such as mice or keyboards). You'll also want a powered USB hub.

A typical USB OTG adapter will look like this:

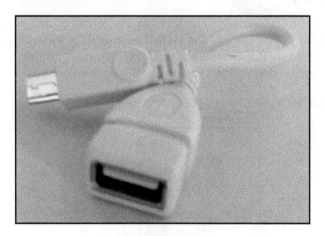

Micro-USB OTG adapter

How to do it...

A USB OTG cable is really a must-have when starting out with the RPZ. It converts the micro-USB male connections to a standard USB female connection. With that and a powered USB hub, you will have no problem connecting a keyboard, mouse, USB storage, or devices such as Wi-Fi or Bluetooth. We will look at different ways of implementing more low-profile things such as Wi-Fi later, but a hub is the easiest way to get started.

All you need to do here is connect your OTG adapter to your Raspberry Pi Zero, and then, your powered USB hub to the other end of the OTG adapter. On your hub, connect your keyboard and mouse. Before too long, we will have the hub filled with peripherals, and then we will look at better ways to access (and accessorize!) the Raspberry Pi Zero.

Connecting to displays and changing the configuration settings

The Raspberry Pi Zero is as capable as its predecessors, offering full HDMI video output. The ports are miniaturized, but that doesn't stop you from connecting your Zero to an LCD monitor. Here's how!

Getting ready

Now that you have your USB set up, your final step is getting video output. If you went with the video RCA hack, you can use the HDMI port or RCA video to get going. For HDMI, you'll need a micro-HDMI to standard HDMI adapter (and standard HDMI cable), or an HDMI cable that has one end micro and the other end standard.

A typical standard-to-micro HDMI adapter looks like this:

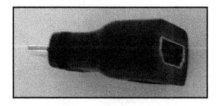

Standard-to-micro HDMI adapter

We now have our HDMI adapter and cable connected, the SD card installed, and the USB OTG adapter ready to go:

Pi connected to USB OTG and HDMI

How to do it...

1. Confirm that the SD card is inserted and that your video and USB connections are set, and connect the micro-USB power to an adapter. If you started with NOOBS, you will be taken to the OS selection screen. Right now, there isn't very much to select from. The primary reason is that the Raspberry Pi Zero doesn't yet have Internet capability, so a list of available operating systems cannot be retrieved. For now, it is as easy as clicking on the checkbox for Raspbian and the **Install** button in the top left. From there, you are a few minutes from your new Raspberry Pi Zero desktop!

2. Once you click on **Install**, NOOBS takes care of the rest and sets up a brand new default Raspbian system on your SD card. The system will start quickly and take you right to the installation screen:

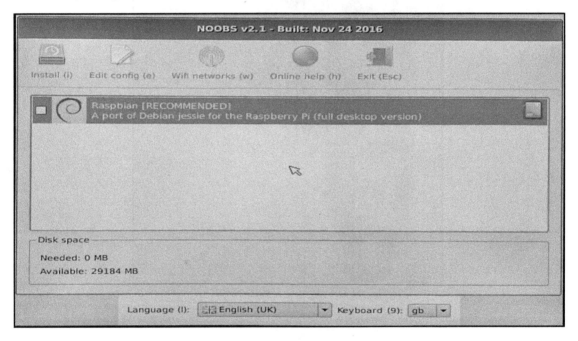

NOOBS OS selection screen

3. When you select **Install**, NOOBS will take care of the rest and prepare your card with the Raspbian operating system:

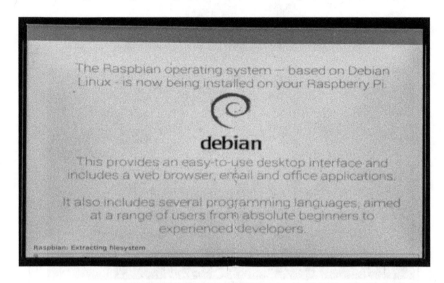

NOOBS Raspbian setup

4. After this is complete, the installer will have you click to reboot, after which you will be taken right into Raspbian.

 If you started by using a Raspbian image instead of NOOBS, you will jump right into Raspbian Linux, skipping over the NOOBS setup section.

Initial Pi configuration

1. The first thing you want to jump into is initial configuration. The fastest way to start that is by opening a terminal window. That's the little computer screen icon three icons to the right of the **Menu** button:

The Terminal icon is just to the right of the File Cabinet

Click on that and type this command:

```
sudo raspi-config
```

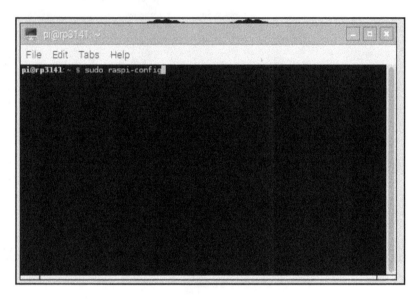

The Terminal screen – you'll be here a lot

2. If you are prompted for a password, the initial password for user `pi` is `raspberry`. The Raspberry Pi configuration tool contains several options:

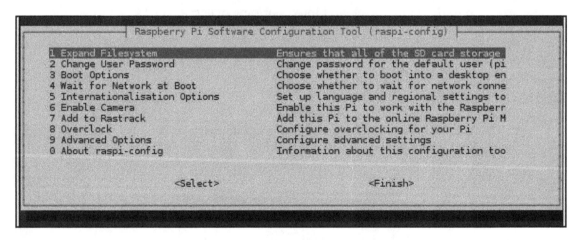

raspi-config main options

3. Let's start with option 1, **Expand Filesystem**. This will extend all of the space that is available on the SD card after making the image. After you select it, the screen will move back to the terminal, run some more commands, and come back to the configuration utility with a report:

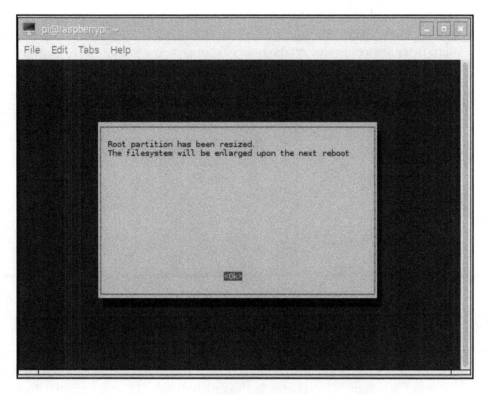

Partition resize success

4. Next, let's change the default password of the pi user. Select the second option, and you will be prompted to enter and verify a new password.

It is a very smart move to change the default user for pi or deactivate that user entirely. As you start playing with your Pi and making it more accessible to the Internet, you also make it more susceptible to hackers and bots. Since everyone knows the default login and password to a Raspbian installation, leaving them as the default when having them open to the Internet will almost certainly lead to unauthorized access and your work being stolen, altered, or destroyed.

Another good option to take care of right away are Internationalization options. You can set your local time zone and keyboard type in this section. You'll know right away whether your Pi is set to the wrong keyboard layout when you start trying special characters.

5. Finally, before rebooting, let's go into **Advanced Options** and pick the fourth option, **SSH**. Enable the SSH server. This will allow you to use the Raspberry Pi Zero from any computer on the network, once you get it on the network:

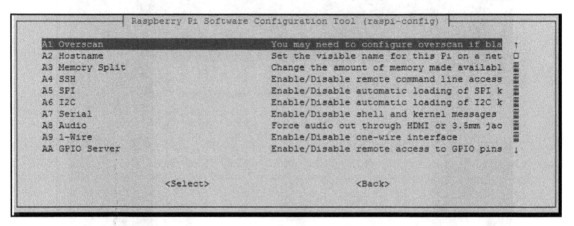

Advanced options menu

The table below shows the options available in raspi-config and what they are used for:

Number	Raspi-config option	Function	Notes
1	Expand Filesystem	Extends all available space on the SD card	Run after initial boot
2	Change User PW	Changes the password for the `pi` user	Run after initial boot
3	Boot Options	Gives you different options to boot to desktop, with or without login	Covered in the next section
4	Wait for Network @ Boot	Waits to boot the Pi until a network has become available	Recommend keeping set to **No**
5	Internationalization Options	Settings for locale, time zone, and keyboard	Run after initial boot

6	Enable Camera	Enables the camera port on the Raspberry Pi	Enable if you have a camera
7	Add to Rastrack	Adds your Raspberry Pi to the Rastrack database	Optional, register at http://rastrack.co.uk
8	Overclock	Increase the maximum speed of the processor	Covered in next section; sadly doesn't work on the Zero
9	Advanced Options	Several different advanced configuration options	Enable SSH after initial boot.
0	About raspi-config	Information about the configuration utility	

Logging in to the RPZ desktop for the first time, creating users, and rebooting

We've taken care of the initial configuration; let's wrap up this chapter by covering a few finishing touches in the configuration, creating users, and giving them power!

How to do it...

1. After you select Finish on the `raspi-config` tool, it will ask whether you'd like to reboot. Select **Yes**, and the Raspberry Pi Zero will begin its power-down process. When it starts back up, it will take you right back to the Raspbian desktop. You can reboot the Pi anytime with this command:

```
sudo reboot now
```

2. **Boot Options**: After your reboot completes, reopen the Terminal screen and run `sudo raspi-config` again. Select the third option, **Boot Options**. There are four different boot mode options to choose from:

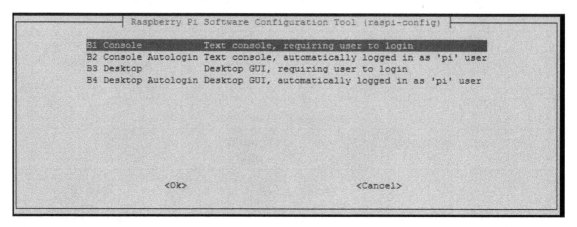

```
┌──────┤ Raspberry Pi Software Configuration Tool (raspi-config) ├──────┐
│                                                                       │
│      B1 Console            Text console, requiring user to login      │
│      B2 Console Autologin Text console, automatically logged in as 'pi' user │
│      B3 Desktop            Desktop GUI, requiring user to login       │
│      B4 Desktop Autologin Desktop GUI, automatically logged in as 'pi' user │
│                                                                       │
│                                                                       │
│                                                                       │
│                                                                       │
│                                                                       │
│              <Ok>                              <Cancel>               │
│                                                                       │
└───────────────────────────────────────────────────────────────────────┘
```

The Boot Options menu

3. Here, you can choose to start the Raspbian desktop or just boot into a command-line interface. It also gives you choices on requiring logins or not; if automatic login is chosen, you won't need to enter the password, so if you want a little bit of security, select one of the options that require the user to log in. My preference is **Text console, requiring user to login**, because it gives you a bit of security and requires less CPU and memory than running the desktop. If I need the desktop, it is simple to start it with `startx`. You can do a lot with Linux just from the command line, so a lot of the time, the desktop GUI isn't necessary.

4. **Overclocking**: Option 8, **Overclocking**, returns a rather un-fun message to the user. I'm not sure whether this is the latest version of Raspian's `raspi-config` program or whether it applies to both the Raspberry Pi Zero and the Raspberry Pi 3, but the same message was returned on both.

   An attempt to overclock from `raspi-config` does not return an optimistic response:

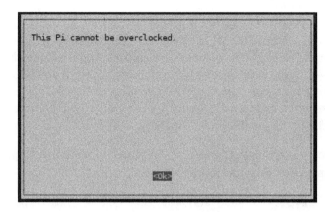

No overclock for you!

It was discovered in late 2015 that overclocking options on the Raspberry Pi Zero only caused it to slow down, so the latest version of `raspi-config` does not assist with overclocking. This doesn't mean it is impossible, however-just not advised.

5. Open the following file:

```
$ sudo grep arm /boot/config.txt
#uncomment to overclock the arm. 700 MHz is the
default.
#arm_freq=800
```

6. This does hint that overclocking is still possible at startup using the `config.txt` file. Commenting out `arm_freq=800` in the `/boot/config.txt` file to a higher frequency should work, although the Raspberry Pi community suggests that it doesn't, and perhaps even reduces performance. Even more interestingly, looking at the running settings of a Raspberry Pi Zero suggests that it is already being overclocked to 1 GHz, compared to the former setting of 700 MHz on older Raspberry Pi models:

```
$ cat
/sys/devices/system/cpu/cpu0/cpufreq/scaling_cur_freq
1000000
$ cat
/sys/devices/system/cpu/cpu0/cpufreq/scaling_max_freq
1000000
$ cat
/sys/devices/system/cpu/cpu0/cpufreq/
scaling_available_frequencies
700000 1000000
```

This output suggests that it is already running at 1 GHz and has options to run from 700 MHz to 1 GHz. You can play around with overclocking, and I suppose it was possible to push the B+ Pis to the 1.1 GHz range- you will probably see too much instability from setting it to anything much higher than that. If it becomes unusable, you should be able to recover by commenting out your `arm_freq` change in the `config.txt` file from a stable machine. Now let's work on creating new users:

7. Creating new users is very easy on Raspbian. Here, we will create one named `rpz` with a home directory located in `/home/rpz`:

```
pi@raspberrypi:~ $ sudo adduser rpz --home /home/rpz
Adding user `rpz' ...
Adding new group `rpz' (1002) ...
Adding new user `rpz' (1002) with group `rpz' ...
Creating home directory `/home/rpz' ...
Copying files from `/etc/skel' ...
Enter new UNIX password:
Retype new UNIX password:
passwd: password updated successfully
Changing the user information for rpz
Enter the new value, or press ENTER for the default
        Full Name []: Raspberry Pi Cookbook
        Room Number []:
        Work Phone []: 123-456-7890
        Home Phone []: 234-456-7890
        Other []:
Is the information correct? [Y/n] y
```

8. This will create the new user's home directory and prompt you for the password. Once you have this set up, you can log on as this user. This will give the user their own home directory in `/home/username` and the ability to execute applications. The users are stored in a file called `/etc/passwd`.

9. To look at your user, you can look at the end of this file:

```
pi@rpz14101:~ $ cat /etc/passwd | tail -5
lightdm:x:109:114:Light Display
Manager:/var/lib/lightdm:/bin/false
pulse:x:110:116:PulseAudio
daemon,,,:/var/run/pulse:/bin/false
rtkit:x:111:118:RealtimeKit,,,:/proc:/bin/false
ed:x:1001:1001::/home/ed:/bin/bash
rpz:x:1002:1002:Raspberry Pi Cookbook,,123-456
-7890,234-456-7890:/home/rpz:/bin/bash
```

10. The last entry is the user just created:

```
rpz:x:1002:1002:Raspberry Pi Cookbook,,123-456-
7890,234-456-7890:/home/rpz:/bin/bash
```

This breaks down to fields separated by a colon (`:`):

- `rpz` is the name
- `x` indicates that there is an encrypted password stored in the `/etc/shadow` file
- `1002` is the user ID
- `1002` is also the group ID, automatically generated when the user was created
- The next few fields are user ID Information
- `/home/rpz` is the home directory-the location the user will start in when they log on
- `/bin/bash` is the default command shell-the shell that the user will use when logging in.

There's more...

Before logging on as your new user, you might want to give them the ability to do superuser things, like the `pi` account does. Let's take a look at how to give your new user more powers!

What is this `sudo` thing anyway? If you are new to Linux, it probably seems strange to see a lot of these commands start with `sudo`. This command means `superuser-do`, which puts the command in a temporary elevated state. `sudo` is intended to prevent regular users from being able to do something they shouldn't (such as formatting a disk or deleting a filesystem), but it gives certain users powers to do those things if they specifically ask for elevation. It also logs attempts at trying to run things with elevated permissions that users were not given permission to do. It should become more clear as we move through the cookbook, but if you find yourself typing a command, failing, and then typing it again with `sudo` when you realize your mistake, you are already living the life of many experienced Linux users.

To give your user the ability to run as a superuser, use the `visudo` tool:

```
sudo visudo
```

This opens an edit window of the sudoers file, which will allow you to give your new user special permissions. Look down to where the pi user is already set up, and add rpz ALL=(ALL) ALL, like this:

```
#includedir /etc/sudoers.d
pi ALL=(ALL) NOPASSWD: ALL
   rpz ALL=(ALL) ALL
```

This gives your user the same permissions as the pi user, but requires that you enter a password when executing something that requires elevated permissions. This way, you can prevent the unauthorized execution of things that only a superuser should execute.

You can try logging in as our new user and trying to sudo. The touch command creates an empty file wherever you tell it to. If you don't have permissions to write, the touch command will fail. We will try logging on as our rpz user and trying touch with and without sudo, in a directory that requires elevated permission to write to. Use the su command to log on as another user:

```
pi@rpz14101:~ $ sudo su - rpz
rpz@rpz14101:~ $ touch /opt/testsudo.deleteme
touch: cannot touch '/opt/testsudo.deleteme':
Permission denied
rpz@rpz14101:~ $ sudo touch /opt/testsudo.deleteme
[sudo] password for rpz:
rpz@rpz14101:~ $ ls /opt
minecraft-pi  pigpio  sonic-pi  testsudo.deleteme
vc  Wolfram
```

Excellent! You now have superuser abilities (but remember, Spider-Man, with great power comes great responsibility), and whoever is executing them needs to know your password (which is only you, of course). If you'd prefer to keep the permissions the same as the pi user, you can sudo visudo the permissions again and set your user's settings to NOPASSWD: ALL, just like for the pi user.

There is a collection of user and group commands you can use beyond adduser: addgroup, usermod, and userdel are all good things to put in your administrator's toolbox. For pretty much any Linux command, adding --help (for example, useradd --help) or prefixing with man (man useradd) will provide you with instructions and options for what you can do with it:

```
rpz@rpz14101:~ $ useradd --help
Usage: useradd [options] LOGIN
       useradd -D
       useradd -D [options]
Options:
```

```
-b, --base-dir BASE_DIR        base directory for
the home directory of the
                               new account
-c, --comment COMMENT          GECOS field of the
new account
-d, --home-dir HOME_DIR        home directory of
the new account
-D, --defaults                 print or change
default useradd configuration
-e, --expiredate EXPIRE_DATE   expiration date of
the new account
-f, --inactive INACTIVE        password inactivity
period of the new account
-g, --gid GROUP                name or ID of the
primary group of the new account
-G, --groups GROUPS            list of
supplementary groups of the new account
-h, --help                     display this help
message and exit
-k, --skel SKEL_DIR            use this alternative
skeleton directory
-K, --key KEY=VALUE            override
/etc/login.defs defaults
-l, --no-log-init              do not add the user
 to the lastlog and faillog databases
-m, --create-home              create the user's
home directory
-M, --no-create-home           do not create the
user's home directory
-N, --no-user-group            do not create a
group with the same name as the user
-o, --non-unique               allow to create
users with duplicate (non-unique) UID
-p, --password PASSWORD        encrypted password
of the new account
-r, --system                   create a system
account
-R, --root CHROOT_DIR          directory to chroot
into
-s, --shell SHELL              login shell of the
new account
-u, --uid UID                  user ID of the new
account
-U, --user-group               create a group with
the same name as the user
-Z, --selinux-user SEUSER      use a specific
SEUSER for the SELinux user mapping
```

2
Setting Up Physical and Wireless Connections

In this chapter, we will cover the following recipes:

- Controlling the RPZ from the UART GPIO port using the console cable
- Adding a Wi-Fi dongle over USB OTG
- Hacking RPZ hardware to add a permanent Wi-Fi dongle
- Setting up dynamic and static IP addresses for the RPZ
- Pinging from another computer over same network
- SSHing your RPZ from your desktop computer
- Sharing a screen on your desktop computer
- Copying different files to and from your home network
- Adding USB functions to Raspbian Jessie
- Using a virtual serial adapter on USB OTG
- Programming over a virtual Ethernet modem on USB OTG
- Making your RPZ a USB mass storage device

Introduction

Now that we have our operating system running, we can really start to thinking about the portability advantages this Raspberry Pi Zero can bring. We'll start talking to the Raspberry Pi Zero, get it on the network, and look at the unique features and modes you get with the Zero's small form factor.

Controlling the RPZ from the UART GPIO port using the console cable

If you already have a computer that you use at home, the Raspberry Pi Zero will probably not be serving as a replacement. Wouldn't it be nice if you could work with the Zero through your own home computer? Then you only need one mouse, one keyboard, and one monitor. This recipe will show you how to use the Raspberry Pi Zero's UART GPIO to communicate with a USB-to-serial interface. Becoming familiar with this interface is great for troubleshooting (for example, when USB isn't working or you don't have a monitor nearby) and is one many different ways you can interact with your Zero.

 What is a UART and a GPIO? **UART** stands for **Universal Asynchronous Receiver/Transmitter**. Basically, that means it is a communication device understood by a lot of different devices, and it talks back and forth and doesn't wait for an acknowledgement. **GPIO** stands for **General Purpose Input/Output** and is the set of communication connections that can be configured to interact with various different things, from LCD screens to humidity monitors to microphones. We'll be exploring GPIO a lot more in later recipes.

Getting ready

For this recipe, you will start using your Raspberry Pi Zero's GPIO port. Out of the box, your Zero will not have a header on its GPIO connections-this way, if you have a specific purpose in mind for your board that requires keeping a very low profile, wires can be soldered directly to the GPIO holes.

If you don't have a specific project in mind for your Zero (yet), then attaching a header is the way to go. They are quite inexpensive and available at the same places you would find a Raspberry Pi. You can attach a male or female header, and they are available in both 0- and 90-degree positions. A female header combined with an Adafruit Raspberry Pi Cobbler and a breadboard makes for an ideal prototyping setup.

A 90-degree header, Adafruit Cobbler, and breadboard make the perfect starter lab for your Zero:

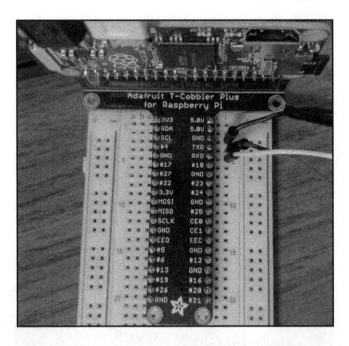

As you get into the Internet of Things and want to try making your Raspberry Pi do more things, inevitably, you will need to take up soldering. While it is fun and pretty easy to learn, you don't want to give it your first try on your Raspberry Pi Zero header. Find a hacker friend with some soldering experience to help you your first time, or find a local tech user group: there is always someone happy to help. There are also great videos and guides on the Internet, but I can promise it is a little bit harder than many of the videos make it look. Don't break your Pi with a soldering disaster!

For this recipe, you will also need a USB-to-serial dongle. With this, you can communicate between any computer with a USB port and your Raspberry Pi Zero. The Adafruit Raspberry Pi Starter Pack includes a USB-to-serial cable, a choice of headers, and the Raspberry Pi Cobbler-everything you need to get going. There are a lot of different choices available, all around the $10-$15 range. When you start getting more into hardware and microcontrollers, you will find yourself needing one of these regularly.

There are a few kinds of serial dongles; Adafruit's is perfect for something like this: one end attaches to your computer's USB port, and the other to your Raspberry Pi Zero's GPIO:

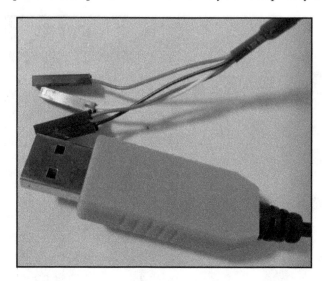

Another old favorite is the USB BUB:

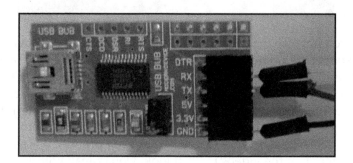

How to do it...

1. First, let's take a look at the configuration of the GPIO pins:

   Look for the hole with the square around it. This is pin 1 on all Raspberry Pi GPIO headers. The pin to its right is 2, below it 3, and so on:

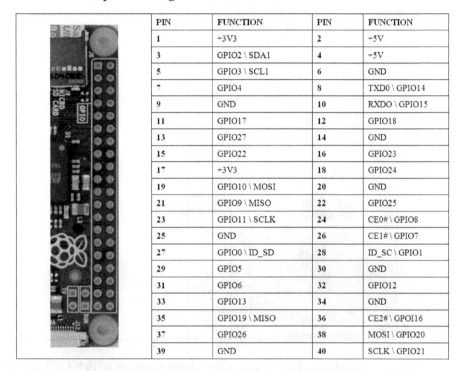

PIN	FUNCTION	PIN	FUNCTION
1	+3V3	2	+5V
3	GPIO2 \ SDA1	4	+5V
5	GPIO3 \ SCL1	6	GND
7	GPIO4	8	TXD0 \ GPIO14
9	GND	10	RXD0 \ GPIO15
11	GPIO17	12	GPIO18
13	GPIO27	14	GND
15	GPIO22	16	GPIO23
17	+3V3	18	GPIO24
19	GPIO10 \ MOSI	20	GND
21	GPIO9 \ MISO	22	GPIO25
23	GPIO11 \ SCLK	24	CE0# \ GPIO8
25	GND	26	CE1# \ GPIO7
27	GPIO0 \ ID_SD	28	ID_SC \ GPIO1
29	GPIO5	30	GND
31	GPIO6	32	GPIO12
33	GPIO13	34	GND
35	GPIO19 \ MISO	36	CE2# \ GPOI16
37	GPIO26	38	MOSI \ GPIO20
39	GND	40	SCLK \ GPIO21

   While you will get more familiar with several of these in the course of reading the book, the ones we use for this recipe are:

   - 6 GND (Ground)
   - 8 TXD0 (Transmit Data)
   - 10 RXD0 (Receive Data)

2. Connect the black wire of the USB-to-serial cable to pin 6, the green cable to 8, and the white cable to 10. The red wire is not connected for this recipe. A typical USB to Serial connection to your Raspberry Pi Zero will resemble this:

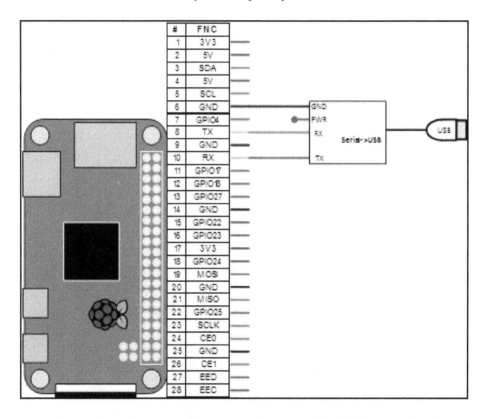

 Your wire colors may vary, depending on which USB-to-serial device you are using. Also, depending on your Operating System, you may need to install the appropriate USB driver.

3. If you are connecting your Raspberry Pi Zero to another Linux machine (or even another Raspberry Pi!), there are several ways to begin communicating with the Raspberry Pi Zero. First, identify which port your serial cable is connected to. If there aren't any other devices connected, it should be /dev/ttyUSB0. An easy method to identify the port is to plug it in and run dmesg | epgrep 'serial|ttyU*|ttyS*'. Your output should be something like this:

```
$ dmesg | egrep 'serial|ttyU|ttyS'
[    0.000000] Kernel command line: 8250.nr_uarts=0
dma.dmachans=0x7f35 bcm2708_fb.fbwidth=640
bcm2708_fb.fbheight=480 bcm2709.boardrev=0xa02082
bcm2709.serial=0xfd550dda
smsc95xx.macaddr=B8:27:EB:55:0D:DA bcm2708_fb.fbswap=1
bcm2709.uart_clock=48000000 vc_mem.mem_base=0x3dc00000
vc_mem.mem_size=0x3f000000  dwc_otg.lpm_enable=0
console=ttyS0,115200 console=tty1 root=/dev/mmcblk0p7
rootfstype=ext4 elevator=deadline fsck.repair=yes
rootwait
[    5.342786] usbcore: registered new interface
driver usbserial
[    5.342987] usbcore: registered new interface
driver usbserial_generic
[    5.343113] usbserial: USB Serial support
registered for generic
[    5.347321] usbserial: USB Serial support
registered for pl2303
[    5.352416] usb 1-1.5: pl2303 converter now
attached to ttyUSB0
```

The dmesg command returns an ordered list of the events that have occurred on the computer. One of the most recent events will be your connecting the USB. The last line of the output shows ttyUSB0, which corresponds to the "device" /dev/ttyUSB0. This device is the communication path to your Zero, and with a terminal program, you will be able to use this command to control it. Pretty much every Linux distribution is going to have screen, minicom, or the Python miniterm.py script available by default. Any one of these will work for talking to your Raspberry Pi Zero.

4. The simplest command to get on your Raspberry Pi Zero over serial is this:

```
screen /dev/ttyUSB0
```

You may need to provide the speed and duplex, depending on your setup. The Raspberry Pi serial connection default is 115200, 8 Bits, No Parity, One Stop Bit (typically referred to as 8N1)

This will replace your terminal window with a terminal window from the Raspberry Pi Zero. Anything you enter from this point will be sent to and executed on the Zero. To exit the terminal and return to your host machine, type Ctrl + A, followed by `K`. Minicom and `miniterm.py` are a little more robust and feature-rich than `screen`, but they all pretty much do the same thing.

Sometimes, you will see some strange characters and undecipherable mangled text come in when you open the serial connection. You haven't hacked into the Matrix (or have you?); it is just the serial connection getting itself figured out. Usually, entering a few characters and hitting *Enter* a few times clears it up and gets text into human-readable format.

5. If you are using Windows, PuTTY is the perfect open source program for connecting over serial ports and, later on in the cookbook, SSH. Once you connect your Pi to your Windows computer, you need to identify which COM port it is on. It will come online as a new device in **Device Manager**, and then you just need to select **Serial** and the COM number:

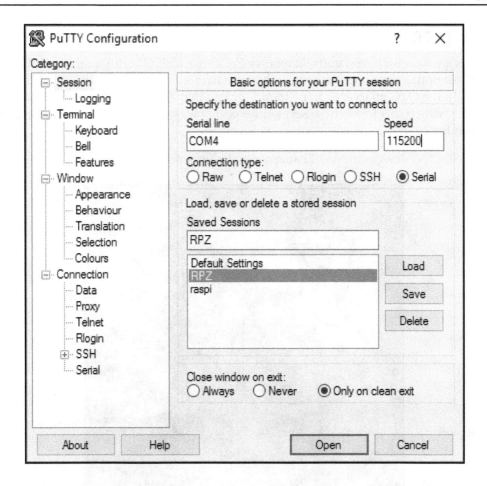

Adding Wi-Fi dongle over USB OTG

An easy way to communicate with your Pi and get your little computer connected to the Internet is connecting it to a USB Wi-Fi adapter. Once you have your Raspberry Pi Zero connected to Wi-Fi, we can get it to interact with pretty much anything that lives on your home network.

Getting ready

For this recipe, you will need your Raspberry Pi Zero, a USB OTG adapter, and a USB Wi-Fi device. Most of this equipment comes with any starter kit and is inexpensive to buy individually-the OTG adapters can be found for less than $5 and Wi-Fi dongles are $10-$15. It is still amazing that a lot of these accessories cost at least as much as the computer they are needed for!

A small USB OTG dongle and Wi-Fi adapter make for a pretty small setup:

You do need to add power, but even with that, you maintain a very small footprint for what will be an Internet-enabled computer.

The embedded Linux site (`elinux.org`) has a comprehensive listing of tested and compatible Wi-Fi cards. If you don't use one from the list, behavior may be unpredictable or the device may not work at all. The list also identifies which ones can be used without a powered USB hub. Another important note about that list is whether the driver for the card is preinstalled or not-if you pick one that is preinstalled, then your Raspberry Pi should recognize it immediately. If not, you'll need to get the driver files onto your Pi first.

Of course, if you have one laying around (as many hardware geeks do), try that first: many devices will work, or can be configured to, without too much trouble.

Finally, you'll want to know your Wi-Fi network's SSID and password so you can authenticate your Zero.

How to do it...

If you have a Wi-Fi dongle that is listed as preinstalled on Raspbian, this should be a very easy recipe. Using the USB-serial connection you established in the previous recipe, we can get Wi-Fi configured:

1. Start with the `lsusb` command to see whether it has been recognized by your Raspberry Pi Zero:

```
pi@rpz14101:/usr/share/ppp$ lsusb
Bus 001 Device 012: ID 0bda:8176 Realtek
Semiconductor
Corp. RTL8188CUS 802.11n WLAN Adapter
Bus 001 Device 002: ID 05e3:0608 Genesys Logic, Inc.
USB-2.0 4-Port HUB
Bus 001 Device 001: ID 1d6b:0002 Linux Foundation
2.0
root hub
```

2. Here at the top of the list is our Wi-Fi device. If your device showed up, it should be pretty easy to get yourself connected to your wireless network. If not, check `dmesg` to see whether something went wrong. This is the command:

```
dmesg | grep -I usb | tail -20
```

This command instructs the Pi to search the logs for anything containing usb or USB, and return the most recent 20 lines. If the following test run, first a USB dongle with power issues was attached, followed by a working dongle. You can see the difference between a USB device that attached correctly versus one that experienced an error:

```
pi@rpz14101:/usr/share/ppp$ dmesg | grep -i usb | tail
-20
[ 4222.016769] usb 1-1.3: device not accepting address
7, error -32
[ 4222.017187] usb 1-1-port3: unable to enumerate USB
device
[ 8456.015076] usb 1-1: reset high-speed USB device
number 2 using dwc_otg
[ 8456.515070] usb 1-1.3: new full-speed USB device
number 8 using dwc_otg
[ 8456.595063] usb 1-1.3: device descriptor read/64,
error -32
[ 8456.785087] usb 1-1.3: device descriptor read/64,
error -32
[ 8456.975074] usb 1-1.3: new full-speed USB device
number 9 using dwc_otg
[ 8457.055082] usb 1-1.3: device descriptor read/64,
error -32
[ 8457.245079] usb 1-1.3: device descriptor read/64,
error -32
[ 8457.435082] usb 1-1.3: new full-speed USB device
number 10 using dwc_otg
[ 8457.855082] usb 1-1.3: device not accepting address
10, error -32
[ 8457.935163] usb 1-1.3: new full-speed USB device
number 11 using dwc_otg
[ 8458.355084] usb 1-1.3: device not accepting address
11, error -32
[ 8458.355431] usb 1-1-port3: unable to enumerate USB
device
[29178.281722] usb 1-1.3: new high-speed USB device
number 12 using dwc_otg
[29178.383627] usb 1-1.3: New USB device found,
idVendor=0bda, idProduct=8176
[29178.383667] usb 1-1.3: New USB device strings:
Mfr=1, Product=2, SerialNumber=3
[29178.383690] usb 1-1.3: Product: 802.11n WLAN
Adapter
[29178.383710] usb 1-1.3: Manufacturer: Realtek
[29178.383732] usb 1-1.3: SerialNumber: 000000000000
```

3. If your device won't get picked up by your Raspberry Pi Zero, you can search for your error message on the Internet to see whether someone has experienced the same thing, or, ideally, use a spare USB Wi-Fi dongle or one you can borrow (it's probably not something wrong with your Pi). Most compatible USB dongles will attach without incident and are ready to get connected to your Wi-Fi network. Running `ifconfig` should show the interface, but without any connection information:

```
pi@rpz14101:/usr/share/ppp$ ifconfig
lo         Link encap:Local Loopback
       inet addr:127.0.0.1  Mask:255.0.0.0
       inet6 addr: ::1/128 Scope:Host
       UP LOOPBACK RUNNING  MTU:65536  Metric:1
       RX packets:1992 errors:0 dropped:0
overruns:0 frame:0
       TX packets:1992 errors:0 dropped:0
overruns:0 carrier:0
       collisions:0 txqueuelen:1
       RX bytes:161808 (158.0 KiB)  TX bytes:161808
       (158.0 KiB)
wlan0      Link encap:Ethernet  HWaddr
00:13:ef:80:0b:41
       inet addr:192.168.2.119  Bcast:192.168.2.255
Mask:255.255.255.0
       inet6 addr: fe80::a577:b1b7:a7a7:8a60/64
Scope:Link
       UP BROADCAST RUNNING MULTICAST  MTU:1500
Metric:1
       RX packets:20 errors:0 dropped:10000
overruns:0 frame:0
       TX packets:55 errors:0 dropped:0 overruns:0
carrier:0
       collisions:0 txqueuelen:1000
```

4. Now we just need to find and connect to our network. This is very easy to do from the command line. To search for available networks, we use the `iwlist` command:

```
sudo iwlist wlan0 scan | grep SSID | sort | uniq
```

This command asks your Wi-Fi adapter, `wlan0`, to scan for available networks. This outputs a lot of information, so we've piped it to the `grep` command to filter out the data we don't need in order to connect. The sort and `uniq` commands sort the SSIDs by name and remove any duplicates:

```
pi@rpz14101:~ $ sudo iwlist wlan0 scan | grep SSID
| sort | uniq
                    ESSID:""
                    ESSID:"141FAST"
                    ESSID:"FBI Surveillance Van 3"
                    ESSID:"bullies"
                    ESSID:"HOME-7068-2.4"
                    ESSID:"L78MH"
                    ESSID:"NETGEAR45"
```

Hopefully, you'll see the network you want to connect to. If not, you may have to look into your signal from your router. Timing can be a factor too, as SSIDs are broadcast on an interval. Give the command a few tries if nothing comes up the first time.

5. Once you've found it, you just need to add it to the list of available SSIDs for your Raspberry Pi Zero to use. For this, we'll edit the `wpa_supplicant.conf` file, located in `/etc/wpa_supplicant/wpa_supplicant.conf`. Initially, it should be mostly empty, like this:

```
pi@rpz14101:~ $ sudo cat
/etc/wpa_supplicant/wpa_supplicant.conf
ctrl_interface=DIR=/var/run/wpa_supplicant
GROUP=netdev
update_config=1
country=US
```

6. We will add some lines to this file for the SSID to be used. The format is as follows:

```
network = {
    ssid="MYSSID"
    psk="My SSID Password"
}
```

Add this to the file, save it, and then run this:

```
sudo ifdown wlan0; sudo ifup wlan0
```

7. Finally, check `ifconfig` again. Your `wlan0` interface should now show an IP address and additional information it needs to work on the Wi-Fi network:

```
pi@rpz14101:/usr/share/ppp$ ifconfig
lo        Link encap:Local Loopback
          inet addr:127.0.0.1  Mask:255.0.0.0
          inet6 addr: ::1/128 Scope:Host
          UP LOOPBACK RUNNING  MTU:65536  Metric:1
          RX packets:1992 errors:0 dropped:0
          overruns:0 frame:0
          TX packets:1992 errors:0 dropped:0
          overruns:0 carrier:0
          collisions:0 txqueuelen:1
          RX bytes:161808 (158.0 KiB)  TX bytes:161808
          (158.0 KiB)
wlan0     Link encap:Ethernet  HWaddr
00:13:ef:80:0b:41
          inet addr:192.168.2.119  Bcast:192.168.2.255
          Mask:255.255.255.0
          inet6 addr: fe80::a577:b1b7:a7a7:8a60/64
          Scope:Link
          UP BROADCAST RUNNING MULTICAST  MTU:1500
          Metric:1
          RX packets:20 errors:0 dropped:10000
          overruns:0 frame:0
          TX packets:55 errors:0 dropped:0 overruns:0
          carrier:0
          collisions:0 txqueuelen:1000
          RX bytes:3466461 (3.3 MiB)  TX bytes:115712
          (113.0 KiB)
```

That's it! Your Raspberry Pi Zero is now on your Wi-Fi network, much like any other computer, tablet, cell phone, or any other wireless, internet-enabled device you have in your home.

Hacking RPZ hardware to add up permanent Wi-Fi dongle

The USB dongle solder hack is considered one of the very first hacks shared in the community after the release of the Raspberry Pi Zero. With such a small form factor and USB OTG connectors, many hackers didn't like the idea of adding to the size of the board with an adapter and then tacking on a USB dongle. This recipe shows you how to attach an uncased Wi-Fi adapter to the Raspberry Pi Zero to keep your footprint still small enough to fit a mints tin.

Getting ready

This is another soldering hack, and not necessarily for the faint of heart. You'll need a compatible USB Wi-Fi dongle, but it is important to make sure to check the compatibility list on https://www.elinux.org to ensure that your dongle is both compatible and does not require additional power. Since we will be soldering this one right to the Zero, it will need to be able to get all of the power it needs from the incoming USB 5V port.

A great way to test whether you have the right equipment is to set it up with the USB OTG dongle in the previous recipe. If you can get your Wi-Fi set up with only the Wi-Fi and OTG dongles (and no supplemental power), then it should work fine when soldered directly to the board. You can even set up your SSID beforehand so that it will come right up after you've finished the soldering and started up the board again.

How to do it...

1. First, carefully remove the case from your Wi-Fi dongle. This will result in just a small board with four connectors. The adapter is really just a very small board and its casing, as shown in this before-and-after picture:

2. The connectors are for Power, Transmit, Receive, and Ground. The power and ground wires will attach to PP1 and PP6. The Transmit and Receive will connect to PP22 and PP23. Use short, equal lengths of wire to solder the two together, and be sure to twist the Transmit and Receive wires.

3. Here is how we will connect the adapter to the Pi Zero:

4. This will connect to the test pads on the Raspberry Pi Zero here:

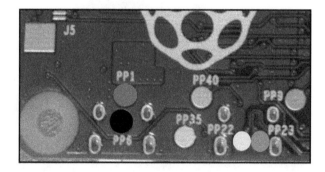

5. You'll want to make the data wires as short as possible, the same length, and twisted, just like the inside of a network cable.

6. With the Raspberry Pi Zero's power detached, solder the connecters together. My approach to soldering with test points is heavy preparation.

7. First, put a small bit of solder onto each test pad and on each cupper strip of the Wi-Fi card.

8. Next take the wires you will be using to solder, and apply solder to the wires themselves.

9. Finally, when you get to attaching the wires to the connection points, the solder from both should bond everything together nicely. Be careful not to use too much, as solder running across the test pads or connections will cause a short, and they can be a true pain to clean off.

After your connections have been made, start up your Pi Zero and see how things work! You should see your device when running `lsusb`, and if you configured your Wi-Fi before soldering, `ifconfig` should show an active `wlan0` connection with IP addresses. If not, follow the instructions from the previous recipe, and you will be up and running!

Whether you decided to go with USB OTG or solder the Wi-Fi adapter directly to your board, your Raspberry Pi Zero can now be accessible from pretty much anywhere you have a Wi-Fi network. Now that we're on the network, we will start moving into recipes to make you a true power user!

 If you have your Wi-Fi dongle in, remove it first. It will be easier to test your recipe, and easy to configure.

If soldering onto the board isn't your thing, that's OK too. This cookbook doesn't require it, and we are going to experiment with Wi-Fi over the GPIO bus later, so we aren't finished with hacking the Raspberry Pi Zero and Wi-Fi devices.

Setting Up dynamic and static IP address for RPZ

Now that we have our Raspberry Pi Zero on the network, let's look a little closer at what we can do with the networking. Everything should have connected to your Wi-Fi network thanks to **DHCP (Dynamic Host Allocation Protocol)**. DHCP takes incoming requests from devices to be added to the network. It has a pool of IP addresses on the network that it will "lease" to the device for a period of time. After the lease expires, the device may renew (and, depending on the DHCP server rules, will get a new or the same address), or the address will be returned to the available pool. This makes it easy to add machines to a network without keeping track of individual addresses assigned to devices. When your Raspberry Pi Zero connected to your Wi-Fi network, by default, it would have been assigned at least one IP address: an IPv4 address (four sets of numbers between 0 and 255, as in `192.168.17.250`), and/or a newer IPv6 address (8 sets of hexadecimal numbers between 0 and FFFF, as in `fda5:eec5:fae1: fda5:eec5:fae1:ffff`).

An IP address works very much like a phone number-any device on your home network or any device that can be seen from the Internet will have an IP address associated with it. On the Internet, the device will have a unique IP, much like a phone number. Just like every friend you have has a different phone number, every device has its own IP address. Internal, or private, networks work like phone number extensions inside an office. There may be one number you dial to get to the office, but inside, each employee might get their own internal number.

The **DNS** (**domain name system**) is much like an Internet phone book. It ties an address, such as `www.yahoo.com`, to an IP address, such as `50.51.200.222`. This way, humans can remember names of places instead of individual IP addresses.

Sometimes, however, it is ideal for a device to have a known, permanent IP address, and on a home network, IPv4 is a lot easier to remember. Most home networks have an address in the form of `192.168.x.x`, known as a private address, which gives you plenty of room to assign permanent, or static, IP addresses to some devices while letting others get assigned automatically. In this recipe, we will explore the options for both.

One important note: In this recipe, we will look at how to set up DHCP and static IP from the command line (the hard way). If you plan on using your Raspberry Pi Zero frequently with X Windows or a VNC server, we will look at a way to set this up from the Raspbian desktop as well, which has been documented to override the command-line settings.

Getting ready

Whether you've soldered your Wi-Fi adapter to the Pi or have it connected via a USB OTG dongle, you are ready to go. You should keep your serial connection available in case you make a change that results in the loss of your network connection. We can run through all of this configuration using the console connection established in the first recipe of this chapter.

How to do it...

1. First, let's take another look at your network configuration using `ifconfig`:

```
pi@rpz14101:~$ ifconfig
lo          Link encap:Local Loopback
        inet addr:127.0.0.1  Mask:255.0.0.0
        inet6 addr:  ::1/128 Scope:Host
        UP LOOPBACK RUNNING  MTU:65536  Metric:1
        RX packets:1992 errors:0 dropped:0
        overruns:0 frame:0
        TX packets:1992 errors:0 dropped:0
        overruns:0 carrier:0
        collisions:0 txqueuelen:1
        RX bytes:161808 (158.0 KiB)  TX bytes:161808
        (158.0 KiB)
wlan0       Link encap:Ethernet  HWaddr
00:13:ef:80:0b:41
        inet addr:192.168.2.119  Bcast:192.168.2.255
Mask:255.255.255.0
        inet6 addr:  fe80::a577:b1b7:a7a7:8a60/64
Scope:Link
        UP BROADCAST RUNNING MULTICAST  MTU:1500
Metric:1
        RX packets:14761 errors:0 dropped:17582
overruns:0 frame:0
        TX packets:826 errors:0 dropped:0 overruns:0
carrier:0
        collisions:0 txqueuelen:1000
        RX bytes:5874864 (5.6 MiB)  TX bytes:228064
(222.7 KiB)
```

The first entry, `lo`, should always come up when this command is run. This is called the **loopback adapter** and is the *home* of the device. If I am on the device and no other adapter or address is present, I can always use `127.0.0.1` to have the Pi Zero talk to itself. This isn't something you'll need to worry about, but it is something you will see on any Linux computer you work with.

The second entry, `wlan0`, is the Wi-Fi adapter. The second line is the IPv4 address, and the third is the IPv6 one. As you can see, my IPv4 address follows the `192.168.x.x` standard.

2. Next, we will look at how and where DHCP or static addressing are configured. You'll find that file in `/etc/network/interfaces`:

```
pi@rpz14101:~$ cat /etc/network/interfaces
# interfaces(5) file used by ifup(8) and ifdown(8)
# Please note that this file is written to be used          with
dhcpcd
# For static IP, consult /etc/dhcpcd.conf and 'man
dhcpcd.conf'
# Include files from /etc/network/interfaces.d:
source-directory /etc/network/interfaces.d
auto lo
iface lo inet loopback
iface eth0 inet manual
allow-hotplug wlan0
iface wlan0 inet manual
wpa-conf /etc/wpa_supplicant/wpa_supplicant.conf
```

3. We want to look closely at the lines starting with `iface` here. Our Wi-Fi adapter has this entry:

```
iface wlan0 inet manual
```

The part of the command we want to focus on here is `manual`. This setting means *manual configuration*, which means that something else takes care of the configuration, or it is handled manually by the user. On the Raspbian OS, it doesn't seem to make much difference once you have things configured to this point, but you can change the setting to `dhcp` to specifically tell the interface to work as a DHCP client.

4. Change this line in your `/etc/network/interfaces` file:

```
iface wlan0 inet manual
```

Make it this:

```
iface wlan0 inet dhcp
```

Restarting your network adapter with `sudo ifdown wlan0; sudo ifup wlan0` will return messages that a message is being sent to the DHCP server:

```
pi@rpz14101:~$ sudo ifdown wlan0; sudo ifup wlan0
Internet Systems Consortium DHCP Client 4.3.1
Copyright 2004-2014 Internet Systems Consortium.
All rights reserved.
```

```
For info, please visit
https://www.isc.org/software/dhcp/
Listening on LPF/wlan0/00:13:ef:80:0b:41
Sending on   LPF/wlan0/00:13:ef:80:0b:41
Sending on   Socket/fallback
DHCPDISCOVER on wlan0 to 255.255.255.255 port 67          interval

DHCPREQUEST on wlan0 to 255.255.255.255 port 67
DHCPOFFER from 192.168.2.1
DHCPACK from 192.168.2.1
bound to 192.168.2.119 -- renewal in 36084
seconds.
```

6

5. Now, let's say you want to assign your Raspberry Pi Zero a permanent address so you will always know what the address is. Generally speaking, you will want to keep the first three *octets* in your network address the same as before. So, my DHCP address is `192.168.2.119`, but I want to give it a static address. The address I should choose should be anything available between `192.168.2.1` and `192.168.2.254`, and it can't already be in use by another device on the network. To do this, I have to enter a lot more information: DHCP figures out a lot of things for you. Let's say I want my IP address to always be `192.168.2.42`. My `/etc/network/interfaces` file is currently as follows:

```
allow-hotplug wlan0
iface wlan0 inet dhcp
wpa-conf /etc/wpa_supplicant/wpa_supplicant.conf
```

It will change to this:

```
allow-hotplug wlan0
iface wlan0 inet static
address 192.168.2.42
netmask 255.255.255.0
gateway 192.168.2.1
wpa-conf /etc/wpa_supplicant/wpa_supplicant.conf
```

Restarting with `sudo ifdown wlan0; sudo ifup wlan0` will restart the interface with the new static IP address:

```
wlan0     Link encap:Ethernet  HWaddr
00:13:ef:80:0b:41
          inet addr:192.168.2.42  Bcast:192.168.2.255
Mask:255.255.255.0
          inet6 addr: fe80::a577:b1b7:a7a7:8a60/64
          Scope:Link
          UP BROADCAST RUNNING MULTICAST  MTU:1500  Metric:1
```

```
RX packets:20 errors:0 dropped:97297 overruns:0
frame:0
TX packets:42 errors:0 dropped:1 overruns:0
carrier:0
collisions:0 txqueuelen:1000
RX bytes:37298989 (35.5 MiB)   TX bytes:14776826
(14.0 MiB)
```

Now you know how to set up your Raspberry Pi Zero with a dedicated IP address or leverage your home network's DHCP service to take care of the details for you.

There are a lot of reports about the Raspberry Pi tools available in the GUI overriding your network settings that you have modified in the `/etc/network/interfaces` file. I didn't run into an issues with it myself, but the best approach is to stick to either the command-line tool or the GUI tool, but if you make edits in both, you are bound to run into some service conflicts.

Pinging from another computer over same network

Now that we have our computer on the network, we want to make sure other computers are able to contact it. The `ping` command is one of the first tests to tell whether your computer can be contacted. The command sends a small test packet of data to another computer's IP address or hostname and waits to hear a response. If it does, it tells you how long it took for the response to come back. If it doesn't, it tells you it is not receiving a response.

Some computer systems have firewalls that do not allow ICMP ECHO attempts. This means that even though the computer is available on the network, attempts to ping it will fail. On the default configuration of Raspbian, `ping` commands are allowed, so attempts to ping your Pi should succeed.

Getting ready

As long you as you know your IP address (whether it was dynamically assigned using DHCP or you assigned a static IP from the previous recipe), you should be able to contact it from your network. The easiest way to do this is by looking at `ifconfig`. From your serial terminal connection, and if you followed one of the previous recipes to add Wi-Fi connectivity, `ifconfig` should report the IP address of your Raspberry Pi Zero:

```
pi@rpz14101:~$ ifconfig
lo          Link encap:Local Loopback
            inet addr:127.0.0.1  Mask:255.0.0.0
            inet6 addr: ::1/128 Scope:Host
            UP LOOPBACK RUNNING  MTU:65536  Metric:1
            RX packets:264 errors:0 dropped:0 overruns:0
            frame:0
            TX packets:264 errors:0 dropped:0 overruns:0
            carrier:0
            collisions:0 txqueuelen:1
            RX bytes:21840 (21.3 KiB)  TX bytes:21840
            (21.3 KiB)
wlan0       Link encap:Ethernet  HWaddr
00:13:ef:80:0b:41
inet addr:192.168.2.119  Bcast:192.168.2.255
Mask:255.255.255.0
inet6 addr: fe80::a577:b1b7:a7a7:8a60/64 Scope:Link
UP BROADCAST RUNNING MULTICAST  MTU:1500  Metric:1
RX packets:212682 errors:0 dropped:54847 overruns:0
frame:0
TX packets:19599 errors:0 dropped:1 overruns:0
carrier:0
collisions:0 txqueuelen:1000
RX bytes:34267586 (32.6 MiB)  TX bytes:1911492 (1.8
MiB)
```

The `wlan0` interface is the one I set up in the previous recipe. The `inet addr` field shows my Raspberry Pi Zero's IP address. This is the one I want to try and contact.

How to do it...

1. `ping <IP address>`, like this, for example:

   ping `192.168.2.119`

2. On a Windows machine, you can execute `ping` via the command line (Windows + R followed by `cmd`). Below is a shot of a typical successful response:

```
C:\WINDOWS\system32\cmd.exe                          —    □    ✕

C:\Users\Ed>ping 192.168.2.119

Pinging 192.168.2.119 with 32 bytes of data:
Reply from 192.168.2.119: bytes=32 time=132ms TTL=64
Reply from 192.168.2.119: bytes=32 time=8ms TTL=64
Reply from 192.168.2.119: bytes=32 time=60ms TTL=64
Reply from 192.168.2.119: bytes=32 time=78ms TTL=64

Ping statistics for 192.168.2.119:
    Packets: Sent = 4, Received = 4, Lost = 0 (0% loss),
Approximate round trip times in milli-seconds:
    Minimum = 8ms, Maximum = 132ms, Average = 69ms

C:\Users\Ed>
```

3. Trying `192.168.2.120`, which isn't assigned to anything on my home network, will show a failed ping:

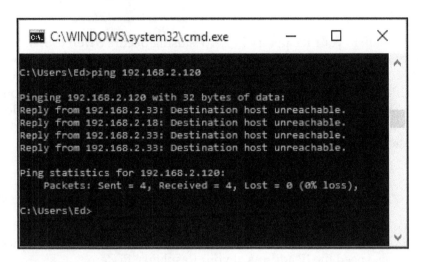

This means that there is nothing responding from that IP address, which could mean it is down, off, or blocked by a firewall. The command `ping /?` will give you all available options for the Windows `ping` command. By default, the Windows `ping` tries four times and reports the results.

In an OSX or Linux terminal, the `ping` utility will continue trying to reach the address and report back the response time (or whether it failed). Breaking the utility with *Ctrl + C* will stop it.

Running `ping -help` will give you a list of all the options, and `man ping` will give you a more detailed document of what is possible. A few favorite flags of administrators are the following:

ping -c 5 192.168.2.70

This will try to ping 5 times and then stop.

ping -i 2 192.168.2.70

This will send a ping command every 2 seconds.

SSHing your RPZ from your desktop computer

The ideal way to talk to your Raspberry Pi Zero is using **Secure SHell (SSH)**. This gives you a secure, encrypted channel to talk to your Pi from anywhere on the network. For example, let's say you want your Pi to collect temperature information from your attic and make it available on your home network. You don't want to drag a monitor, mouse, and keyboard up to your attic every time you want to make a change-you want to do it from your regular home computer! If you have your RPZ using Wi-Fi, on the network, and ping-able, the next step is to work with it remotely over SSH. Here's how.

Getting ready

If you are using a Windows machine, PuTTY is the way to go, just like a serial connection. If you are on OSX or Linux, SSH should be installed and available using any terminal window. You'll also need the IP address of your Raspberry Pi Zero.

If you ran through the earlier recipe to enable SSH using the `rasp-config` utility covered in `Chapter 1`, *Kick-Start your Raspberry Pi Zero*, then you should be set to go.

How to do it...

1. Talking to your Raspberry Pi Zero over SSH is quite simple. On OSX or Linux, use this command:

    ```
    ssh pi@192.168.2.118
    ```

    You will be prompted for your password; after entering it, you will be in your Zero's terminal.

2. On Windows, open PuTTY and enter the address in the **Host Name** box. Select `SSH` for the connection type. Click on **Open**, and PuTTY will open the terminal window. You can also **Save** the session to connect quickly in the future.

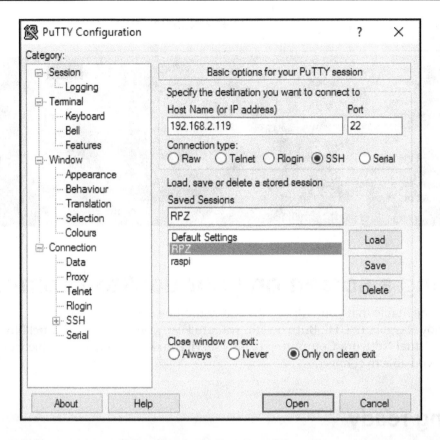

At this point, you are connected remotely to your Raspberry Pi over an encrypted connection. If your network speeds are acceptable, you should find this to be a much faster connection than the USB-serial connection used earlier. The serial connection is great for troubleshooting, especially when you can't see your Pi Zero on the network. Once that's functioning normally, you'll probably find the SSH terminal the fastest and easiest way to get connected, especially if you don't want your keyboard and monitor connected to your Raspberry Pi Zero (they are much harder to carry in your bag that way).

Once you are connected, you can use it just like you used the serial connection. You'll find that you probably want to use this one, as your home network is probably quite a bit faster than your direct serial connection. If you have your Wi-Fi adapter connected, you can put your Raspberry Pi Zero anywhere it can get power and is within reach of a known Wi-Fi network.

Here is what a typical successful SSH connection would look like:

```
Using username "pi".
pi@192.168.2.119's password:

The programs included with the Debian GNU/Linux system are free software;
the exact distribution terms for each program are described in the
individual files in /usr/share/doc/*/copyright.

Debian GNU/Linux comes with ABSOLUTELY NO WARRANTY, to the extent
permitted by applicable law.
Last login: Sun Jul 24 07:43:10 2016
pi@rpz14101:
```

Sharing a screen on your desktop computer

While it is inevitable that you will use the command line a lot when using Linux, a lot of people enjoy Raspbian's GUI. But you still want to keep your Zero in the attic! No problem at all: the Virtual Network Computing (VNC) service makes the GUI available from anywhere you able to connect.

Getting ready

Stay connected to your Raspberry Pi Zero with your SSH terminal. On your home computer, you will need a VNC viewer application. I love the VNC Viewer Chrome extension, and it is available on any platform.

How to do it...

1. First, you need to install a VNC server on your Raspberry Pi Zero. To install it on Raspbian, type the following:

   ```
   sudo apt-get install tightvncserver
   ```

2. Once it's installed, starting it is as simple as typing `vncserver`:

   ```
   $ vncserver
   New 'X' desktop is rpz14101:1
   Starting applications specified in
   ```

```
/home/pi/.vnc/xstartup
Log file is /home/pi/.vnc/rpz14101:1.log
```

3. The first time you start a server, it will prompt you for a password. This is the password that you will use to connect using the VNC viewer. The VNC session you create will be for the user that started it, so if you initialized it from the `pi` user as in the previous example, VNC connections in it will also be for the `pi` user, if you are logged on as root, VNC will connect as root, and so on.

4. Now your Zero is available on the network over VNC. Any kind of device that can run a VNC viewer application will be able to use X Windows on the Pi. The VNC server returns the device name and a port instead of the IP address. To connect, we will use this format:

```
<IP Address>:<Desktop number>
```

Here's an example:

```
192.168.2.119:1
```

We'll use the same address we found with `ifconfig` and used to ping and SSH to our Raspberry Pi Zero.

5. Once you are connected, it works just like being directly connected to the Zero over HDMI. This way, you can use the Raspberry Pi Zero no matter where you or the Zero are located. If you need the command line, SSH is the ideal tool, but if you are using GUI tools such as Scratch, need to look something up with a browser, or write a song with Sonic Pi, the VNC connection will be the choice for you.

 Because of the Raspberry Pi Zero's size, some sacrifices had to be made. It uses an older CPU, which is quite a bit slower overall than the Raspberry Pi 2 or 3. If you are planning to use the GUI a lot, you might want to use one of the larger, faster models. The Raspberry Pi Zero is perfectly capable, but it won't be nearly as much fun playing Minecraft Pi over VNC as it would be on a Raspberry Pi 3.

6. Logging on using a VNC viewer is as simple as providing the IP address and desktop number:

7. You'll be prompted for the password you created when you set up the VNC server, and then you are ready to go!

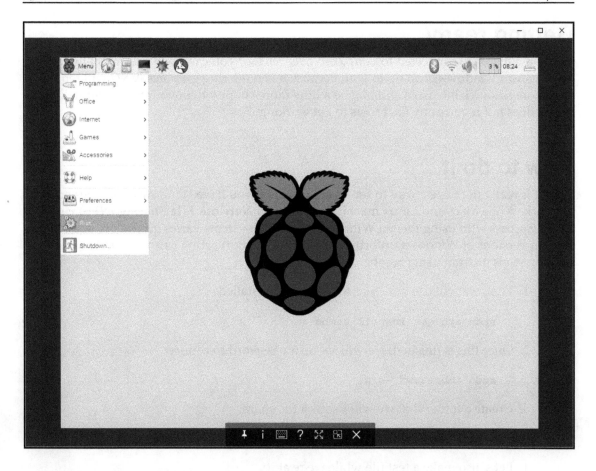

Copying different files to and from your home network

Now that your Raspberry Pi Zero is sitting comfortably on your home network, it can work as a central part of it and interact with the other computers using it. This will show you how to set up a file share on your Raspberry Pi that can interact with the computers on your home network.

Getting ready

You can either stay connected to your Zero over SSH, or you can open a terminal in your VNC viewer window-it's all up to you. Because it is rendering graphics, VNC will tend to be a more resource intensive and maybe a little more choppy than your SSH terminal; this recipe does not require any GUI tools to get working.

How to do it...

Samba is really the easiest way to set up a file share if you have Windows machines on your network. While Macs and Linux machines work with **Network File Sharing (NFS)** very easily, success with using this on Windows operating systems varies quite a bit. Most Home Edition versions of Windows unfortunately do not support acting as an NFS client, but nothing stops us from using Samba:

1. First, we will use `apt-get` to get Samba installed:

   ```
   sudo apt-get install samba
   ```

2. Once this is finished, we will set up a password to connect:

   ```
   sudo smbpasswd -a pi
   ```

3. Create a folder that we will use as a file share:

   ```
   mkdir /home/pi/share
   ```

4. Let's also make a test file while we're at it:

   ```
   touch /home/pi/share/helloNetwork.yes
   ```

5. Now we just need to tell the Samba service about this new share. Open the `/etc/samba/smb.conf` using your favorite editor:

   ```
   sudo vi /etc/samba/smb.conf
   ```

6. To the end of the file, add your share information:

   ```
   [share]
   path = /home/pi/share
   valid users = pi
   read only = no
   ```

7. Save the file, and then restart Samba:

```
sudo service smbd restart
```

8. Once Samba restarts, it will pick up the new share you entered into the smb.conf file. You can check for errors by running this command:

```
testparm
```

9. A truncated version of the expected output is displayed here:

```
pi@rpz14101:~ $ testparm
Load smb config files from /etc/samba/smb.conf
Processing section "[homes]"
Processing section "[printers]"
Processing section "[print$]"
Processing section "[share]"
Loaded services file OK.
Server role: ROLE_STANDALONE
Press enter to see a dump of your service definitions
...
[share]
        path = /home/pi/share
        valid users = pi
        read only = No
```

10. If there is anything wrong, this utility should tell you. Otherwise, you should see the new share you just created. If you want to connect from a Linux or Mac computer, the address will be in this format:

```
smb://<IP_Address>/shareName
```

11. In my case, it is this:

```
smb://192.168.2.42/share
```

On a Windows machine, you connect to \\IP_Address\ShareName, as in \\192.168.2.42\share.

A login prompt should appear; use the name and password you provided in `smbpasswd`:

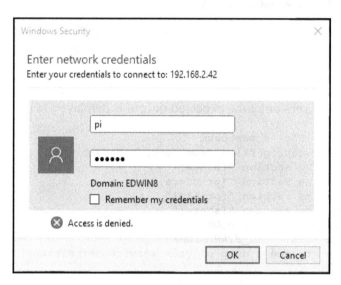

12. If all went well, you should see the file you created earlier:

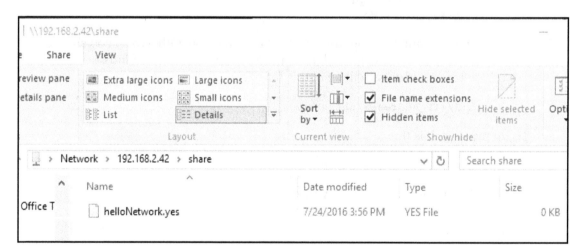

Now you can read and write into and out of that folder. This is a great way to copy a backup of files you've created on your Raspberry Pi Zero in case you decide you want to start with a fresh SD card. For future recipes where we will write programs and scripts, we will work in this directory so that it is easy to make a backup.

Adding USB functions to Raspbian Jessie

The latest release of Raspbian Jessie added some wonderful hacks that make the Raspberry Pi both an ideal test device and at the same time the most inexpensive awesome little Linux server you could fit into a box of mints. With the next series of hacks, we will use the USB port to connect as a serial device, a network device, or even a mass storage device (like a USB flash drive). The possibilities grow with every release!

If you are using Mac OS X, you should be all set-the Bonjour services come installed. If on Windows, Apple's Bonjour print services will be the only installation you need to get things working. Finally, on Linux, `avanti-daemon` needs to be installed, which it is by default as of Ubuntu 14.04.

 The USB OTG functions are only available on the Raspberry Pi Zero. The reason for this is that the USB port is connected directly to the processor for the Zero but runs through a USB hub on its larger siblings. This is an RPZ-only hack!

Getting ready

For this recipe, you can work directly over your SSH connection to your Raspberry Pi, or you can shut down the Pi, put the SD card into another computer, and edit the files there.

How to do it...

1. First, let's make sure our OS, service, and applications are up to date. First, run these two commands:

```
sudo apt-get update
sudo apt-get upgrade
```

> If there are things that need to be updated to the latest version, these commands will take care of it for you. We will dive into the `apt-get` command later on in the book. If you are using a Raspbian build newer than `2016-06-15`, then the kernel updates are already installed.

 To set things up for the next bunch of recipes, we are going to be looking in the Raspberry Pi Zero's `/boot` volume, specifically, the `config.txt` and `cmdline.txt` files. These files are used at startup to get the Pi Zero configured and booted.

I recommend first making a backup of the files. This way, if you do something wrong that causes the Pi not to start up, you can just put the SD card in a computer and copy the original file back:

```
sudo cp /boot/config.txt /boot/config.txt.bak
sudo cp /boot/cmdline.txt /boot/cmdline.txt.bak
```

2. Now we can go ahead and edit our original files. The command is as follows:

```
sudo nano /boot/config.txt
```

3. To the very end of the file, add the following and save:

```
dtoverlay=dwc2
```

This sets up the `config.txt` file for USB OTG access. In the following recipes, we will make additional configuration changes to leverage some of the unique capabilities of our Raspberry Pi Zero.

Using a virtual serial adapter on USB OTG

Some of the coolest hacks that are available on the Raspberry Pi Zero are to do with getting it to work with other computers using a single USB cable. In this recipe, we will create a "virtual" serial adapter, so instead of connecting with a specialized USB-to-serial adapter/cable, we can create the same connection using a standard regular-to-micro USB cable. I can carry around the Pi Zero and a cable in my backpack, and any time I need a Linux terminal, I just need a machine with a keyboard and a screen to plug into.

Getting ready

All you need to do to be set up here is perform the USB OTG previous functions recipe. After making the change, you can connect your Pi to any computer from the micro-USB connection. For most desktops, you won't even need additional power to run the Pi; it will all work over the one connection.

How to do it...

This is the most finicky file you will have to edit. Be very careful not to make any mistakes, as it will probably stop your Zero from starting until you fix it (fortunately, you made a backup copy earlier, right?):

1. The unedited version of the file should look something like this:

```
pi@rpz14101:~$ sudo cat /boot/cmdline.txt
dwc_otg.lpm_enable=0 console=serial0,115200
console=tty1 root=/dev/mmcblk0p2 rootfstype=ext4
elevator=deadline fsck.repair=yes rootwait
```

2. We're going to add one piece after `rootwait` to make the Pi ready for serial connections over USB:

```
pi@rpz14101:~$ sudo cat /boot/cmdline.txt
dwc_otg.lpm_enable=0 console=serial0,115200
console=tty1 root=/dev/mmcblk0p2 rootfstype=ext4
elevator=deadline fsck.repair=yes rootwait
modules-
load=dwc2,g_serial
```

3. Finally, you will enable the configuration service for the port in order to allow serial communication:

```
pi@rpz14101:~ $ sudo systemctl enable
getty@ttyGS0.service
Created symlink from
/etc/systemd/system/getty.target.wants/
getty@ttyGS0.service to
/lib/systemd/system/getty@.service.
```

4. After this, unplug your Raspberry Pi Zero, and reconnect it to a computer with a USB-to-micro cable. Connect using the USB power, not the power port. If you use a powered USB port on your computer, you shouldn't need to add additional power either. Once the Zero has a chance to boot up, you should see the following come up in Device Manager on a Windows system:

5. On Linux or Max OS X, you should be able to find a new device just like you found the real serial device in the first recipe of this chapter. With PuTTY, you'll use the same serial connection, but with the COM port specified for Pi USB to serial, like this:

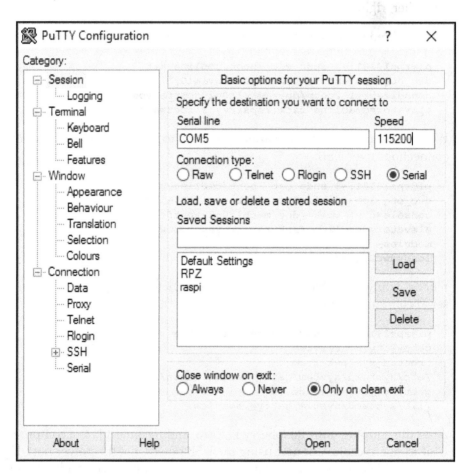

6. Clicking on **Open** should get you to your familiar Raspberry Pi Zero terminal window:

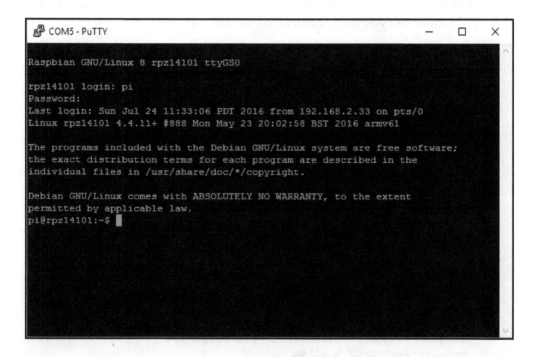

```
Raspbian GNU/Linux 8 rpz14101 ttyGS0

rpz14101 login: pi
Password:
Last login: Sun Jul 24 11:33:06 PDT 2016 from 192.168.2.33 on pts/0
Linux rpz14101 4.4.11+ #888 Mon May 23 20:02:58 BST 2016 armv6l

The programs included with the Debian GNU/Linux system are free software;
the exact distribution terms for each program are described in the
individual files in /usr/share/doc/*/copyright.

Debian GNU/Linux comes with ABSOLUTELY NO WARRANTY, to the extent
permitted by applicable law.
pi@rpz14101:~$
```

Programming over a virtual Ethernet modem on USB OTG

This is my favorite way to connect to the Raspberry Pi Zero. Not only can you operate it with a single USB cable, but you can get it attached to the network and be able to communicate with other machines and the Internet.

Getting ready

The same as the last recipe, if you have the USB OTG functions installed and a regular-to-micro USB cable, you are ready to go.

How to do it...

Just like the last recipe, be careful with the edits to cmdline.txt. You can make this change from the serial connection you made before, reboot, and go!

1. The unedited version of the file should look something like this:

```
pi@rpz14101:~$ sudo cat /boot/cmdline.txt
dwc_otg.lpm_enable=0 console=serial0,115200
console=tty1 root=/dev/mmcblk0p2 rootfstype=ext4
elevator=deadline fsck.repair=yes rootwait
```

If you're coming from the previous recipe, it will look like this:

```
pi@rpz14101:~$ sudo cat /boot/cmdline.txt
dwc_otg.lpm_enable=0 console=serial0,115200
console=tty1 root=/dev/mmcblk0p2 rootfstype=ext4
elevator=deadline fsck.repair=yes rootwait
modules-load=dwc2,g_serial
```

2. We want our new configuration to look like this:

```
pi@rpz14101:~$ sudo cat /boot/cmdline.txt
dwc_otg.lpm_enable=0 console=serial0,115200
console=tty1 root=/dev/mmcblk0p2 rootfstype=ext4
elevator=deadline fsck.repair=yes rootwait
modules-load=dwc2,g_ether
```

3. After you make the change, you can use sudo reboot. You'll see the COM device disappear from the device manager and should see a new device come up in the **Network Adapters** tree:

4. Now, you can connect your Raspberry Pi through your USB cable using SSH:

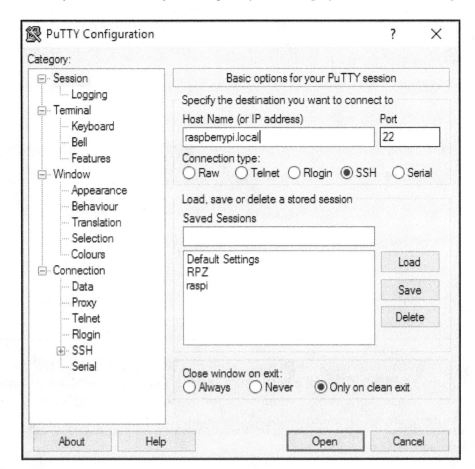

If the Bonjour service is running on Windows (or `avanti-daemon` on Linux), you should be able to SSH to `raspberrypi.local`.

The default hostname for the Raspberry Pi is `raspberrypi`. If you changed the name of your Zero in `raspi-config` or using the `hostname` command, the connection will be `hostname.local`. For instance, if I change my Raspberry Pi Zero's name to `rpz14101`, then I will SSH to `rpz14101.local`.

Another great thing about using SSH to connect the Raspberry Pi Zero is if you configure your host machine's network adapter to allow Internet sharing, your Zero can communicate with the Internet! On Windows, go to **Network connections** in **Control Panel,** select the adapter that's connected to your home network, and enable **Internet Connection Sharing**. Here's where you can find the option in Windows:

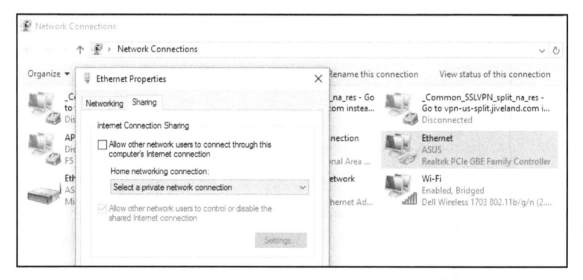

On OS X go to System Preferences -> Sharing -> Internet Sharing and Choose the "RNDIS/Ethernet Gadget." Check the box to start sharing. On Linux machines, it varies by distro and version, check the docs or community forums for Internet Connection Sharing.

With this setting, your Pi Zero can use your host computer's adapter to talk to other devices on the home network or over the Internet.

Making your RPZ a USB mass storage device

This last hack makes it possible to use your Raspberry Pi Zero as a mass storage device. While at first it doesn't seem like much more than turning it into a flash drive, depending on what you are doing, and what else you are doing with your Raspberry Pi Zero, you can make your Raspberry Pi Zero be recognized as a USB flash drive to other computers.

Getting ready

Since we will be using the USB connection for a mass storage device, we should connect to the Raspberry Pi Zero using the USB-to-serial adapter and the GPIO pins, as shown in the first recipe of this chapter. You can make your modifications here, connect your USB and Raspberry Pi together, reboot, and work with the Pi as a flash drive or as the little computer you're used to.

How to do it...

1. We're going to add one piece after `rootwait` to make the Pi enabled for USB mass storage. You've seen this in the previous recipes:

   ```
   pi@rpz14101:~$ sudo cat /boot/cmdline.txt
   dwc_otg.lpm_enable=0 console=serial0,115200
   console=tty1 root=/dev/mmcblk0p2 rootfstype=ext4
   elevator=deadline fsck.repair=yes rootwait
   modules-load=dwc2,g_mass_storage
   ```

   This change should be pretty familiar, but to finish setting up your Zero as a storage device, you need to create a space that acts as storage. Most USB flash drives are formatted using FAT32, one of the more common formatting standards available.

2. Let's make a mini "filesystem" for our Zero flash drive:

   ```
   sudo dd if=/dev/zero of=/opt/cookbook.share bs=1M1
   count=512
   ```

3. Then, we will format this into a FAT32 system with the `mkfs.fat` command:

   ```
   sudo mkfs.fat /opt/cookbook.share
   ```

4. Set permissions:

   ```
   sudo chwon 755 /opt/cookbook.share
   ```

5. Finally, reboot and connect your USB cable:

   ```
   sudo reboot
   ```

6. At first your computer will probably not recognize your Pi as a mass storage device. Reconnect over your serial connection and log in. After login, activate the device with this:

```
sudo modprobe g_mass_storage
file=/opt/cookbook.share stall=0
```

7. On a Windows machine, you will probably see drivers loading, and then you will see a new icon under USB devices:

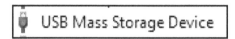

8. From, here, looking at disk management, we will see we have a new, initialized volume:

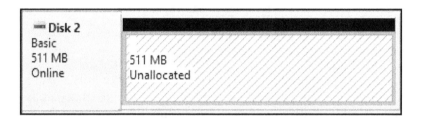

9. From here, it is all yours: format a new simple volume, name it, give it a drive letter, and it will be ready to go! Back on the Raspberry Pi, you can see the initialization of the USB driver in the logs:

```
pi@rpz14101:~$ dmesg | tail -n 20
[   14.017876] i2c /dev entries driver
[   15.469264] bcm2835-wdt 20100000.watchdog:
Broadcom BCM2835 watchdog timer
[   15.541326] gpiomem-bcm2835 20200000.gpiomem:
Initialised: Registers at 0x20200000
[   15.761343] EXT4-fs (mmcblk0p2): re-mounted.        Opts:
(null)
[   18.711165] systemd-journald[105]: Received
request to flush runtime journal from PID 1
[   20.907976] Installing knfsd (copyright (C)
1996 okir@monad.swb.de).
[   21.160769] Adding 102396k swap on /var/swap.
Priority:-1 extents:1 across:102396k SSFS
[   80.621706] random: nonblocking pool is
initialized
[ 1605.922774] Mass Storage Function, version:
```

```
2009/09/11
[ 1605.922809] LUN: removable file: (no medium)
[ 1605.922989] LUN: file: /opt/cookbook.share
[ 1605.923005] Number of LUNs=1
[ 1605.923520] g_mass_storage gadget: Mass Storage
Gadget, version: 2009/09/11
[ 1605.923548] g_mass_storage gadget: userspace
failed to provide iSerialNumber
[ 1605.923562] g_mass_storage gadget:
g_mass_storage ready
[ 1605.923607] dwc2 20980000.usb:
dwc2_hsotg_enqueue_setup: failed queue (-11)
[ 1605.926714] dwc2 20980000.usb: bound driver
g_mass_storage
[ 1606.099808] dwc2 20980000.usb: new device is
high-speed
[ 1606.115562] dwc2 20980000.usb: new address 12
[ 1606.147599] g_mass_storage gadget: high-speed
config #1: Linux File-Backed Storage
```

There's more...

Let's say you don't want to pick between virtual serial or virtual Ethernet, but want both! For this, there is an OTG option called g_multi. There is quite a long list of options you can use to make your Raspberry Pi Zero act like a variety of USB devices: a webcam, a printer, or even a MIDI device!

You'll inevitably run into situations where things don't work exactly as described. There are a few ways to tackle this. First, check the Raspberry Pi forums and search for the problems you are experiencing: it is likely that you aren't the only one. The Raspberry Pi community is active in helping other users figure things out. Another approach is to start clean. If you have an extra SD card, put a fresh copy of Raspbian on it and try your hack again. It's possible that all of the prior changes and updates are causing a conflict in some way. If you have your Samba share set up, it is easy enough to copy anything you might want to keep on your current SD card before starting fresh.

3
Programming with Linux

Now that we have our operating system installed and our Raspberry Pi Zero on our home network, we can dive into some basic Linux commands. You will find knowing these commands useful any time you are working on a Linux machine. In this chapter, we'll start prepping with some Linux recipes:

- Navigating a filesystem and viewing and searching the contents of a directory
- Creating a new file, editing it in an editor, and changing ownership
- Renaming and copying/moving the file/folder into a new directory
- Installing and uninstalling a program
- Downloading a file from the Internet and deleting a file
- Changing to root and using superpowers
- Extracting a zipped file and zipping it back
- Searching executed code from the terminal's history
- Changing RPZ configuration settings from the command line
- Checking running processes and killing a process running in the background
- Creating our first shell program and automating a process
- Syncing with NTC servers to update the current time
- Running a background process in Linux
- Setting a file to run automatically on startup
- Using crontab to run a script automatically at predefined intervals

Navigating a filesystem and viewing and searching the contents of a directory

If you aren't already a Linux or Mac user, getting around the filesystem can seem pretty alien at first. Truly, if you've only used Windows Explorer, this is going to seem like a strange, alien process. Once you start getting the hang of things, though, you'll find that getting around the Linux filesystem is easy and fun.

Getting ready

The only thing you need to get started is a client connection to your Raspberry Pi Zero. I like to use SSH, but you can certainly connect using the serial connection or a terminal in X Windows.

How to do it...

1. If you want to find out where you are in the filesystem, use `pwd`:

    ```
    pi@rpz14101:~$ pwd
    /home/pi
    ```

    This tells me I'm in the `/home/pi` directory, which is the default home directory for the pi user. Generally, every user you create should get a `/home/username` directory to keep their own files in. This can be done automatically with user creation and the `adduser` command.

2. To look at the contents of the directory you are in, use the `ls` command:

    ```
    pi@rpz14101:~$ ls
    Desktop    Downloads  Pictures  python_games  share      Videos
    Documents  Music      Public    Scratch       Templates
    ```

3. To look in another directory, simply specify the directory you want to list (you may need to use `sudo` depending on where you are looking):

```
pi@rpz14101:~$ sudo ls /opt/
cookbook.share  pigpio  sonic-pi            vc
minecraft-pi    share   testsudo.deleteme   Wolfram
```

4. This is a nice quick summary of what files are in the directory, but you will usually want a little more information about the files and directories. The `ls` command has a ton of options, all of which can be displayed with `ls -help` and explained in more detail with `man ls`. Some of the best ones to know are as follows:

   - `-a` show all files (regular and hidden)
   - `-l` show long format (more file information, in columns)
   - `-h` human readable (turns bytes into MB or GB as appropriate)
   - `-t` or `-tr` order in time order, or reverse time order

5. My typical command when I start looking in a directory is this one:

   `ls -ltrh`

6. This produces all non-hidden files, with human-readable sizes, in column format, and the newest file at the bottom:

```
pi@rpz14101:~$ ls -ltrh /opt/
total 513M
drwxr-xr-x 7 root root 4.0K May 27 04:11 vc
drwxr-xr-x 3 root root 4.0K May 27 04:32 Wolfram
drwxr-xr-x 3 root root 4.0K May 27 04:34 pigpio
drwxr-xr-x 4 root root 4.0K May 27 04:36 minecraft-pi
drwxr-xr-x 5 root root 4.0K May 27 04:36 sonic-pi
-rw-r--r-- 1 root root    0 Jul  4 13:41 testsudo.deleteme
drwxr-xr-x 2 root root 4.0K Jul  9 13:05 share
-rwxr-xr-x 1 root root 512M Jul 24 17:53 cookbook.share
```

7. One last trick: if you need this format but there are a lot of files in the directory you are searching, you will see a ton of text scroll by. Maybe you just need the most recent or largest files? We can do this with a pipe (`|`) and the `tail` command. Let's take a directory with a lot of files, such as `/usr/lib/`. To list the five most recently modified files, I can pipe `ls -ltrh` to the `tail` command:

```
pi@rpz14101:~$ ls -ltrh /usr/lib/ | tail -5
lrwxrwxrwx  1 root root   22 May 27 04:40
```

```
libwiringPiDev.so -> libwiringPiDev.so.2.32
drwxr-xr-x  2 root root 4.0K Jun  5 10:38 samba
drwxr-xr-x  3 root root 4.0K Jul  4 22:48 pppd
drwxr-xr-x 65 root root  60K Jul 24 15:48 arm-linux-
gnueabihf
drwxr-xr-x  2 root root 4.0K Jul 24 15:48 tmpfiles.d
```

8. What about the five largest files? Instead of the t in -ltrh, I can use S:

```
pi@rpz14101:~$ ls -lSrh /usr/lib/ | tail -5
-rw-r--r--  1 root root 2.8M Sep 17  2014 libmozjs185.so.1.0.0
-rw-r--r--  1 root root 2.8M Sep 30  2014 libqscintilla2.so.11.3.0
-rw-r--r--  1 root root 2.9M Jun  5  2014 libcmis-0.4.so.4.0.1
-rw-r--r--  1 root root 3.4M Jun 12  2015 libv8.so.3.14.5
-rw-r--r--  1 root root 5.1M Aug 18  2014 libmwaw-0.3.so.3.0.1
```

9. A little creative piping and you can find exactly the file you are looking for. If not, another great tool for exploring the filesystem is tree. This gives a pseudo-graphical tree that shows how the files are structured in the system. It produces a lot of text, especially if you have it print an entire directory tree. If just looking into directory structures, you can use tree with the -d flag for directories only. The -L flag will reduce how deep you dive into nested directories:

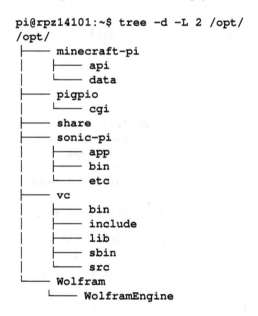

```
pi@rpz14101:~$ tree -d -L 2 /opt/
/opt/
├── minecraft-pi
│   ├── api
│   └── data
├── pigpio
│   └── cgi
├── share
├── sonic-pi
│   ├── app
│   ├── bin
│   └── etc
├── vc
│   ├── bin
│   ├── include
│   ├── lib
│   ├── sbin
│   └── src
└── Wolfram
    └── WolframEngine
```

10. Last, we will look at a couple of searching utilities, `find` and `grep`. The `find` command is a powerful function that finds files in whatever directories you specify. It is great for trying to find that mystery piece of software that installed itself in an odd place or the needle-in-a-haystack file in a directory that contains hundreds of files. For example, if I were to run `tree` in the `/opt/sonic-pi/` directory, it would run on for several seconds, and thousands of files would shoot by. I, however, am only interested in finding files with `cowbell` in the name. I can use the `find` command to look for it:

```
pi@rpz14101:~$ find /opt/sonic-pi/ -name *cowbell*
/opt/sonic-pi/etc/samples/drum_cowbell.flac
```

When looking for anything with `cowbell` in the filename, the `find` command returns the exactly location of anything that matches. There are tons of options for using the `find` command; start with `find -help`, and then try `man find` when you want to get really deep.

11. The `grep` command can be used in a couple different ways when searching for files, and it is one of those commands you will find yourself using constantly while both loving and hating its awesome power. Let's say you need to find something *inside* of a file –`grep` is the tool for you. It can also find things like `find` can, but generally, `find` is more efficient at finding filename patterns than `grep` is.

12. If I use `grep` to look for cowbells in my `sonic-pi` directory, I'll get a different, and more colorful, output. Running `grep -r -i cowbell /opt/sonic-pi/*` will return something similar to the screenshot below

```
pi@rpz14101:~$ grep -r -i cowbell /opt/sonic-pi/*
/opt/sonic-pi/app/server/sonicpi/lib/sonicpi/synths/synthinfo.rb:                    :drum_cowbell,
Binary file /opt/sonic-pi/app/server/native/raspberry/extra-ugens-jessie/StkUGens.so matches
Binary file /opt/sonic-pi/app/server/native/raspberry/extra-ugens-wheezy/StkUGens.so matches
Binary file /opt/sonic-pi/app/gui/qt/qrc_info_files.o matches
/opt/sonic-pi/app/gui/qt/help/samples_item_454.html:sample <span class="symbol">:drum_cowbell</span>
Binary file /opt/sonic-pi/app/gui/qt/sonic-pi matches
/opt/sonic-pi/app/gui/qt/book/Sonic Pi - Samples.html:sample <span class="symbol">:drum_cowbell</span>
/opt/sonic-pi/app/gui/qt/info/CHANGELOG.html:    <li><a href="#v2.10">v2.10 'Cowbell'</a>, 15th April, 2016</li>
/opt/sonic-pi/app/gui/qt/info/CHANGELOG.html:<h2 id="version-210---cowbell">Version 2.10 - 'Cowbell'</h2>
/opt/sonic-pi/app/gui/qt/info/CHANGELOG.html:<p><em>"I gotta have more cowbell!"</em> - The Bruce Dickinson</p>
/opt/sonic-pi/app/gui/qt/info/CHANGELOG.html:including a full tabla set and a cowbell.</p>
/opt/sonic-pi/app/gui/qt/info/CHANGELOG.html:    <li>Add new samples: <code>:drum_cowbell</code>, <code>:drum_ro
ll</code>, <code>:misc_cros</code>,
/opt/sonic-pi/etc/samples/README.md:* `:drum_cowbell` - http://freesound.org/people/Neotone/sounds/75338/
```

Wrapping your search string in double quotes is a good practice to stick to in the long run. In this case, we would use `grep -r -i "cowbell" /opt/sonic-pi/*`. When moving into more complex regular expressions, and strings that use special characters, the double-quotes will help a lot.

We don't see the file with `cowbell` in the name like we did using `find`, but we find every file that contains `cowbell` inside of it. The `-r` flag tells `grep` to delve into subdirectories, and `-i` tells it to ignore cases with `cowbells` (so `Cowbell` and `cowbell` are both found, as shown in the screenshot).

13. As you use Linux more often, both `find` and `grep` become regularly used tools for administration and file management. This won't be the last time you use them!

Creating a new file, editing it in an editor, and changing ownership

There are a lot of different text editors to use on a Linux system from the command line. The program vi is the Ubuntu default, and the program you will find installed on pretty much any Linux system. Emacs is another popular editor, and lots of Linux users get quite passionate about which one is better. My preference is vim, which is generally known as vi improved. The `nano` text editor is another one that is commonly installed on Linux distros, and it is one of the most lightweight editors available.

Getting ready

For this recipe, we will work with vi, since that's definitely going to be installed on your system. If you want to try out vim, you can install it using this:

```
sudo apt-get install vim
```

How to do it...

1. First we will go to our share directory:

```
cd /home/pi/share
```

2. Then, we will create an empty file using the `touch` command:

   touch ch3_touchfile.txt

   > If you use the `ls` command from the previous directory, you can see that the size of the file is 0. You can also display the contents of the file with the `cat` command, which will return nothing in this case. The `touch` command is a great way to test whether you have permissions to create files in a specific directory.

3. You can also create a new file with the editor itself:

   vi ch3_vifile.txt

   > This will open the vi editor with a blank file named `ch3_vifile.txt`:

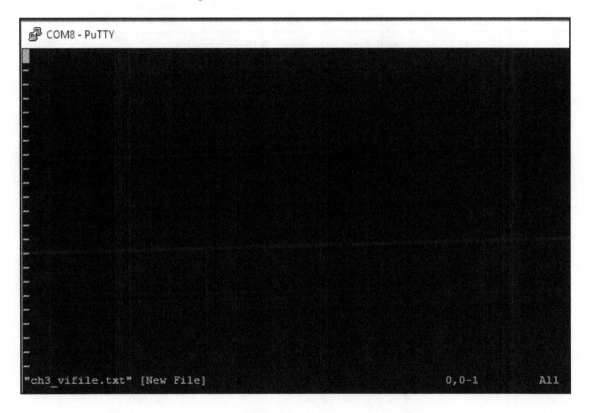

Using vi or vim (or Emacs) for the first time is completely different from using something like OpenOffice or Microsoft Word. Vi works in two modes: insert (or edit) and command. Once you learn how to use command mode, vi becomes a very efficient editor for working on scripts in Bash or Python. Edit mode, more or less, is the mode where you can type and edit text like a regular WYSIWYG editor. The reason behind this was that vi was originally only a file viewer, it was later on that editing capabilities were added to the program. There are books written on becoming a power user of vi, well beyond the scope of this book. The table below is a good list of basic commands you'll want to be familiar with:

Command	Function
I	Insert into edit mode – switches to edit mode at the cursor location, to insert text.
a	Append into edit mode – switches to edit mode after the cursor location, to append text
ESC	Exit insert mode switch back to View Mode
o	Create a line below the cursor and switch to edit mode
O	Create a line above the cursor and switch to edit mode
dd	Remove line and put in buffer
yy	Copy line and put in buffer
p	Paste buffer line to line below cursor
:w	Write / save file
:wq	Save file and quit
:q!	Quit without saving
G	Go to end of file
1G	Go to first line of file
/	Search for string
:help	Open help file

Getting a handle on the basics is the best place to start:

1. With the empty file, you can jump into edit mode by pressing the i or a keys. The editor will switch to insert mode, as shown by the — **INSERT** — in the bottom left of the screen. Then you can you start typing in your text:

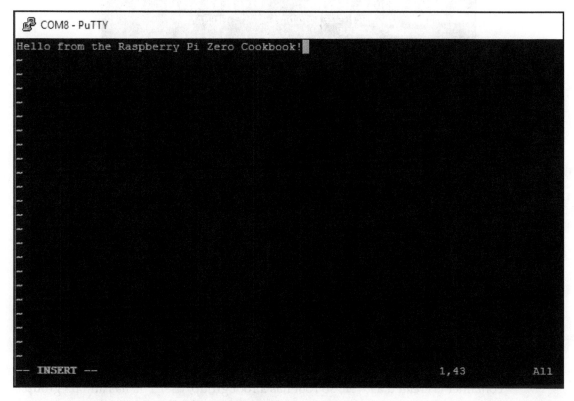

2. To get out of insert mode, press the *Esc* key. The :w command will save the file, and the :q command will quit. You can combine them, so :wq saves the file and quits. You can verify that the contents were saved with the cat command:

```
pi@rpz14101:~$ cat ch3_vifile.txt
Hello from the Raspberry Pi Zero Cookbook!
```

Let's take another look at the `ls` command and some of the information the `-l` format includes. We will take a look at the files we've created so far in this recipe. If we execute ls – ltrh *.txt in the ch3 directory, we will see output similar to below:

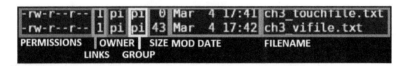

Understanding the output of ls

The table below describes the output from the image

Column	Example Output	Meaning
Permissions	-rw-r-r-	The read / write / execute permissions for the file for `usergroupworld`.
Links	1	The number links associated to the file
Owner	pi	The user that owns the file
Group	pi	The group that owns the file
Size	43	The size of the file, in bytes
Mod Date	Mar 4 17:41	The timestamp when the file was last modified
Filename	ch3_vifile.txt	The name of the file.

3. We can see that since we made the files as the `pi` user, the owner of the file and the group owner are `pi`. By default, when a new user is created, a group container is created as well, so root has a root group, user `rpz` has an `rpz` group, and so on. We can change the ownership settings of a file with the `chown` command. Be careful, since you can take away your own access, though you can always `sudo` your way back. The `chmod` command will change who is allowed to do what with a file. Let's look at ownership changes and what impact they will have with a few examples:

```
pi@rpz14101:~ $ ls -ltrh *.txt
-rw-r--r-- 1 pi pi  0 Jul 25 13:28 ch3_touchfile.txt
-rw-r--r-- 1 pi pi 43 Jul 25 13:28 ch3_vifile.txt
pi@rpz14101:~ $ cat ch3_vifile.txt
Hello from the Raspberry Pi Zero Cookbook!
pi@rpz14101:~ $ sudo chown root:root ch3_vifile.txt
pi@rpz14101:~ $ cat ch3_vifile.txt
```

```
cat: ch3_vifile.txt: Permission denied
pi@rpz14101:~ $ sudo cat ch3_vifile.txt
Hello from the Raspberry Pi Zero Cookbook!
pi@rpz14101:~ $ sudo chown rpz:pi ch3_vifile.txt
pi@rpz14101:~ $ cat ch3_vifile.txt
cat: ch3_vifile.txt: Permission denied
pi@rpz14101:~ $ sudo chmod 750 ch3_vifile.txt
pi@rpz14101:~ $ cat ch3_vifile.txt
Hello from the Raspberry Pi Zero Cookbook!
pi@rpz14101:~ $ sudo chown root:root ch3_vifile.txt
pi@rpz14101:~ $ cat ch3_vifile.txt
cat: ch3_vifile.txt: Permission denied
pi@rpz14101:~ $ sudo chmod 755 ch3_vifile.txt
pi@rpz14101:~ $ cat ch3_vifile.txt
Hello from the Raspberry Pi Zero Cookbook!
```

The chmod values are documented very well, and with a little practice, you can get your file permissions and ownership set up in a way that is both secure and easy to work with.

Renaming and copying/moving the file/folder into a new directory

A common activity on any filesystem is the practice of copying and moving files, and even directories, from one place to another. You might do it to make a backup copy of something, or you might decide that the contents should live in a more appropriate location. This recipe will explore how to manipulate files in the Raspbian system.

Getting ready

If you are still in your terminal from the last recipe, we are going to use the same files from the previous recipe. We should have the ownership back to pi:pi; if not, run the following:

```
sudo chown pi:pi /home/pi/share/*.txt
```

 If you are in a directory and want to operate on a file, you can reference just the file or use "./" to indicate the current directory. In this recipe, we will refer to the full path that we want to operate on. If you are already in the /home/pi directory (also designated by "~/" you can alternatively run this command without the path, as in: sudo chown pi:pi ./share/*.txt or sudo chown pi:pi ~/share/*.txt

How to do it...

1. First, let's make a new directory. We'll put it under the /home/pi/share/ folder so it is accessible to other computers on your home network. To make a directory, use the mkdir command:

    ```
    pi@rpz14101:~$ mkdir /home/pi/share/ch3
    ```

2. We can look at the new directory with the ls command:

    ```
    pi@rpz14101:~$ ls -ltrh /home/pi/share/
    total 4.0K
    -rw-r--r-- 1 pi pi    0 Jul 24 15:56 helloNetwork.yes
    drwxr-xr-x 2 pi pi 4.0K Jul 25 13:06 ch3
    ```

3. A great flag to go with the mkdir command is -p. This will allow you to create directories and subdirectories in one command. Without it, if I try to create a subdirectory that doesn't already exist, I'll get an error:

    ```
    pi@rpz14101:~$ mkdir /home/pi/share/ch3/nested/folders
    mkdir: cannot create directory
    '/home/pi/share/ch3/nested/folders': No such file or
    directory
    ```

4. With the -p flag, it works without a problem:

    ```
    pi@rpz14101:~$ mkdir -p /home/pi/share/ch3/nested/folders
    ```

5. The tree command shows the structure of our ch3 directory:

    ```
    pi@rpz14101:~$ tree /home/pi/share
    /home/pi/share
    ├── ch3
    │   └── nested
    │       └── folders
    └── helloNetwork.yes
    3 directories, 1 file
    ```

6. Now, let's move our files to our new ch3 directory. The copy and move commands - cp and mv, respectively – are the tools we will use. Copying a file from one place to another is as simple as indicating the file's source and destination. The following command will make a copy of vifile.txt and save it as vifile.txt.copy in the /home/pi/share/ch3/ directory:

```
cp /home/pi/share/ch3_vifile.txt
/home/pi/share/ch3/ch3_vifile.txt.copy
```

> We can copy files as well as directories and their contents as long as you have enough disk space.

7. To move or rename a file, we use the mv command. This takes the file given in the source and moves it to the destination provided. As simple as the cp command, let's move all of our files to the share directory:

```
mv /home/pi/share/ch3_vifile.txt
/home/pi/share/ch3/ch3_vifile.txt.moved
mv /home/pi/share/ch3_touchfile.txt
/home/pi/share/ch3/ch3_touchfile.txt
```

8. If we look at the tree of our share directory, we will see everything nicely organized:

```
pi@rpz14101:~$ tree /home/pi/share/
/home/pi/share/
├── ch3
│   ├── ch3_touchfile.txt
│   ├── ch3_vifile.txt.copy
│   ├── ch3_vifile.txt.moved
│   └── nested
│       └── folders
└── helloNetwork.yes
3 directories, 4 files
```

Installing and uninstalling a program

We've installed a few programs throughout the book so far, but have yet to delve into the apt-get command and the family of software-installation utilities. Now, we will learn how to install and uninstall any program available for Raspbian as well as how to search for new software and run updates.

Getting ready

Stay in your terminal window, and get ready to install some applications!

How to do it...

1. The `apt-*` commands are a suite of utilities that allow you to do various things with installed packages. To install a package, we use the `apt-get` tool, and the `install` command, like this:

   ```
   sudo apt-get install <packagename>
   ```

2. Let's install something cool – how about a Matrix screensaver? It is super easy and works great from the command line. To look for a package, we use the `apt-cache search` command. `apt-cache` is another tool in the `apt-*` family of utilities, and it checks the software database for matches.

3. Running `sudo apt-cache search matrix` results tons of results! The word "matrix" is a little too popular for us computer and math nerds – we have matrixes everywhere! It would take forever to go through that list to find what we are looking for. Fortunately, we can take advantage of `grep`, which we touched on in an earlier recipe, to narrow down our results. One of the fun things about using Linux and the command line is the ways you can chain commands to do cool things:

   ```
   pi@rpz14101:~ $ sudo apt-cache search matrix | grep "The Matrix"
   cmatrix - simulates the display from "The Matrix"
   wmmatrix - View The Matrix in a Window Maker dock application
   ```

4. That's a bit more manageable! We could also have narrowed the list using this command:

   ```
   sudo apt-cache search "The Matrix"
   ```

5. This returns fewer results than before, but a few more than the `grep` command. Whichever way you find it, we see that the `cmatrix` package is the one we are looking for. Installing is as simple as running this:

   ```
   pi@rpz14101:~ $ `
   Reading package lists... Done
   Building dependency tree
   Reading state information... Done
   Suggested packages:
     cmatrix-xfont
   The following NEW packages will be installed:
     cmatrix
   0 upgraded, 1 newly installed, 0 to remove and 0 not
   upgraded.
   ```

```
Need to get 16.2 kB of archives.
After this operation, 27.6 kB of additional disk space
will be used.
Get:1 http://mirrordirector.raspbian.org/raspbian/
jessie/main cmatrix armhf 1.2a-5 [16.2 kB]
Fetched 16.2 kB in 1s (15.3 kB/s)
Selecting previously unselected package cmatrix.
(Reading database ... 121906 files and directories
currently installed.)
Preparing to unpack .../cmatrix_1.2a-5_armhf.deb ...
Unpacking cmatrix (1.2a-5) ...
Processing triggers for man-db (2.7.0.2-5) ...
Setting up cmatrix (1.2a-5) ...
```

6. After that, we are ready to go! Channel your inner Neo and run this command:

   ```
   cmatrix -s -b
   ```

7. You should be in the Matrix!

8. Try it on your serial and SSH connections, and even in the terminal on VNC: you'll notice differences in the rendering behavior.

> There are literally thousands of software packages available to install in the repositories of our awesome open source communities. Pretty much anything you think a computer should be able to do, someone, or a group of people, has worked on a solution and pushed it out to the repositories. We will be using `apt-get` a lot throughout this cookbook; it is one of the commands you'll find yourself using all the time as you get more interested in Raspberry Pis and the Linux operating system.
>
> Running `sudo apt-get update` will check all repositories to see whether there are any version updates available. Here, you can see all of the locations it checks to see whether there is anything new for Raspbian:

```
pi@rpz14101:~ $ sudo apt-get update
Get:1 http://archive.raspberrypi.org jessie InRelease
[13.2 kB]
Get:2 http://mirrordirector.raspbian.org jessie
InRelease [14.9 kB]
Get:3 http://archive.raspberrypi.org jessie/main armhf
Packages [144 kB]
Get:4 http://mirrordirector.raspbian.org jessie/main
armhf Packages [8,981 kB]
Hit http://archive.raspberrypi.org jessie/ui armhf
Packages
Ign http://archive.raspberrypi.org jessie/main
Translation-en_GB
Get:5 http://mirrordirector.raspbian.org
jessie/contrib armhf Packages [37.5 kB]
Ign http://archive.raspberrypi.org jessie/main
Translation-en
Get:6 http://mirrordirector.raspbian.org jessie/non-
free armhf Packages [70.3 kB]
Ign http://archive.raspberrypi.org jessie/ui
Translation-en_GB
Ign http://archive.raspberrypi.org jessie/ui
Translation-en
Get:7 http://mirrordirector.raspbian.org jessie/rpi
armhf Packages [1,356 B]
Ign http://mirrordirector.raspbian.org jessie/contrib Translation-en_GB
Ign http://mirrordirector.raspbian.org jessie/contrib Translation-en
Ign http://mirrordirector.raspbian.org jessie/main Translation-en_GB
Ign http://mirrordirector.raspbian.org jessie/main Translation-en
Ign http://mirrordirector.raspbian.org jessie/non-free
```

```
Translation-en_GB
Ign http://mirrordirector.raspbian.org jessie/non-free Translation-en
Ign http://mirrordirector.raspbian.org jessie/rpi
Translation-en_GB
Ign http://mirrordirector.raspbian.org jessie/rpi Translation-en
Fetched 9,263 kB in 34s (272 kB/s)
Reading package lists... Done
```

 The Raspberry Pi Zero is focused on affordability and size. One of the things it lacks is a lot of speed. Even with a new Raspbian Download, the update command can take quite a while (30 minutes or more). Once you start the command, it is a perfect time to stretch, get some coffee, or hack away at other things.

9. After updating, `apt-get upgrade` will look at the versions of everything you have installed and upgrade anything to the latest version if there is one available. Depending on how many updates you have, this can take quite a while:

```
pi@rpz14101:~ $ sudo apt-get upgrade
Reading package lists... Done
Building dependency tree
Reading state information... Done
Calculating upgrade... Done
The following packages will be upgraded:
dpkg-dev gir1.2-gdkpixbuf-2.0 initramfs-tools
libavcodec56 libavformat56 libavresample2
libavutil54 libdevmapper-event1.02.1
libdevmapper1.02.1 libdpkg-perl
python-picamera python3-picamera raspberrypi-kernel
raspberrypi-net-mods ssh tzdata xarchiver
40 upgraded, 0 newly installed, 0 to remove and 0 not
upgraded.
Need to get 57.0 MB of archives.
After this operation, 415 kB of additional disk space
will be used.
Do you want to continue? [Y/n] y
Get:1 http://archive.raspberrypi.org/debian/
jessie/main nodered armhf 0.14.5 [5,578 kB]
...
Adding 'diversion of /boot/overlays/w1-gpio.dtbo to
/usr/share/rpikernelhack/overlays/w1-gpio.dtbo by
rpikernelhack'
...
run-parts: executing /etc/kernel/postrm.d/initramfs-
tools 4.4.11-v7+ /boot/kernel7.img
Preparing to unpack .../raspberrypi-net-
mods_1.2.3_armhf.deb ...
```

```
Unpacking raspberrypi-net-mods (1.2.3) over (1.2.2) ...
Processing triggers for man-db (2.7.0.2-5) ...
...
Setting up libssl1.0.0:armhf (1.0.1t-1+deb8u2) ...
Setting up libxml2:armhf (2.9.1+dfsg1-5+deb8u2) ...
...
Removing 'diversion of /boot/overlays/w1-gpio-pullup.dtbo to
/usr/share/rpikernelhack/overlays/w1-gpio-pullup.dtbo by rpikernelhack'
...
Setting up raspberrypi-net-mods (1.2.3) ...
Modified /etc/network/interfaces detected. Leaving
unchanged and writing new file as interfaces.new.
Processing triggers for libc-bin (2.19-18+deb8u4) ...
Processing triggers for initramfs-tools (0.120+deb8u2) ...
```

You don't really have to understand the details of what's going on during the upgrade, and it will let you know if there were any problems at the end (and often what to do to fix them). Regularly updating and upgrading will keep all of your software current with all of the latest bug fixes and security patches.

There's more...

1. You can also add and remove software from the GUI. If you log on to your Pi, either directly to a monitor or over VNC Server (a recipe we covered earlier), you can find the **Add / Remove Software** option under **Menu** | **Preferences**:

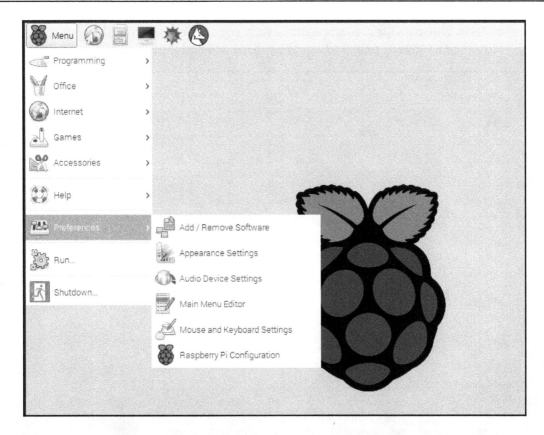

The `PiPackages` utility makes it very easy to find software when you only have a general idea of what you are looking for. While you can do the same things with the `apt` commands, if you are browsing, this is a little easier on the eyes.

2. The utility provides categorizations so you don't have to scroll through every package. Clicking on a package provides a detailed description:

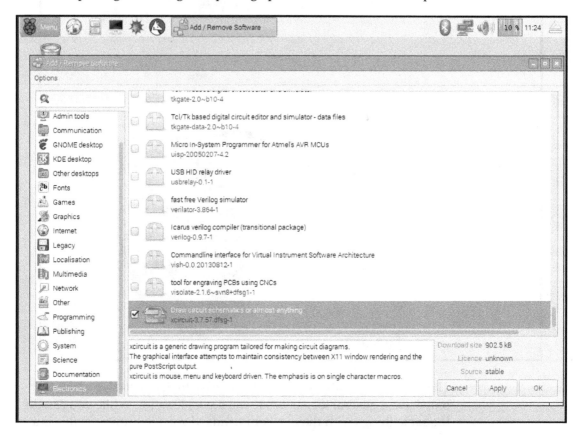

3. Simply check the box and click on **Apply** or **OK**, and the software will be installed. Now you can install software on your Raspberry Pi Zero from the command line or GUI.

Downloading a file from the Internet and deleting a file

Most computer users have downloaded files using their favorite browser: sometimes, pictures, video, or music, and other times, other applications and setup programs. In Linux, this is certainly possible from a browser in the GUI, but there are ways to download files using the command line too!

As useful a feature this is, it is easy to download a lot until you've run out of space to store your files. We will also cover the commands to help you clean things up. What could be more fun that learning a command that can wipe out your entire system?

Getting ready

If you are still in your SSH or serial window, you are ready to go.

How to do it...

The two commands that are built into most Linux systems are `curl` and `wget`. They are both good. Linux can never have one of anything. Generally speaking, `wget` has more options and is good for downloads and web scraping. We'll take a quick look at both:

1. A spot to check out the curl command is `wrrt.in`.
2. Running `curl wttr.in/Moon` returns the current phase of the moon, ASCII style:

```
pi@rpz14101:    curl wttr.in/Moon
                       .------
                  .--'   o
               .-'    .      o
            .-'@    @@@@@@@
           /@@@    @@@@@@@@@
        ./    o  @@@@@@@@@@
       /@@   o   @@@@@@@@@@
      /@@@@       @@@@@@@
     |@@@@@@
     /@@@@@   O   `.-./   .      Last Quarter +
     | @@@@       --`-'          0 21:57:24
     |@ @@@        `             New Moon -
     |       @@   @                5 23:46:40
     \   . @         @@@
      |      @@     @@@@@
      \      @@@@   @\@@
       \  o  @@       \ \
        `\          .\.-.
          \           `_-'
           `-.   o    / |
            `-.      /
               `--.'
                  `------
Check new Feature: wttr.in/Moon or wttr.in/Moon@2016-Mar-23 to see the phase of the Moon
Follow @igor_chubin for wttr.in updates
pi@rpz14101:
```

3. If you `curl` a regular website, you will probably see a lot of HTML code-not right away with `https://www.google.com`, however:

```
pi@rpz14101:~ $ curl google.com
<HTML><HEAD><meta http-equiv="content-type"
content="text/html;charset=utf-8">
<TITLE>301 Moved</TITLE></HEAD><BODY>
<H1>301 Moved</H1>
The document has moved
<A HREF="http://www.google.com/">here</A>.
</BODY></HTML>
```

4. If we add the `-L` flag to our command, it will follow the redirects seen in the previous step. To get a nice wall of HTML text instead, type this:

```
pi@rpz14101:~ $ curl -L google.com
```

5. Another fun `curl` is to find definitions through `http://www.dict.org/bin/Dict`. Take a look at the next example:

```
pi@rpz14101:~/share/ch3 $ curl dict://dict.org/d:raspberry
220 pan.alephnull.com dictd 1.12.1/rf on Linux 4.4.0-
1-amd64 <auth.mime> <12202445.3330.1469742211@pan.alephnull.com>
250 ok
150 1 definitions retrieved
151 "Raspberry" gcide "The Collaborative International
Dictionary of English v.0.48"
Raspberry Rasp"ber*ry (r[a^]z"b[e^]r*r[y^]; 277), n. [From E.
    rasp, in allusion to the apparent roughness of the fruit.]
    (Bot.)
    (a) The thimble-shaped fruit of the {Rubus Idaeus} and other
        similar brambles; as, the black, the red, and the white
        raspberry.
    (b) The shrub bearing this fruit.
        [1913 Webster]
    Note: Technically, raspberries are those brambles in which
          the fruit separates readily from the core or
          receptacle, in this differing from the blackberries, in
          which the fruit is firmly attached to the receptacle.
          [1913 Webster]
  .
250 ok [d/m/c = 1/0/16; 0.000r 0.000u 0.000s]
221 bye [d/m/c = 0/0/0; 0.000r 0.000u 0.000s]
```

   Try out the same thing with pi!

6. The `wget` command is the alternative to `curl`. It has more recursion options, but basic use is more or less the same. Let's download the source code for the classic 1970s mainframe game Star Trek. With the `wget` command, it is as simple as `wget http://www.almy.us/files/sstsrc.zip`:

```
pi@rpz14101:~ $ cd /home/pi/share/ch3/
pi@rpz14101:~/share/ch3 $ wget http://www.almy.us/files/sstsrc.zip
--2016-07-28 14:52:54--  http://www.almy.us/files/sstsrc.zip
Resolving www.almy.us (www.almy.us)... 72.167.232.227
Connecting to www.almy.us (www.almy.us)|72.167.232.227|:80...
connected.
HTTP request sent, awaiting response... 200 OK
Length: 98800 (96K) [application/zip]
Saving to: 'sstsrc.zip'
sstsrc.zip
100%[==============================================>]  96.48K   568KB/s
in 0.2s
    2016-07-28 14:52:54 (568 KB/s) - 'sstsrc.zip' saved [98800/98800]
```

7. An `ls` command will show you that you now have the `sstsrc.zip` file in your folder. Hold on to that file; we will be using (and installing) it in a later recipe.

Changing to root and using superpowers

We've touched upon `sudo` briefly and used it in some recipes, and now it is time to cover this essential command more deeply. There are also ways to become the root user and run whatever you want without having to prefix everything with `sudo`.

Getting ready

Stay in your terminal!

How to do it...

1. Any time someone needs elevated permissions to do something, such as installing a program or changing another user's password, if they have the appropriate permissions, they may use `sudo` to execute such commands. We've used `apt-get` several times, and if you forgot to use `sudo`, you will recognize these messages:

```
pi@rpz14101:~/share/ch3 $ apt-get install postgresql
E: Could not open lock file /var/lib/dpkg/lock - open
(13: Permission denied)
E: Unable to lock the administration directory
(/var/lib/dpkg/), are you root?
```

2. Running the command again with `sudo` will sort out the issue. Instead of retyping the entire command, you can also use this trick, which runs the previous command as `sudo`:

```
pi@rpz14101:~/share/ch3 $ sudo !!
sudo apt-get install postgresql
Reading package lists... Done
Building dependency tree
Reading state information... Done
The following extra packages will be installed:
  libpq5 postgresql-9.4 postgresql-client-9.4 postgresql-client-common
postgresql-common ssl-cert
```

```
Suggested packages:
  postgresql-doc oidentd ident-server locales-all postgresql-doc-9.4
openssl-blacklist
The following NEW packages will be installed:
  libpq5 postgresql postgresql-9.4 postgresql-client-9.4 postgresql-
client-common postgresql-common ssl-cert
0 upgraded, 7 newly installed, 0 to remove and 2 not upgraded.
Need to get 4,639 kB of archives.
After this operation, 22.3 MB of additional disk space will be used.
Do you want to continue? [Y/n] y
```

3. If you find you are doing a lot of things that require elevated access and are sick of forgetting to put in `sudo`, you can also log on as the root user. Of course, you just have to remember to `sudo` this one last time, using `sudo su - root`:

```
pi@rpz14101:~/share/ch3 $ sudo su - root
root@rpz14101:~# echo NOW I CAN DESTROY EVERYTHING
NOW I CAN DESTROY EVERYTHING
root@rpz14101:~# apt-get install postgresql-contrib
Reading package lists... Done
Building dependency tree
Reading state information... Done
The following extra packages will be installed:
  postgresql-contrib-9.4
Suggested packages:
  libdbd-pg-perl
The following NEW packages will be installed:
  postgresql-contrib postgresql-contrib-9.4
0 upgraded, 2 newly installed, 0 to remove and 2 not upgraded.
Need to get 444 kB of archives.
After this operation, 1,727 kB of additional disk space will be used.
Do you want to continue? [Y/n]
```

4. As long as you are the root user, you don't need to put in `sudo` for anything. Keep in mind, however, that the things you save will be in the `/root/` directory and only accessible by the root user, so when you go back to being the `pi` user (you can log out with *Ctrl + D*), you will need to `sudo` to get those files back.

5. The `su` command stands for "substitute user." This gives the current user permission to work as another user on the system. I don't just have the ability to substitute myself with root (if I have the permissions)-I can become any user I want:

```
pi@rpz14101:~/share/ch3 $ sudo su - rpz
rpz@rpz14101:~ $
```

Extracting a zipped file and zipping it back

Another way to reduce your overall file size footprint is by using techniques for archiving and compressing one or many files into a single, relatively small file. There are several ways to do this, which we will explore in this recipe.

Getting ready

Stay in the terminal, return to being the pi user, and go to your /home/pi/share/ch3 directory. If you followed the recipe on using wget, you should have a Star Trek ZIP file in there named sstsrc.zip. You can find it using the ls command. If you didn't download it before, first make sure you have zip installed, and then grab your zip file using the commands below:

```
sudo apt-get install zip
cd /home/pi/share/ch3/
wget http://www.almy.us/files/sstsrc.zip
```

How to do it…

The sstsrc.zip file is known as a source file; it contains the code to compile a program on any machine. We're going to unzip this file and compile it to run on our Raspberry Pi Zero! Then, we are going to take our compiled code and zip it back up. There are several different utilities for this: zip and unzip get the job done, and generally are readable on any operating system (even though your compiled game will only work on devices with the same chip as the Raspberry Pi Zero):

1. First, let's unzip our source file with the unzip command:

```
pi@rpz14101:~/share/ch3 $ unzip sstsrc.zip
Archive:  sstsrc.zip
   creating: sstsrc/
  inflating: sstsrc/ai.c
  inflating: sstsrc/battle.c
   creating: __MACOSX/
   creating: __MACOSX/sstsrc/
  inflating: __MACOSX/sstsrc/._battle.c
  inflating: sstsrc/buildforwindows.txt
  inflating: __MACOSX/sstsrc/._buildforwindows.txt
  inflating: sstsrc/events.c
  inflating: __MACOSX/sstsrc/._events.c
  inflating: sstsrc/finish.c
```

```
inflating:  __MACOSX/sstsrc/._finish.c
inflating:  sstsrc/makefile
inflating:  sstsrc/moving.c
inflating:  sstsrc/osx.c
inflating:  __MACOSX/sstsrc/._osx.c
inflating:  sstsrc/planets.c
inflating:  sstsrc/reports.c
inflating:  sstsrc/setup.c
inflating:  __MACOSX/sstsrc/._setup.c
inflating:  sstsrc/sst.bak
inflating:  sstsrc/sst.c
inflating:  __MACOSX/sstsrc/._sst.c
inflating:  sstsrc/sst.doc
inflating:  sstsrc/sst.h
inflating:  __MACOSX/sstsrc/._sst.h
inflating:  __MACOSX/._sstsrc
```

2. Then we will jump into the directory and look at the files:

```
pi@rpz14101:~/share/ch3 $ cd sstsrc/
pi@rpz14101:~/share/ch3/sstsrc $ ls
ai.c       buildforwindows.txt  finish.c  moving.c  planets.c  setup.c
sst.c      sst.h
battle.c   events.c             makefile  osx.c     reports.c  sst.bak
sst.doc
```

3. It is as easy as that to decompress a file. Not only does it handle collections of files, but it also can significantly reduce the total size, making transferring much faster. Now, we are going to compile the game, test it, and then zip it back up so our other Raspberry Pi Zero friends can play! The make command handles the compilation instructions in the directory. It is well beyond the scope of this cookbook to cover makefiles and gcc; for now, you just need to type make:

```
pi@rpz14101:~/share/ch3/sstsrc $ make
cc -O -DSCORE -DCAPTURE -DCLOAKING -Wno-unused-result -c sst.c
cc -O -DSCORE -DCAPTURE -DCLOAKING -Wno-unused-result -c finish.c
cc -O -DSCORE -DCAPTURE -DCLOAKING -Wno-unused-result -c reports.c
cc -O -DSCORE -DCAPTURE -DCLOAKING -Wno-unused-result -c setup.c
cc -O -DSCORE -DCAPTURE -DCLOAKING -Wno-unused-result -c osx.c
cc -O -DSCORE -DCAPTURE -DCLOAKING -Wno-unused-result -c moving.c
cc -O -DSCORE -DCAPTURE -DCLOAKING -Wno-unused-result -c battle.c
cc -O -DSCORE -DCAPTURE -DCLOAKING -Wno-unused-result -c events.c
cc -O -DSCORE -DCAPTURE -DCLOAKING -Wno-unused-result -c ai.c
cc -O -DSCORE -DCAPTURE -DCLOAKING -Wno-unused-result -c planets.c
gcc  -o sst sst.o finish.o reports.o setup.o osx.o moving.o battle.o
events.o ai.o planets.o -lm
```

4. If we look inside the directory again, we will see there are several new files created. The `sst` file is the one we are interested in; this is the final executable created from the compilation process:

```
pi@rpz14101:~/share/ch3/sstsrc $ ls
ai.c       battle.o              events.o  makefile  osx.c       planets.o
setup.c    sst.bak  sst.h
ai.o       buildforwindows.txt   finish.c  moving.c  osx.o       reports.c
setup.o    sst.c    sst.o
battle.c   events.c              finish.o  moving.o  planets.c   reports.o
sst        sst.doc
```

5. Before we repackage it, let's test it out! We can execute the `sst` file with `./sst`. Engage!

```
pi@rpz14101:~/share/ch3/sstsrc $ ./sst
-SUPER- STAR TREK
Latest update-21 Sept 78
Would you like a regular, tournament, or frozen game?regular
Would you like a Short, Medium, or Long game? short
Are you a Novice, Fair, Good, Expert, or Emeritus player?novice
Please type in a secret password (9 characters maximum)-makeitso
It is stardate 3200. The Federation is being attacked by
a deadly Klingon invasion force. As captain of the United
Starship U.S.S. Enterprise, it is your mission to seek out
and destroy this invasion force of 3 battle cruisers.
You have an initial allotment of 7 stardates to complete
your mission.  As you proceed you may be given more time.
You will have 4 supporting starbases.
Starbase locations-  8 - 1   1 - 1   6 - 6   2 - 6
The Enterprise is currently in Quadrant 8 - 4  Sector 7 - 5
Good Luck!
COMMAND>
```

6. Hooray! `QUIT` will get you out right away, unless you decide you need to spend some time further investigating or conquering the galaxy. Now, let's zip up this directory so we can send it to our friends. The `cd..` command will take us down one directory, back to the `/home/pi/share/ch3` folder:

```
pi@rpz14101:~/share/ch3 $ zip sst_rpz.zip ./sstsrc/*
  adding: sstsrc/ai.c (deflated 66%)
  adding: sstsrc/ai.o (deflated 45%)
  adding: sstsrc/battle.c (deflated 67%)
  adding: sstsrc/battle.o (deflated 53%)
  adding: sstsrc/buildforwindows.txt (deflated 17%)
  adding: sstsrc/events.c (deflated 67%)
```

```
adding: sstsrc/events.o (deflated 48%)
adding: sstsrc/finish.c (deflated 70%)
adding: sstsrc/finish.o (deflated 61%)
adding: sstsrc/makefile (deflated 40%)
adding: sstsrc/moving.c (deflated 67%)
adding: sstsrc/moving.o (deflated 52%)
adding: sstsrc/osx.c (deflated 51%)
adding: sstsrc/osx.o (deflated 54%)
adding: sstsrc/planets.c (deflated 68%)
adding: sstsrc/planets.o (deflated 57%)
adding: sstsrc/reports.c (deflated 67%)
adding: sstsrc/reports.o (deflated 52%)
adding: sstsrc/setup.c (deflated 65%)
adding: sstsrc/setup.o (deflated 51%)
adding: sstsrc/sst (deflated 51%)
adding: sstsrc/sst.bak (deflated 64%)
adding: sstsrc/sst.c (deflated 65%)
adding: sstsrc/sst.doc (deflated 67%)
adding: sstsrc/sst.h (deflated 64%)
adding: sstsrc/sst.o (deflated 57%)
```

7. If we take a look at the last two files in that directory, we see our new zip file, `sst_rpz.zip`:

```
pi@rpz14101:~/share/ch3 $ ls -ltrh | tail -2
drwx------ 2 pi pi 4.0K Jul 28 15:37 sstsrc
-rw-r--r-- 1 pi pi 230K Jul 28 16:24 sst_rpz.zip
```

8. This is the zip file we can share with our fellow Raspberry Pi Zero owners. We can verify the contents using the `unzip` utility again:

```
pi@rpz14101:~/share/ch3 $ unzip -l sst_rpz.zip
Archive:  sst_rpz.zip
  Length      Date    Time    Name
---------  ---------- -----   ----
    17047  2013-11-10 16:15   sstsrc/ai.c
    10820  2016-07-28 15:37   sstsrc/ai.o
    36506  2013-11-17 18:38   sstsrc/battle.c
    30492  2016-07-28 15:37   sstsrc/battle.o
      126  2015-08-29 12:50   sstsrc/buildforwindows.txt
    21506  2013-11-11 06:55   sstsrc/events.c
    16848  2016-07-28 15:37   sstsrc/events.o
    17621  2013-11-11 06:59   sstsrc/finish.c
    20484  2016-07-28 15:37   sstsrc/finish.o
      340  2014-01-03 14:57   sstsrc/makefile
    25574  2014-01-03 14:39   sstsrc/moving.c
    21172  2016-07-28 15:37   sstsrc/moving.o
```

```
    731    2015-08-28 13:16    sstsrc/osx.c
   1344    2016-07-28 15:37    sstsrc/osx.o
  13385    2013-09-20 08:56    sstsrc/planets.c
  15452    2016-07-28 15:37    sstsrc/planets.o
  13986    2014-01-03 14:39    sstsrc/reports.c
  15376    2016-07-28 15:37    sstsrc/reports.o
  18427    2015-06-26 09:15    sstsrc/setup.c
  16828    2016-07-28 15:37    sstsrc/setup.o
 125360    2016-07-28 15:37    sstsrc/sst
  16813    2015-12-24 13:08    sstsrc/sst.bak
  16812    2015-12-24 13:08    sstsrc/sst.c
  67778    2014-01-03 18:10    sstsrc/sst.doc
  12807    2015-08-28 13:13    sstsrc/sst.h
  14768    2016-07-28 15:37    sstsrc/sst.o
 ----------                    -------
 568403                        26 files
```

Warp speed to the next recipe!

Searching executed code from the terminal's history

Linux users aren't necessarily fond of a lot of typing. Fortunately, there are a few built-in tools that make working in the command line at least as efficient as working from a GUI desktop. Seeing what you've done before can save you from having to type it again and can also help you figure out where things went wrong or how to do it over again.

Getting ready

You want to be in the same SSH or serial terminal you've been using.

How to do it...

1. The easiest way to get history is the up arrow on the keyboard. Pressing it once will show the last command, twice is two commands ago, and so on. While not the fastest way to look at history, it is good when you want to run something again.

2. The other way is to use the `history` command. With this, you can see every command the user tried to run. This will be a very long list, so it is good to pipe into `less`, `head`, or `tail`.

3. Running `history | less` will take you to a vi-like window that lets you easily scroll up and down through the history (or any text you send to it). To look at the most recent entries, I would pipe to `tail`; for example, here are the last several entries in my history:

```
pi@rpz14101:~/share/ch3 $ history | tail -n 9
  481  zip sst_src.zip ./sstsrc/*
  482  ls
  483  zip sst_rpz.zip ./sstsrc/*
  484  ls
  485  ls -ltrh | tail -2
  486  rm sst_src.zip
  487  ls -ltrh | tail -2
  488  unzip --help
  489  unzip -l sst_rpz.zip
```

4. If you have administrator rights, you can also `sudo su - <user>` and run `history` to see what was run for that user. Another great tool is always `grep`; you can pipe to that and look for specific commands, such as software installations:

```
pi@rpz14101:~/share/ch3 $ history | grep "apt-get install"
   45  sudo apt-get install /media/pi/A8A2-9948/firmware-
  ralink_0.43_all.deb
   77  sudo apt-get install screen
  352  sudo apt-get install vim
  354  sudo apt-get install curl wget
  355  sudo apt-get install cmatrix
```

Changing RPZ configuration settings from the command line

Now that we are quickly becoming command-line masters, let's see what sort of hacking we can do with the Raspberry Pi configuration. We've done a little of this before with the USB OTG hacks; let's find out what other interesting settings we can change in the system.

Getting ready

We're going to continue working from the terminal and do a few things that aren't possible in `raspi-config`.

How to do it...

1. The key file to edit the Raspberry Pi Zero's startup configuration is `/boot/config.txt`. Let's take a look at the entire file. We have already edited that to enable USB OTG gadget functionality, but there are a ton of settings that can be added to it. Let's add the following to the `config.txt` file. It is a good idea to make a backup copy if you haven't already. Append the following settings to the bottom of the `config.txt` file:

   gpu_mem=96

2. After rebooting, the GPU memory will be increased from the default of 64 MB to 96 MB. This gives a little more memory for rendering graphics, and adjusting these settings can improve the video quality of your Raspberry Pi Zero. The Raspberry Pi Foundation documentation has dozens of different settings you can change in `config.txt`. You can see the settings in place using the `vcgencmd` command:

   pi@rpz14101:~ $ /opt/vc/bin/vcgencmd get_mem gpu
   gpu=96M

3. As you might expect, the remainder of the Zero's 512 MB goes to serving the CPU:

   pi@rpz14101:~ $ /opt/vc/bin/vcgencmd get_mem arm
   arm=416M

As Raspbian is updated, these settings can change, and the documentation on the Raspberry Pi site for `config.txt` properties is extensive, so when you really start hacking away at your startup config, make sure and have that page bookmarked. Also, be sure to have your work backed up (including your last working `config.txt` file) in case you configure yourself into disaster.

There's more...

There are many different ways to configure your Raspberry Pi, or any Linux system, to start up. One cool thing is making changes to the Message of the Day:

1. Let's add some pizzazz to our Raspberry Pi Zero's login screen with some ASCII text. There are plenty of text-to-ASCII-image websites that create them for you. I went with the "Money RPZ" look for my ASCII text. Open the /etc/motd file with your favorite text editor (you will need to also use sudo to write this file) and add the following text:

```
$$$$$$$  $$$$$$$ $$$$$$$$
$$   __$$ $$   __$$____$$   |
$$  |  $$ |$$  |  $$  |    $$  /
$$$$$$$  |$$$$$$$  |  $$  /
$$   __$$< $$   ____/  $$  /
$$  |  $$ |$$  |        $$  /
$$  |  $$ |$$  |        $$$$$$$$
 __|   __|__|         _____|
```

2. Now save that file and reboot, or log out and back in. If all went well, you should have your new, exciting login screen:

```
Using username "pi".
pi@rpz14101.local's password:
$$$$$$$\   $$$$$$$\ $$$$$$$$\
$$   __$$\ $$   __$$\\____$$   |
$$  |  $$ |$$  |  $$  |    $$  /
$$$$$$$  |$$$$$$$  |   $$  /
$$   __$$< $$   ____/   $$  /
$$  |  $$ |$$  |         $$  /
$$  |  $$ |$$  |      $$$$$$$$\
\__|   \__|\__|       _____|
Last login: Thu Jul 28 20:44:5
pi@rpz14101:  
```

With a little practice, you can have your message of the day show you about anything, A last great startup setting is configuring aliases. Let's say I don't want to type `ls -ltrh` every time I want to get a directory listing or `/home/pi/share/ch3/rpz_temp.sh` when I want to know the temperature. The `.bash_aliases` stored in `/home/pi/` will take aliases and interpret them for you. Add the following lines to `.bash_aliases` (you may need to make a new file):

```
alias ll='ls -ltrh'
alias rpzt='vcgencmd measure_temp'
alias moon='curl wttr.in/Moon'
```

3. Save the file and then run this command:

```
source ~/.bash_profile
```

4. Now, just type `rpzt` or `moon`, and see what happens! Think of all the shortcuts you can make!

Checking running processes and killing a process running in the background

There are times using Linux when there's a problem with a particular application or service, and other times when you aren't sure an application or service is running. This recipe will look at how to observe the state of running processes and how you can kill these processes from the command line.

Getting ready

Your familiar old terminal window is all you'll need. Let's kill some things!

How to do it...

The first command most Linux users know when looking at system activity is `top`. Running `top` provides a nice table that shows system load, memory usage, and running processes. It also shows how much CPU and memory any individual process is using. This updates continuously (and is configurable with the `-d` flag) and is a great way to see what's happening on your Raspberry Pi Zero.

A typical `top` output will look something like this:

```
top - 16:40:40 up  8:30,  2 users,  load average: 0.07, 0.10, 0.16
Tasks: 125 total,   1 running, 124 sleeping,   0 stopped,   0 zombie
%Cpu(s):  1.0 us,  0.3 sy,  0.0 ni, 98.4 id,  0.0 wa,  0.0 hi,  0.3 si,  0.0 st
KiB Mem:    445112 total,   398452 used,    46660 free,    19612 buffers
KiB Swap:   102396 total,       20 used,   102376 free.   256752 cached Mem

  PID USER      PR  NI    VIRT    RES    SHR S  %CPU %MEM     TIME+ COMMAND
21312 pi        20   0    5100   2492   2088 R   1.0  0.6   0:00.23 top
  579 pi        20   0   12196   3032   2296 S   0.3  0.7   0:30.58 sshd
    1 root      20   0    5376   3748   2660 S   0.0  0.8   2:35.88 systemd
    2 root      20   0       0      0      0 S   0.0  0.0   0:00.03 kthreadd
    3 root      20   0       0      0      0 S   0.0  0.0   0:11.07 ksoftirqd/0
    5 root       0 -20       0      0      0 S   0.0  0.0   0:00.00 kworker/0:0H
    7 root      20   0       0      0      0 S   0.0  0.0   0:00.01 kdevtmpfs
    8 root       0 -20       0      0      0 S   0.0  0.0   0:00.00 netns
    9 root       0 -20       0      0      0 S   0.0  0.0   0:00.00 perf
   10 root      20   0       0      0      0 S   0.0  0.0   0:00.03 khungtaskd
   11 root       0 -20       0      0      0 S   0.0  0.0   0:00.00 writeback
   12 root       0 -20       0      0      0 S   0.0  0.0   0:00.00 crypto
   13 root       0 -20       0      0      0 S   0.0  0.0   0:00.00 bioset
   14 root       0 -20       0      0      0 S   0.0  0.0   0:00.00 kblockd
   16 root       0 -20       0      0      0 S   0.0  0.0   0:00.00 rpciod
   17 root      20   0       0      0      0 S   0.0  0.0   0:01.30 kswapd0
   18 root      20   0       0      0      0 S   0.0  0.0   0:00.00 fsnotify_mark
```

The other tool commonly used in Linux systems is the `ps` command. This is a versatile command that shows all kinds of information on system processes and their states. The `ps all` command shows all running processes:

```
pi@rpz14101:~/share/ch3 $ ps all
```

Your output will look something like this:

```
pi@rpz14101:                 ps all
F   UID   PID  PPID PRI  NI    VSZ   RSS WCHAN   STAT TTY       TIME COMMAND
4     0   469     1  20   0   4040  1676 -       Ss+  tty1      0:00 /sbin/agetty --noclear tty1 linux
4     0   470     1  20   0   7260  3012 -       Ss   ?         0:00 /bin/login --
4  1000   562   470  20   0   6488  4344 wait    S    ttyAMA0   0:01 -bash
0  1000   581   579  20   0   6572  4476 wait    Ss   pts/0     0:08 -bash
0  1000  9923     1  20   0  26804 13728 poll_s  S    ?         4:08 Xtightvnc :1 -desktop X -auth /home/pi/.Xauth
0  1000  9927     1  20   0   1900  1076 wait    S    ?         0:00 /bin/sh /home/pi/.vnc/xstartup
0  1000  9930  9927  20   0  51144 10348 poll_s  Sl   ?         0:00 /usr/bin/lxsession -s LXDE-pi -e LXDE
1  1000  9958     1  20   0   3680  1732 poll_s  S    ?         0:00 /usr/bin/dbus-launch --exit-with-session x-se
0  1000  9980  9930  20   0  20640  9380 poll_s  S    ?         0:05 openbox --config-file /home/pi/.config/openbo
0  1000  9981  9930  20   0  46856 14620 poll_s  Sl   ?         0:01 lxpolkit
0  1000  9982  9930  20   0  84596 19292 poll_s  Sl   ?         1:34 lxpanel --profile LXDE-pi
0  1000  9984  9930  20   0  75676 14944 poll_s  Sl   ?         0:02 pcmanfm --desktop --profile LXDE-pi
1  1000 10035     1  20   0   1900   632 wait    S    ?         0:00 /bin/sh /usr/bin/start-pulseaudio-x11
0  1000 10037 10035  20   0   5784  2072 poll_s  S    ?         0:00 /usr/bin/xprop -root -spy
0  1000 20959   562  20   0   4328  2436 poll_s  S+   ttyAMA0   0:00 man zip
0  1000 20968 20959  20   0   3704  1828 wait_w  S+   ttyAMA0   0:00 pager -s
0  1000 22154   581  20   0   4272  1840 -       R+   pts/0     0:00 ps all
```

Once of the columns you'll notice in both the output of ps and top is the PID, or Process ID. Each individual program that is running on your Raspberry Pi Zero is assigned a unique number. For as long as this process is running without interruption, it will have that PID assigned to it. The other common piece of information is for Users, with top you are shown the user name, and in ps the User ID (UID) is given. User ID and Name mapping can be identified looking at the passwd file (try `cat /etc/passwd`).

1. Now, we will create a process that runs in the background continuously. The `watch` command runs something over and over; we will have it run the `ps` command and send the output to escape (`&`). This will return control of the terminal to us instead of displaying the output of the command over and over:

```
pi@rpz14101:~/share/ch3 $ watch 'ps -ef' &
[1] 22159
```

2. We can use the `ps -ef` command, which is an extended output of the `ps` command, and look for our `watch` command. If you do it quickly, it will show as `stopped` because the `watch` command has not started executing anything yet. Running it again should only show the running process:

```
pi@rpz14101:~/share/ch3 $ ps -ef | grep watch
pi         22159    581   0 16:51 pts/0     00:00:00 watch ps -ef
pi         22163    581   0 16:51 pts/0     00:00:00 grep --color=auto watch
[1]+  Stopped                    watch 'ps -ef'
pi@rpz14101:~/share/ch3 $ ps -ef | grep watch
pi         22159    581   0 16:51 pts/0     00:00:00 watch ps -ef
pi         22165    581   0 16:51 pts/0     00:00:00 grep --color=auto watch
```

3. To stop this command from continuing to execute, we use the `kill` command. It often requires `sudo` permissions, but in our case, it will let us run `kill`, since we created the process:

```
pi@rpz14101:~/share/ch3 $ kill 22159
pi@rpz14101:~/share/ch3 $ ps -ef | grep watch
pi         22159    581   0 16:51 pts/0     00:00:00 watch ps -ef
pi         22171    581   0 16:51 pts/0     00:00:00 grep --color=auto watch
```

4. Oddly, we see that the `watch` command is still running. Some commands and services cannot be killed with a `kill` command. By default, the `kill` command is "friendly" and won't stop something it thinks it shouldn't. Fortunately, there is a flag in `kill`, `-9`, which never fails. We can see here that `kill -9` removes the `watch` command from my process list:

```
pi@rpz14101:~/share/ch3 $ kill -9 22159
[1]+  Killed                  watch 'ps -ef'
pi@rpz14101:~/share/ch3 $ ps -ef | grep watch
pi       22175   581  0 16:51 pts/0    00:00:00 grep --color=auto watch
```

Always be careful with `kill` and definitely with `kill -9`. If you kill the wrong thing, you can crash your system or kill your application that was running perfectly fine. You really only need to use it if your application or service won't close or stop gracefully.

Creating our first shell program and automating a process

The **Bourne Again shell**, or **bash**, is a common terminal for Linux users to control their computers. One of the great things about it is it can be written into longer scripts, which do multiple things, or make decisions based on certain information, which makes what would be a long, manual task virtually effortless. Let's go over a practical example of writing a shell script to make our life easier.

Getting ready

The terminal window you've been working in is your shell. In fact, every command you type is more or less a one-line script! We'll only need a connection and our favorite text editor.

If you are still in the `ch3` directory, you are ready to go. If not, you can get there with this:

```
cd /home/pi/share/ch3/
```

How to do it...

Here is another recipe we can use later, and it fulfils a practical purpose. We're going to take a reading on the Raspberry Pi Zero's built-in temperature sensor and output the value with the time. We'll save this process to a file named `rpz_temp.sh`:

1. Open a text editor and enter the following script:

```
#!/bin/bash
TEMP=`/opt/vc/bin/vcgencmd measure_temp | cut -d "=" -f 2`
DATE=`date`
echo RPZ Temperature at $DATE: $TEMP
```

2. Let's go over each line, as they show some basics on using Bash scripting, which will get you started. The first line indicates this is a Bash script. When executing the file, the presence of this line makes it easy for the shell to know what it's trying to run. The second line sets a variable named TEMP to the results of the following command:

```
/opt/vc/bin/vcgencmd measure_temp | cut -d "=" -f 2
```

> The `vcgencmd` command is a utility that can provide a ton of processor or board information, clock speeds, temperatures, settings, and more. We're going to get the CPU temperature and then split the output with the `cut` command to only return the value of the temperature to the TEMP variable. The third line takes the output of the `date` command and sets it to the DATE variable. Because the commands are inside of grave accents (aka backticks: `` ` ``), Bash knows to return the output of the executed command to the variable. Finally, the last line returns the date and temperature in a friendly format.

3. Save your file and return to the terminal window. Before executing it the first time, you need to give it permission to be executed. We can do this with the `chmod` command:

```
pi@rpz14101:~/share/ch3 $ chmod +x rpz_temp.sh
```

4. Now we can run our new temperature script!

```
pi@rpz14101:~/share/ch3 $ ./rpz_temp.sh
RPZ Temperature at Thu 28 Jul 18:08:00 PDT 2016: 35.8'C
```

Fantastic! You now have a script that returns your Raspberry Pi Zero's temperature. Later on, we will be collecting all kinds of sensor data!

Syncing with NTC servers to update the current time

For data collection, having an accurate timestamp is crucial for capturing time-series data than can be compared to other datasets with consistent timestamps. **Network Time Protocol** (**NTP**) is a network communication standard that is designed to keep all computers communicating with an NTP server accurate within a few milliseconds of each other. By checking the time with the NTP server periodically, you can ensure your network machines are all time synchronized. There are several public servers available on the Internet to use; let's talk to one!

Getting ready

My Raspbian installation already had NTP running; we can validate this from the terminal window. Either way, you can install it with `apt-get`. If your installation has `ntp` already going, you'll get the same message as follows. If not, `apt-get` will take care of it for you.

```
pi@rpz14101:~$ sudo apt-get install ntp
Reading package lists... Done
Building dependency tree
Reading state information... Done
ntp is already the newest version.
0 upgraded, 0 newly installed, 0 to remove and 2 not upgraded.
```

How to do it...

The NTP daemon is a service that periodically checks central NTP servers on the Internet to make sure that the times are synchronized. There is no need to configure the polling interval; the daemon takes care of that for you.

1. Once you've verified that the service is installed, check the status of the service:

```
pi@rpz14101:~$ sudo service ntp status
ntp.service - LSB: Start NTP daemon
   Loaded: loaded (/etc/init.d/ntp)
   Active: active (running) since Thu 2016-07-28 08:35:15 PDT; 8h ago
   CGroup: /system.slice/ntp.service
           └─7885 /usr/sbin/ntpd -p /var/run/ntpd.pid -g -u 106:111
Jul 28 08:35:15 rpz14101 ntpd[7885]: proto: precision = 1.000 usec
Jul 28 08:35:15 rpz14101 ntpd[7885]: Listen and drop on 0 v4wildcard
0.0.0....23
```

```
Jul 28 08:35:15 rpz14101 ntpd[7885]: Listen and drop on 1 v6wildcard :: 
UDP 123
Jul 28 08:35:15 rpz14101 ntpd[7885]: Listen normally on 2 lo 127.0.0.1
UDP 123
Jul 28 08:35:15 rpz14101 ntpd[7885]: Listen normally on 3 usb0
192.168.137....23
Jul 28 08:35:15 rpz14101 ntpd[7885]: Listen normally on 4 lo ::1
UDP 123
Jul 28 08:35:15 rpz14101 ntpd[7885]: Listen normally on 5
usb0 fe80::317b:5...23
Jul 28 08:35:15 rpz14101 ntpd[7885]: peers refreshed
Jul 28 08:35:15 rpz14101 ntpd[7885]: Listening on routing socket on
fd #22 ...es
Jul 28 08:35:15 rpz14101 systemd[1]: Started LSB: Start NTP daemon.
Hint: Some lines were ellipsized, use -l to show in full.
```

2. You can also use `service ntp start`, `service ntp stop`, or `service ntp restart` to start, stop, or restart the service, respectively.

3. The `ntptime` command does a check and returns the confirmed time. The output is relatively verbose, but gives some insight into how much is factored in when synchronizing time across the Internet:

```
pi@rpz14101:~$ ntptime
ntp_gettime() returns code 0 (OK)
   time db452367.99be7ef4  Thu, Jul 28 2016 17:35:51.600, (.600563337),
   maximum error 403526 us, estimated error 4340 us, TAI offset 0
ntp_adjtime() returns code 0 (OK)
   modes 0x0 (),
   offset -6574.282 us, frequency -9.672 ppm, interval 1 s,
   maximum error 403526 us, estimated error 4340 us,
   status 0x6001 (PLL,NANO,MODE),
   time constant 10, precision 0.001 us, tolerance 500 ppm,
```

Running a background process in Linux

While running things from the command line is great, sometimes you want it to run without your intervention. These may be things such as listening services, database engines, or VNC servers that you want to be continuously available but not sitting open in one of your terminal windows. In this recipe, we will look at how to manipulate these services and assess their current status.

Getting ready

There is nothing you need to add for this recipe; we're going to leverage `systemctl`, a common daemon for managing background services. We're going to make sure our PostgreSQL database starts after a reboot; if you haven't installed PostgreSQL yet, you can do that with this command:

```
sudo apt-get install postgresql
```

How to do it...

There are plenty of services that you want to count on starting up automatically after an unexpected reboot, crash, or power loss. If you are hosting a database, its service is usually one that you want to start any time your system does. We can use the `systemctl` utility to make this possible. As with so many Linux utilities, there are several different options:

1. First, let's look at the current status of our installation with `systemctl status postgresql`:

```
pi@rpz14101:~ $ sudo systemctl status postgresql
● postgresql.service - PostgreSQL RDBMS
   Loaded: loaded (/lib/systemd/system/postgresql.service; enabled)
Active: inactive (dead) since Sat 2017-03-04 19:33:54 CET; 3s ago
  Main PID: 584 (code=exited, status=0/SUCCESS)
    CGroup: /system.slice/postgresql.service
Jul 28 19:29:58 rpz14101 systemd[1]: Started PostgreSQL RDBMS.
```

2. Looking at the line that starts with "Active", we see that the service is stopped (inactive). Let's make sure that it starts on the next reboot, with the `enable` command:

```
pi@rpz14101:~ $ sudo systemctl enable postgresql
Synchronizing state for postgresql.service with sysvinit
using update-rc.d...
Executing /usr/sbin/update-rc.d postgresql defaults
Executing /usr/sbin/update-rc.d postgresql enable
```

3. Now let's reboot and see what happens. Run `sudo reboot` and then log back in and check the status again:

```
pi@rpz14101:~ $ sudo systemctl status postgresql
● postgresql.service - PostgreSQL RDBMS
   Loaded: loaded (/lib/systemd/system/postgresql.service; enabled)
   Active: active (exited) since Thu 2016-07-28 20:00:41 PDT; 46s ago
```

```
   Process: 583 ExecStart=/bin/true (code=exited, status=0/SUCCESS)
  Main PID: 583 (code=exited, status=0/SUCCESS)
    CGroup: /system.slice/postgresql.service
Jul 28 20:00:41 rpz14101 systemd[1]: Started PostgreSQL RDBMS.
```

Success! Above we see "Active: inactive" has now changed to "Active: active." Now you know how to get a process to start at startup. Of course, the `disable` command will do the opposite: if you decide you don't want your service to start, then you can ensure it won't by calling `systemctl disable`. The utility also supports the `stop` and `start` commands (and so many more), so you can control your service without having to reboot. Many of the things we've been working with already, such as SSH, are configured by default upon installation, and that's why you can SSH back into your Pi Zero after each reboot!

Setting a file to run automatically on startup

If you take your Raspberry Pi Zero with you a lot, unplug it at night, or reboot often, you don't want to have to start services and programs manually every single time. Linux has a rich set of tools that control what services start up when the Raspberry Pi does.

Getting ready

We're going to make a copy of our temperature script and add a little bit to it. First, make a copy as a new script, called `rpz_startup.sh`. We'll use the `cp` command we learned in an earlier recipe:

```
pi@rpz14101:~/share/ch3 $ cp rpz_temp.sh rpz_start.sh
```

How to do it...

1. This file will have some new variables in it, the format will be slightly different, and we will write it directly to our `rpz_startup.log` file in `/var/log/`. The `TEMP` and `DATE` variables are the same, so you can save yourself the retyping with the copy. The finished script will look like this:

```
#!/bin/bash
TEMP=`/opt/vc/bin/vcgencmd measure_temp | cut -d "=" -f 2`
DATE=`date`
GPU=`/opt/vc/bin/vcgencmd get_mem gpu | cut -d "=" -f 2`
ARM=`/opt/vc/bin/vcgencmd get_mem arm | cut -d "=" -f 2`
```

```
STATUS=`/opt/vc/bin/vcgencmd pm_get_status`
echo RPZ startup at $DATE>>/var/log/rpz_startup.log
echo Current core temperature $TEMP>>/var/log/rpz_startup.log
echo GPU RAM $GPU - CPU RAM $ARM>>/var/log/rpz_startup.log
echo RPZ Status: $STATUS>>/var/log/rpz_startup.log
```

We've added some new variables to log the GPU/ARM memory distribution and system status as well as the date and temperature.

2. Next, we want to make a copy in the /etc/init.d/ folder. This is where the startup scripts live. You'll need to sudo to do it too, since these scripts will start when the Raspberry Pi does. We'll also need to change the permission to allow it to be run. As you can see, I'll be using sudo !! throughout:

```
pi@rpz14101:~/share/ch3 $ cp rpz_start.sh /etc/init.d/
cp: cannot create regular file '/etc/init.d/rpz_start.sh':
Permission denied
pi@rpz14101:~/share/ch3 $ sudo !!
sudo cp rpz_start.sh /etc/init.d/
pi@rpz14101:~/share/ch3 $ sudo chmod +x /etc/init.d/rpz_start.sh
```

The command sudo !! executes the prior command, but with sudo. This is an easy shortcut for when you run a command, but forgot to (or didn't realize you needed) to run as sudo.

3. Finally, we'll register our script to be run at startup:

```
pi@rpz14101:~/share/ch3 $ sudo update-rc.d rpz_start.sh defaults
insserv: warning: script 'rpz_start.sh' missing LSB tags and overrides
```

4. After a reboot, we should see the following in our /var/log/rpz_startup.log file:

```
pi@rpz14101:~ $ cat /var/log/rpz_startup.log
RPZ startup at Thu 28 Jul 20:43:15 PDT 2016
Current core temperature 39.0'C
GPU RAM 96M - CPU RAM 416M
RPZ Status: core=400000000 free=398087909 voltage=1.2v
```

You'll get a new entry every time your power goes out, if your Raspberry Pi Zero's battery dies, or if gremlins are secretly turning it off at night. If you changed your GPU memory to 96 MB in the earlier recipe, it is easy to tell it worked right here in your new startup log.

Using crontab to run a script automatically at predefined intervals

For the last recipe in this chapter, we will look at the popular crontab utility, a service that will execute a command or script at a regular interval of your choosing. It is a vital part of the system administrator's toolbox, and one you'll find a lot of uses for, especially when connecting to sensors and Internet of Things devices.

Getting ready

If you followed the recipe to make the Raspberry Pi Zero temperature script, you are ready to go.

How to do it...

Let's start logging the temperature of the Zero to a text file. We will take a reading every minute and save it in the /var/log/rpz_temp.log file. Over the course of a day, especially on days when you are using the Pi a lot, or it is warmer or cooler where your Pi is located, you should see changes in temperature. The crontab utility is built into pretty much every Linux system, and you don't have to worry about installation for Raspbian. Generally, if you are working with services or things already owned by the root user, using the root crontab will ensure you don't have any permissions issues with what you are executing. You can use sudo or change to the root user-whatever you like more.

1. First, we will create the rpz_temp.log file in the /var/log/ directory. This directory is typically used for system logs, so it makes sense to save it here:

```
pi@rpz14101:~/share/ch3 $ sudo touch /var/log/rpz_temp.log
```

2. The -e flag takes you to the crontab editor, where you can add your tasks. Your first time, it will ask what default text editor you'd like to use:

```
pi@rpz14101:~/share/ch3 $ sudo crontab -e
no crontab for root - using an empty one
Select an editor.  To change later, run 'select-editor'.
  1. /bin/ed
  2. /bin/nano         <---- easiest
  3. /usr/bin/vim.basic
  4. /usr/bin/vim.tiny
Choose 1-4 [2]: 2
```

Crontab files are created for each user, so without sudo, you would create a crontab schedule for the pi user. This is fine, as long as the user executing the process has all of the right permissions (in this case, the pi user cannot write to the /var/log/ directory. Creating a crontab file for root will ensure that execution is performed by a superuser.

3. This will take you into a text editor with an initial crontab file and an example. We're going to add the following to the end of the file:

```
* * * * * /home/pi/share/ch3/rpz_temp.sh>>/var/log/rpz_temp.log
```

4. There are five asterisks, which are used to indicate time intervals to execute the command to the right. The interval settings are for minutes, hours, day of month, month, and day of week. Having it set in the way shown here means to run it every minute. We can change these to actual numbers to control the frequency of execution:

Crontab setting	Execution frequency
15 0 * * *	Execute on the fifteenth minute of midnight hour, daily
15 0 15 * *	Fifteenth minute, midnight, on the Fifteenth of each month
15 0 15 12 *	Fifteenth minute, midnight, on the fifteenth day of the twelfth month
15 * * * 4	Fifteenth minute, every hour, on the fourth day of the week (Thursday)
0 * * * *	Execute on the top of every hour (:00), daily
15 * * * *	Execute on the fifteenth minute of every hour, daily
30 * * * *	Execute on the half hour (:30) of every hour, daily
45 * * * *	Execute on the forty-fifth minute of every hour, daily

5. Running `sudo crontab -l` will show the updated configuration. I also run `sudo service cron reload`, just to ensure that the configs are picked up right away. Running a `cat` of your log file after a few minutes shows our new data already being collected:

```
pi@rpz14101:~/share/ch3 $ cat /var/log/rpz_temp.log
RPZ Temperature at Thu 28 Jul 18:50:01 PDT 2016: 34.7'C
RPZ Temperature at Thu 28 Jul 18:51:01 PDT 2016: 34.7'C
RPZ Temperature at Thu 28 Jul 18:52:02 PDT 2016: 35.8'C
RPZ Temperature at Thu 28 Jul 18:53:01 PDT 2016: 35.8'C
RPZ Temperature at Thu 28 Jul 18:54:01 PDT 2016: 36.3'C
RPZ Temperature at Thu 28 Jul 18:55:01 PDT 2016: 35.8'C
RPZ Temperature at Thu 28 Jul 18:56:01 PDT 2016: 35.8'C
```

6. The `cron` utility will continue adding to this file until I remove the command from the scheduler using `sudo crontab -e` or until I shut down the cron service, which is not recommended. Collect some temperature data for a little while and see how the temperature varies; do you see any patterns?

4

Programming with Python

In this chapter, we will bring the book to a boil with the Python programming language, a standard part of a Raspberry Pi distribution and a favorite of Internet of Things users. We'll try out the following:

- Choosing between Python 2 and 3
- Installing important Python packages
- Creating our first Python program and running loops
- Playing with strings
- Plotting graphs using Python
- Sending an e-mail from a Python script
- Creating a program to log and append data to a CSV file
- Using a Python script to upload data online to a Google spreadsheet interface
- Adding help and parameters to your Python Program

Introduction

There are dozens of different programming languages to choose from, so many that it can become hard to decide which one is best for what you are working on. Each language has pros and cons, often times the more complex the language, the potentially faster it will perform on your system. Python strikes a great balance between performance and ease-of-use. The object-oriented side of Python makes it very easy to re-use code, and the functional programming side makes it intuitive to see how the program will iterate. It also runs on just about any operating system, which gives your programs the benefit of portability. Furthermore, Python has a tremendous user community and hundreds of libraries that make it easy to work with just about anything, whether you want to light an LED, read a sensor, draw a graph or run a website. In this Chapter, we will explore Python in enough depth to get you comfortable using it on your Raspberry Pi Zero.

Choosing between Python 2 and 3

The story of Python 2 and Python 3 is long and full of fairly passionate debate. When Python 3 was released, the intention was to have all of the libraries that make Python 2 good enough to be upgraded to work with version 3. It turned out that many of the differences in the coding standards between the versions made the library upgrades too much work, and in other cases, the authors of these libraries refused to upgrade to Python 3 because they disagreed with the changes that came with the new major version.

If you use Python a lot, you'll probably end up using both, which makes for the least ideal scenario–some libraries are only available with one version or the other, and so you may end up being forced to use both to complete your solutions. We'll explore the pros and cons to each in the next recipe.

Getting ready

For this recipe, we will want to use the GUI, so log on to your Pi over a VNC connection, or if you have it attached to a monitor, log on directly.

How to do it...

1. By default, the Raspbian system has both Python 2 and Python 3 installed. If you just enter `python`, it is set to run Python 2, so you need to be explicit when running Python 3:

```
pi@rpz14101:~ $ python --version
Python 2.7.9
pi@rpz14101:~ $ python2 --version
Python 2.7.9
pi@rpz14101:~ $ python3 --version
Python 3.4.2
```

2. If we look at the **Programming** section under the **Menu**, we see here as well that both versions of IDLE, Python's IDE, are included:

3. IDLE is a perfectly fine GUI editor for Python. Of course, so is vim! Another preinstalled tool for working on many different kinds of code is the Geany programmer's editor. This is designed to work with several different programming languages and has templates to get you started. If I create a new file using the Python template, it sets up the foundation of the Python program, leaving you to do the harder work. Here is the Python starter template:

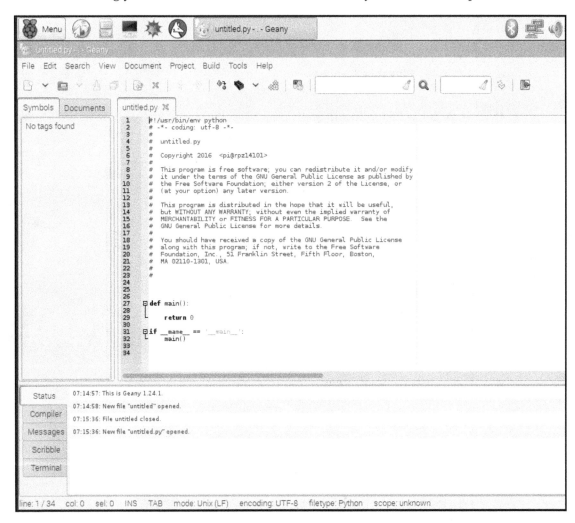

4. Geany is configured to run whatever version is set to run `python`, which in the Zero's case will be Python 2. The IDLE environment is simpler, but it gets the job done:

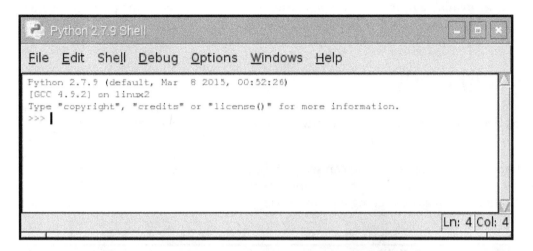

```
Python 2.7.9 Shell

File  Edit  Shell  Debug  Options  Windows  Help

Python 2.7.9 (default, Mar  8 2015, 00:52:26)
[GCC 4.9.2] on linux2
Type "copyright", "credits" or "license()" for more information.
>>>

                                                                  Ln: 4 Col: 4
```

5. The environment you choose to create your programs doesn't matter–in the end, you will have a `program.py` file (or perhaps several files), which will be executed using `python program.py`. As long as you are using version 2 or 3, this file should run on any computer that has Python, anywhere. Some of the examples ahead will be graphing things, so we will work in the GUI for now.

 The **Programming** section in the menu of the Raspbian OS contains several different IDEs for all sorts of different programming languages, including Java and Scratch. The Geany IDE supports many different languages, not only Python, but HTML, PHP, Ruby, and Erlang too. There really isn't anything you can't program on a Raspberry Pi Zero!

For the following recipes, we will work with the default of Python 2 unless we find a good reason to use Python 3. Generally speaking, there are more libraries available in Python 2, which makes it easier to leverage the power of your Pi Zero and communicate with the Internet of Things. Furthermore, while it is clear that the Raspbian builders don't want to be involved in the debate as they have installed both Python 2 and 3, the defaults for `python`, at least today, are Python 2.

Installing important Python packages

One of the things that make Python so easy and fun to work with is the extensive collection of libraries available from central repositories. Let's install some of the packages we will need for the recipes in this cookbook.

Getting ready

For this recipe, you can work from SSH, serial, or a terminal window inside a VNC session. If you decide to use Geany, it has a convenient window at the bottom with a terminal window so you can test your scripts on the fly.

In the following screenshot, you can see that the bottom half of the screen is a normal terminal window, while the Python script is available for editing above it. When you are doing things such as debugging and optimizing, an environment like this can make it a lot easier:

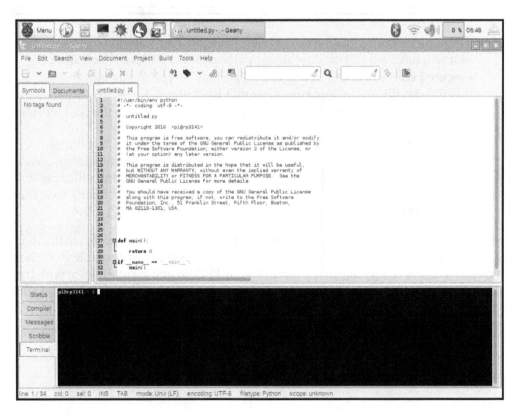

How to do it...

The Python Package Index is a repository of libraries for both Python 2 (`pip`) and Python 3 (`pip3`). The `pip` utility works for Python a lot like `apt-get` works for Linux: it lets you search for, install, uninstall, and upgrade any Python package available in its repositories. For many libraries, we can also search and install with `apt-cache search` or `apt-get`:

1. If we take a look at the Raspbian repositories, we can find Python libraries there as well, all searchable via `apt-cache`:

   apt-cache search python

   This will return a huge list of Python packages available to install. You can pipe that to `grep` to get a more reasonable output, if you know what you are looking for.

2. Here is an example of looking for plotting libraries:

```
pi@rpz14101:            apt-cache search python | grep plot
libplplot-dev - Scientific plotting library (development files)
python-chaco - interactive plotting application toolkit
python-gnuplot - Python interface to the gnuplot plotting program
python-guiqwt - efficient 2D data-plotting library
python-matplotlib - Python based plotting system in a style similar to Matlab
python-matplotlib-data - Python based plotting system (data package)
python-matplotlib-dbg - Python based plotting system (debug extension)
python-matplotlib-doc - Python based plotting system (documentation package)
python-mpld3 - D3 viewer for matplotlib
python-mplexporter - general matplotlib exporter
python-mpltoolkits.basemap - matplotlib toolkit to plot on map projections
python-mpltoolkits.basemap-data - matplotlib toolkit to plot on map projections (data package)
python-mpltoolkits.basemap-doc - matplotlib toolkit to plot on map projections (documentation)
python-plotly - Python plotting library for publication-quality graphs
python-plplot - Python support for PLplot, a plotting library
python-plplot-qt - Scientific plotting library (python qt GUI)
python-pybiggles - Scientific plotting package for Python
python-viper - minimalistic scientific plotter and run-time visualization module
python-wxmpl - Painless matplotlib embedding in wxPython
python3-matplotlib - Python based plotting system in a style similar to Matlab (Python 3)
python3-matplotlib-dbg - Python based plotting system (debug extension, Python 3)
python3-mpld3 - D3 viewer for matplotlib
python3-mplexporter - general matplotlib exporter
python3-plotly - Python 3 plotting library for publication-quality graphs
qtiplot - data analysis and scientific plotting
veusz - 2D scientific plotting application with graphical interface
pi@rpz14101:
```

3. Since we will need it later, let's install Matplotlib, a popular library for easy data visualization:

```
sudo apt-get install python-matplotlib
```

This will take care of installing any dependencies for you, just like installing any application using `apt-get`. Not every library, however, is available in that repository. Looking in the Python Package Index with the `pip` command is another method for library installation.

This is another command that can take a while to complete – there are a lot of libraries and dependencies that will be installed for matplotlib. Another good opportunity to stretch and walk around!

4. Let's install's Google's spreadsheet library, another library we will need later, with the `pip` utility. The Google Spreadsheet API documentation indicates you need to install and/or upgrade two libraries using the following:

```
sudo pip install --upgrade google-api-python-client
sudo pip install google-spreadsheet
```

You'll see a lot of information very similar to what you'd see with an `apt-get` installation.

5. Once this installs, you can also use `pip` to see every package that has been installed in your python library, whether through `pip` or using another method such as `apt-get install`. Try running this:

```
pip list
```

This will return all available Python libraries. You should not only see `google-spreadsheets` and `matplotlib`, but also a lot of other libraries that you didn't install. The Raspbian OS preinstalls several Raspberry Pi-based libraries, which we will be using later.

6. You should see something similar to the following output on your Raspberry Pi Zero:

```
pi@rpz14101:                    pip list
argparse (1.2.1)
chardet (2.3.0)
colorama (0.3.2)
dnspython (1.12.0)
google-api-python-client (1.5.2)
google-spreadsheet (0.0.6)
gpiozero (1.2.0)
html5lib (0.999)
httplib2 (0.9.2)
lxkeymap (0.1)
matplotlib (1.4.2)
mcpi (0.1.1)
mock (1.0.1)
ndg-httpsclient (0.3.2)
nose (1.3.4)
numpy (1.8.2)
oauth2client (3.0.0)
picamera (1.12)
pifacecommon (4.2.1)
pifacedigitalio (3.1.0)
pigpio (1.30)
Pillow (2.6.1)
pip (1.5.6)
pyasn1 (0.1.7)
pyasn1-modules (0.0.8)
pycrypto (2.6.1)
pygame (1.9.2a0)
pygobject (3.14.0)
pyOpenSSL (0.13.1)
pyparsing (2.0.3)
pyserial (2.6)
python-apt (0.9.3.12)
python-dateutil (2.2)
pytz (2012c)
requests (2.4.3)
RPi.GPIO (0.6.2)
rsa (3.4.2)
RTIMULib (7.2.1)
sense-hat (2.1.0)
setuptools (5.5.1)
simplejson (3.8.2)
six (1.8.0)
```

As we go through this cookbook and as you take on your own adventures, you'll find that almost any tool you think you would need is available as a Python library.

Creating our first Python program and running loops

Loops are one the most common programming functions, and very useful when doing things such as collecting readings over and over and reading through log files or sensor data. In this recipe, we will look at the different ways in which Python handles loops.

Getting ready

We're going to work with Raspbian's built-in Geany IDE:

1. Create a new Python program with **File | New (With template) | main.py**. Then, save it as `rpz_log_analysis.py`. We will use add to this program throughout the chapter.

2. If you haven't been logging your own temperature data or Raspberry Pi restarts, it is included in the source code for this book, which you can pull with Git. Make a note of where `rpz_temp.log` and `rpz_startup.log` are (hint: use `find`!), or copy them into the `/var/logs/` directory of your Raspberry Pi Zero.

3. If you want to start with the completed code for this recipe, it is named `rpz_log_analysis_loops.py` in the `/ch4/` directory.

How to do it...

1. Replace the default code below the comment block with this:

```
#!/usr/bin/env python
# COMMENTS BLOCK
# the main function
def main():
        #Execute the summary function
        summary()
        #If the function returns without an error,             return
a 0 for success
        return 0

def summary():
    #Create variables for filenames of log files.
    startuplog = "/var/log/rpz_startup.log"
    templog = "/var/log/rpz_temp.log"
    #Set loop counters to zero
```

```
temprows = 0
rpzstarts = 0
#Open the templog file, and read each line
for row in open(templog):
        #Increment the log file counter
        temprows += 1
#Print results
print "There are " + str(temprows) + " measurements in the file
" + templog
#Loop through startup log file
for row in open(startuplog):
        if row.startswith("RPZ startup"):
                rpzstarts += 1
print "There are " + str(rpzstarts) + " RPZ Startups logged in
file " + startuplog
return 0


if __name__ == '__main__':
main()
```

Tabs are important in Python. The tab character defines an inner code block for functions, loops, and conditions. If you are running a loop, anything you want to happen within that loop has to be one tab indented from where the loop is initialized. This is a bit different from other programming languages, and can take some time to get used to.

2. Let's go over what each section means:

```
# the main function
def main():
    #Execute the summary function
    summary()
    #If the function returns without an error, return a 0 for success
    return 0
```

The main() function is what Python looks for when importing a library or when it is executing itself. This will execute any time you run this file. You can put your entire program into the main() section, but typical Python programs will contain one or more functions that get called from the main() function. For our first program, main() only calls the function, summary().

3. Next, we have this:

```
def summary():
    #Create variables for filenames of log files.
```

```
startuplog = "/var/log/rpz_startup.log"
templog = "/var/log/rpz_temp.log"
#Set loop counters to zero
temprows = 0
rpzstarts = 0
```

> In the beginning of the function, we initialize our variables. First, we identify the location of our Raspberry Pi Zero logs, which you have already been creating yourself or have pulled the samples for from the source code Git repository. If your logs aren't in the `/var/logs/` directory, you can specify their locations by changing the `startuplog` and `templog` variables. The `tmprows` and `rpzstarts` variables are also initialized; these will be used to count the number of temperature readings taken and the number of times your Raspberry Pi Zero has logged startups.

4. Next, we start the first loop by opening our temperature log file and reading through each row. For each row that is read, we increment our counter. As each row is a temperature reading, once we count all the rows, we can output how many readings have been taken:

```
#Open the templog file, and read each line
    for row in open(templog):
            #Increment the log file counter
            temprows += 1
    #Print results
    print "There are " + str(temprows) + "
measurements in the file " + templog
```

5. The startup log file is a little different. If we look at the log of a single startup, several lines are logged:

```
RPZ startup at Sat 20 Aug 20:53:15 PDT 2016
Current core temperature 41.2'C
GPU RAM 96M - CPU RAM 416M
RPZ Status: core=400000000 free=398347658 voltage=1.2v
```

6. If we just counted each line like the previous loop, we would be way off on the number of startups. To account for this, we add an `if` condition inside the loop to only count the lines that start with `RPZ Startup`. This way, even if we add several lines to the startup log, your program will still accurately count the number of times you've logged a startup:

```
#Loop through startup log file
    for row in open(startuplog):
```

```
        if row.startswith("RPZ startup"):
                rpzstarts += 1
    print "There are " + str(rpzstarts) + " RPZ
    Startups logged in file " + startuplog
    return 0
```

7. Once the logs have been read, the loop exits and returns the count of temperature readings and startups to the terminal. Finally, it returns a 0 to let the `main()` function know it finished successfully.

8. The very last part of the program is what tells Python this can be executed by itself:

```
if __name__ == '__main__':
    main()
```

> This is a required part for a Python program for it to execute on its own. When we start using the libraries installed, we will use the `import` command to bring those libraries into our program. Those libraries are really just collections of other Python programs, and when the `import` command is used, Python looks for the library and executes the `main()` function it finds there. If your program can run standalone in that, it doesn't need to be imported into another program to be useful; this block makes it valid. When you get more into Python and start looking at others' programs, this is something you will often see.

9. After entering the code, you can execute it directly from Geany by clicking on the **Run** button:

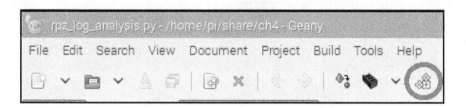

10. Geany will open a terminal window, execute the program, and show you the output:

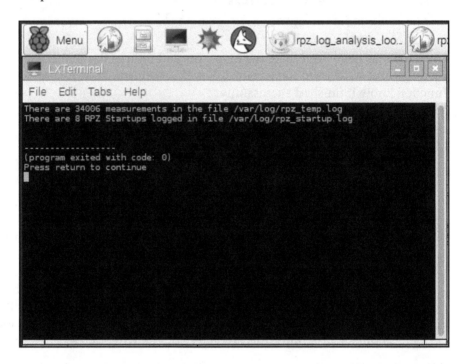

Congratulations! You've started learning loops with a practical program that counts your Raspberry Pi Zero temperature readings and startups. We will make this program more interesting and useful in the following recipes.

You can also create and execute most of the programs right from the command line using your favorite editor and putting `python` before the program you want to run:

```
pi@rpz14101:~/share/ch4 $ python rpz_log_analysis.py
There are 34006 measurements in the file
/var/log/rpz_temp.log
There are 8 RPZ Startups logged in file
/var/log/rpz_startup.log
```

Using a development environment like Geany is nice because it sets up boilerplate code for you and helps you visualize your program, but you can become just as efficient with mastery of command-line tools such as vim and Emacs.

There's more...

There are several ways to use a loop, and though reading through log files is a great way to leverage a loop, you certainly aren't limited to that:

- You can loop something with a counter so that it will only run x times:

```
>>> readings = 5
>>> for x in range(0,readings):
...     print x
...
0
1
2
3
4
```

- You can loop on a condition so that the loop will continue executing until a specific criterion is met:

```
>>> while y>5:
...     print y
...     y-=1
...
10
9
8
7
6
>>>
```

As you get more involved with programming in any language, loops will be one of the most common things you use to build your solutions.

Playing with strings

String manipulation is a common programming task and also important when doing things such as sensor data collection. Python is well equipped for taking a string of characters and modifying it to be more human- or spreadsheet-readable. We're going to take the program we started making in the previous recipe and spice it up to analyze the strings and return some more interesting information!

Getting ready

If you completed the previous recipe, you just need `rpz_log_analysis.py` open. If you've pulled the source code, you can read `rpz_log_analysis_strings.py` to run the completed program from this recipe.

How to do it...

1. We're going to work off of the original code from the last recipe, modify it a bit, and then add to it. Here is the full code below the comment block:

```python
#!/usr/bin/env python
# COMMENTS BLOCK
startuplog = "/var/log/rpz_startup.log"
templog = "/var/log/rpz_temp.log"

def main():
    summary()
    rpztempstats()
    return 0

def summary():
    #create variables for filenames of log files
    temprows = 0
    rpzstarts = 0
    for row in open(templog):
        temprows += 1
    print "There are " + str(temprows) + " measurements
in the file " + templog
    for row in open(startuplog):
        if row.startswith("RPZ startup"):
            rpzstarts += 1
    print "There are " + str(rpzstarts) + " RPZ Startups logged in file
" + startuplog
    return 0

def rpztempstats():
    from time import localtime, strftime, strptime
    maxtemp = 0.0
    totalreadings = 0
    sumreadings = 0
    for row in open(templog):
        data = row.replace("RPZ Temperature at ","").split(": ")
        humandate = data[0]
        pydate = strptime(humandate,'%a %d %b %H:%M:%S %Z %Y')
```

```
        csvdate = strftime('%Y%m%d %H:%M:%S %Z',pydate)
        tempcelcius = float(data[1].split("'")[0])
        if tempcelcius >= maxtemp:
                maxtemp = tempcelcius
                maxtempdate = humandate
        totalreadings += 1
        sumreadings += tempcelcius
    print "Max Temperature of " + str(maxtemp) +
"C on " + maxtempdate
    print "Average Temp: %.2fC" % float(sumreadings/totalreadings)


    return 0
if __name__ == '__main__':
    main()
```

 Depending on your localization settings, your time output may be different.

2. The first thing you'll notice is that we've moved the filename variables out of the `summary()` function and above the `main()` function. This allows the variable to be accessed by any function in the program, so as we add functionality to our Python program, any new function we create will know where the log files are. We've also added a call to a second function in our `main()` function, which will execute after the `summary()` function we created in the previous recipe:

```
def main():
        summary()
        rpztempstats()
        return 0
```

3. We covered how `summary()` works in the previous recipe, so let's take a look at how to leverage strings in the `rpztempstats()` function. We'll start this function with an import:

```
from time import localtime, strftime, strptime
```

This tells Python to pull the `localtime` and `strptime` string/date conversion modules from the time library. We will use these to read the logs and understand the timestamps recorded in them.

4. We're going to be working with the Raspberry Pi Zero temperature logs we
   created earlier (or the sample in the source code), which are in the following
   format:

```
RPZ Temperature at Sun 21 Aug 09:33:02 PDT 2016: 39.0'C
RPZ Temperature at Sun 21 Aug 09:34:01 PDT 2016: 36.3'C
RPZ Temperature at Sun 21 Aug 09:35:01 PDT 2016: 36.9'C
RPZ Temperature at Sun 21 Aug 09:36:01 PDT 2016: 35.8'C
```

5. We just want Python to worry about the date and the temperature–the format
   and text is only there to make it more human friendly. We want to make it more
   computer friendly so that it can return some temperature statistics. We'll utilize
   the same loop in the `templog` we utilized in the last recipe, after initializing our
   variables:

```
maxtemp = 0.0
totalreadings = 0
sumreadings = 0
for row in open(templog):
```

6. In the next line, we perform our first string operations using a combination of
   replace and split. The `replace()` function replaces one found string with
   another. In our case, we want to replace the beginning of our log line so we are
   only left with the date and the temperature. In the same line, we also use the split
   on a colon and a space to turn the date into one field and the temperature into
   another:

```
data = row.replace("RPZ Temperature at ","").split(": ")
```

7. The two fields stored after split will be `data[0]` for the date and `data[1]` for the
   temperature. For clarity, we will set the variable `humandate` to `data[0]`:

```
humandate = data[0]
```

8. The `strptime` function we imported in the beginning is used to take a date string
   and turn it into a Python-understandable timestamp. By setting it to this format,
   we can output it to another format or even leverage Python date functions to
   perform date-based calculations. Here, we are telling `strptime` that the
   `humandate` string is a date represented in the format (Day, DayofMonth, Month,
   Hour:Minute:Second TimeZone Year):

```
pydate = strptime(humandate, '%a %d %b %H:%M:%S %Z %Y')
```

Here, we split the string again:

```
tempcelcius = float(data[1].split("'")[0])
if tempcelcius >= maxtemp:
        maxtemp = tempcelcius
        maxtempdate = humandate
totalreadings += 1
sumreadings += tempcelcius
print "Max Temperature of " + str(maxtemp)
+ "C on " + maxtempdate
print "Average Temp: %.2fC" %
float(sumreadings/totalreadings)
```

9. Executing the program now will return a little more information, and it's
   certainly more useful than a count of readings and startups:

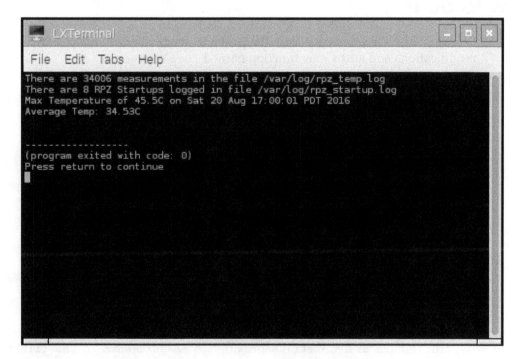

Plotting graphs using Python

Visualization is a key tool to better understanding patterns and correlations. Python is as
great at graphing data as it is with collecting it and manipulating it. This recipe will read in
a range of our Raspberry Pi's temperature log data and render it into a time-series plot.

Getting ready

If you've been following along from the previous recipe, you can continue working in your `rpz_log_analysis.py` file. If you want to see the completed code up to here, you can find it in the `/ch4/` directory named `rpz_log_analysis_plot.py`. This recipe also needs your RPZ temperature logs, either in your `/var/logs/` directory or available at the root of the Git repo.

If you've been using the command line up until now, you'll want to be in your GUI, either directly connected to a monitor or over a VNC connection. You'll need the graphical interface to see your graph!

How to do it...

1. Working with the same code from the previous recipe, we will make a few modifications and add a new function named `rpzplottemp()`:

```
#!/usr/bin/env python
# COMMENTS BLOCK
from pylab import *
startuplog = "/var/log/rpz_startup.log"
templog = "/var/log/rpz_temp.log"

def main():
        summary()
        rpztempstats()
        rpzplottemp(1440)
        return 0

def summary():
        #create variables for filenames of log files
        temprows = 0
        rpzstarts = 0
        for row in open(templog):
                temprows += 1
    print "There are " + str(temprows) + " measurements in the file "
    + templog
    for row in open(startuplog):
                if row.startswith("RPZ startup"):
                        rpzstarts += 1
    print "There are " + str(rpzstarts) + " RPZ Startups logged in file
"
    + startuplog
        return 0
```

```
def rpztempstats():
    maxtemp = 0.0
    totalreadings = 0
    sumreadings = 0
    for row in open(templog):
        data = row.replace("RPZ Temperature at ","").split(": ")
        humandate = data[0]
        tempcelcius = float(data[1].split("'")[0])
        if tempcelcius >= maxtemp:
            maxtemp = tempcelcius
            maxtempdate = humandate
        totalreadings += 1
        sumreadings += tempcelcius
    print "Max Temperature of " + str(maxtemp) + "C on " + maxtempdate
    print "Average Temp: %.2fC" % float(sumreadings/totalreadings)
    return 0

def rpzplottemp(readings):
    import subprocess
    from time import strptime
    grfdt = []
    grftmp = []
    for row in open(templog):
        data = row.replace("RPZ Temperature at ","").split(": ")
        humandate = data[0]
        tempcelcius = float(data[1].split("'")[0])
        grfdt.append(humandate)
        grftmp.append(tempcelcius)
    plt.plot(grftmp[-(readings)::])
    plt.ylabel("Degrees Celcius")
    plt.xlabel("Measurements")
    plt.title("RPZ Temperatures from " + grfdt[-(readings)] + " to "
    + grfdt[-1])
    plt.show()
    return 0
if __name__ == '__main__':
    main()
```

2. The beginning of the program changes very little. We import a new library, `pylab`, which is the collection of calculation and graphical libraries for use with Python. We also call a new function, named `rpzplottemp`, which is the function that will create our graph. You'll also notice the function is taking a parameter of `1440`. This number is sent to the function as the number of readings you'd like to graph. You can adjust this to different ranges to get the last x readings from your logs. `1440` readings is 1 day (1 reading per minute times 60 minutes times 24 hours):

```
from pylab import *
startuplog = "/var/log/rpz_startup.log"
templog = "/var/log/rpz_temp.log"

def main():
        summary()
        rpztempstats()
        rpzplottemp(1440)
        return 0
```

3. The summary and statistics function are the same, and will do the same thing. Let's dive into the plotting function:

```
def rpzplottemp(readings):
```

4. The `subprocess` is a part of the `matplotlib` library, and it will open up our new graph:

```
    import subprocess
```

5. These variables are set to lists; one will be for our date data and the other for our temperature data:

```
    grfdt = []
    grftmp = []
```

6. In this familiar loop, we read our temperature log file, strip it down to a date and temperature, and add each one to the lists we just initialized:

```
for row in open(templog):
        data = row.replace("RPZ Temperature at ","").split(": ")
        humandate = data[0]
        tempcelcius = float(data[1].split("'")[0])
        grfdt.append(humandate)
        grftmp.append(tempcelcius)
```

7. Finally, we leverage the power of our plotting library. We instruct the library to plot the last x readings from the temperature list, `grftmp`. This is going to create the interesting part of our visualization:

```
plt.plot(grftmp[-(readings)::])
```

8. Labeling in `matplotlib` is as easy as identifying your `xlabel` and `ylabel` parameters:

```
plt.ylabel("Degrees Celcius")
plt.xlabel("Measurements")
```

9. Finally, using our date list, we can make a descriptive title for our graph:

```
plt.title("RPZ Temperatures from " + grfdt[-(readings)] + " to "
+ grfdt[-1])
```

10. Once we have provided all of the information we need, we call `show()` to create the graph:

```
plt.show()
return 0
```

11. That's all there is to it! When you execute your program this time, you will see your familiar statistics information, but another window will open with your temperature logs graphed:

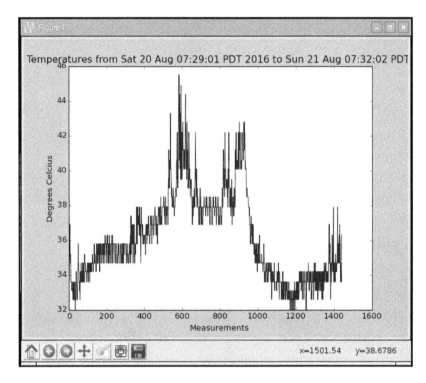

It is as easy as that to make a graph of your temperature logs, and you have many options to improve or modify the way your data is visualized. This is only the beginning!

There's more...

The `matplotlib` documentation is extensive and well written, and shows dozens of different options for different types of graphs, more interactive visualization, and more. We will inevitably be graphing this again later in this cookbook and make a point to explore different features of this awesome Python library.

Sending an e-mail from a Python Script

The ability to send e-mail is the way to have your Raspberry Pi Zero contact you no matter where you are. Python's vast library collection includes one that makes sending e-mail simple. Let's expand our program to e-mail someone with a graph attachment of our Raspberry Pi Zero temperature output. If you have a project where your device is remote but still able to access the Internet, you might want to get a regular e-mail showing how things are working without having to log on.

Getting ready

If you have been following along, you can continue adding to your `rpz_log_analysis.py` program. If you want to see the completed code for this recipe, it is available in the `/ch4/` directory of the Git repository, named `rpz_log_analysis_email.py`.

I used Google's SMTP to send my e-mail. There are a lot of ways you can do it, but this makes it easy to do from pretty much anywhere. All you'll need is a Google account and e-mail.

1. In your Google account settings, under the **Sign-in & Security** section, you can create **App passwords**, which are temporary passwords that you can use for developing applications to use your account. You can generate a password for your Raspberry Pi Zero here:

2. Click on **App passwords**, and, you'll get to your passwords screen:

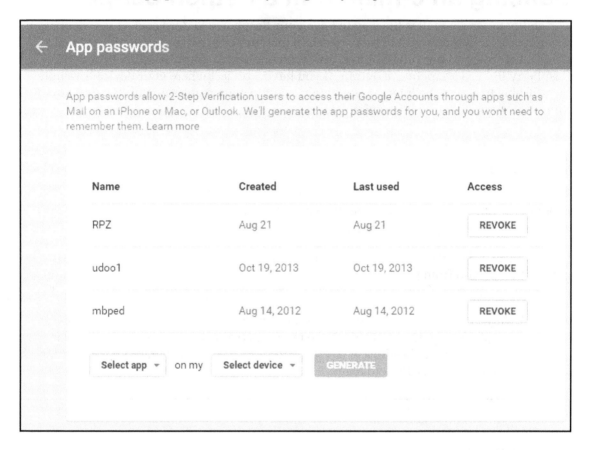

3. You can create a new password for your account by clicking on the **Select app** dropdown. Picking Other allows you to enter your own custom app name, such as RPZ.

4. Clicking on **GENERATE** will display a password that you can use with your Google e-mail to access the SMTP server and send e-mail.

 Many ISPs block outgoing SMTP traffic to reduce spammers and bots and other malicious practices. If you are having problems connecting to Google's SMTP server or sending e-mail through a local one, it could be your ISP's restrictions. If they are blocking outgoing e-mail traffic, they do sometimes provide an SMTP server than you can use and connect to. Troubleshooting networks and ISP firewalls is beyond the scope of this book, but if you've made it this far, you will be able to figure things out.

How to do it...

1. The summary and statistics functions will not change, but we do make some changes to the plotting function to save the graph output to a file. At the beginning of our code, we add the `smtplib` import for our e-mail tools and identify the location where we want to save our temperature graph.

```
#!/usr/bin/env python
# COMMENTS BLOCK
from pylab import *
import smtplib
startuplog = "/var/log/rpz_startup.log"
templog = "/var/log/rpz_temp.log"
graphfile = "/home/pi/share/ch4/rpz_temp_plot.png"
```

2. The `main` function should look very familiar. We've changed the function `rpzplottemp` to receive a second variable, which will indicate whether a picture of the plot should be saved. Setting it to 0 will not save a file, so the functionality will be the same as the previous plotting recipe. Setting it to 1 will save the plot to the filename identified in the `graphfile` variable.

```
def main():
    summary()
    rpztempstats()
    rpzplottemp(1440,0)
    rpzemailgraph(1440)
    return 0
```

3. The `summary` and `rpztempstats` functions are the same as previous recipes, so I've removed the text of the functions for brevity:

```
def summary():

def rpztempstats():
```

4. The `rpzplottemp` function is the first one with changes. In the first line, you can see we've added a `savepng` variable to be passed. The function operates the same way, collecting data from the log file and populating the temperature readings.

```
def rpzplottemp(readings,savepng):
    import subprocess
    from time import strptime
    grfdt = []
    grftmp = []
    for row in open(templog):
```

```
                        data = row.replace("RPZ Temperature at ","").split(": ")
                        humandate = data[0]
                        tempcelcius = float(data[1].split("'")[0])
                        grfdt.append(humandate)
                        grftmp.append(tempcelcius)
                plt.plot(grftmp[-(readings)::])
                plt.ylabel("Degrees Celcius")
                plt.xlabel("Measurements")
                plt.title("RPZ Temperatures from "
              + grfdt[-(readings)] + " to " + grfdt[-1])
```

5. After the loop completes, this is where the function is changed. Previously, the function would show the graph. Here, we tell it first to look at the `savepng` variable passed and, if it is 1, save the file instead of showing it. This will be the file we attach to our e-mail.

```
if savepng == 1:
        plt.savefig(graphfile)
else:
        plt.show()
return 0
```

6. We also have a new function, `rpzemailgraph`, which accepts a number of readings as a parameter. Several e-mail libraries are imported using `from...import`.

```
def rpzemailgraph(readings):
    from email.mime.image import MIMEImage
    from email.mime.multipart import MIMEMultipart
```

7. Next, the plotting function is called, with a directive to save the graph to file. The number of readings coming in from the `email` function is passed on to the plotting function.

```
rpzplottemp(readings,1)
```

8. The remaining code sets up and sends out the e-mail. First, you initialize a `msg` object and populate the `subject`, `to`, and `from` fields:

```
msg = MIMEMultipart()
to = "me@yahoo.com"
frm = "noreply@rpz.local"
msg['Subject'] = "RPZ Temperature Graphs"
msg["From"] = frm
msg["To"] = to
msg.preamble = "Raspberry Pi Zero Temperature Output Graph"
```

9. The next section takes our plot file, reads it into a format compatible with e-mail, and then attaches it to the e-mail with `msg.attach`:

```
rpzgraph = open(graphfile, 'rb')
rpzgraphimg = MIMEImage(rpzgraph.read())
rpzgraph.close()
msg.attach(rpzgraphimg)
```

10. Finally, the server settings and account information are passed, along with some SMTP commands that are used to establish the connection and secure the communication.

```
mailout = smtplib.SMTP('smtp.gmail.com',587)
mailout.ehlo()
mailout.starttls()
mailout.ehlo()
mailout.login('me@gmail.com','MY GOOGLE APP PASSWORD')
mailout.sendmail(frm, to, msg.as_string())
mailout.quit
return 0

if __name__ == '__main__':
    main()
```

11. If everything worked out well, executing your program will send you an e-mail with your temperature graph attached.

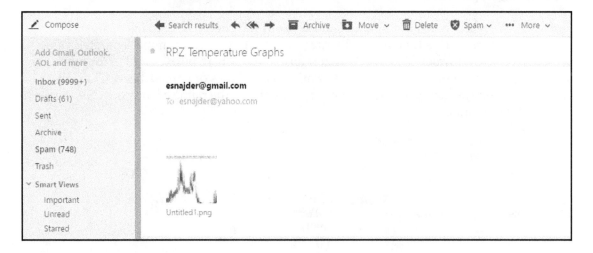

You might want to add the execution of this to a weekly cron job (refer to `Chapter 3`, *Programming with Linux, Using Crontab to run a script automatically at predefined intervals* recipe) and get an e-mail update on the happiness of your Raspberry Pi Zero.

Creating a program to log and append data to a CSV file

A lot of times, we will use the Pi Zero just for data collection and transmission. We can use the power of Python to collect data on our Pi and save it to a CSV file for importing into spreadsheets or databases. Python has a CSV library for precisely this purpose, as a part of its vast collection of data manipulation tools.

Getting ready

If you are continuing with building your `rpz_log_analysis.py` file, then you don't need to do anything more in preparation. If you'd like to see the code up to this point in the recipe, you can find it in the `/ch4/` directory as `rpz_log_analysis_csv.py`.

How to do it...

1. We're going to add another feature to our Raspberry Pi Zero log analysis program. This function will write out our log data into comma separated value, or CSV, format. This is a common format for data to be exported in for migration to other data systems, such as relational databases or spreadsheets. The only thing we change in the beginning is specifying the name of the new CSV file we'll be creating.

```
#!/usr/bin/env python
# COMMENTS BLOCK
from pylab import *
import smtplib
startuplog = "/var/log/rpz_startup.log"
templog = "/var/log/rpz_temp.log"
graphfile = "/home/pi/share/ch4/rpz_temp_plot.png"
csvfile = "/home/pi/share/ch4/rpz_temps.csv"
```

2. For this recipe, let's also comment out the other functions we've made so when we run it here, it will only make the CSV file. We're going to improve the way we handle this in a couple of recipes, but for now, just add a # in front of the functions you don't want to execute.

```
def main():
        #summary()
        #rpztempstats()
        #rpzplottemp(1440,0)
        #rpzemailgraph(1440)
        rpztempcsvexport()
        return 0
```

3. Because we aren't calling any other functions, we really only need to look at the new `rpztempcsvexport` function. We will need the `strptime` function to convert our string to a time and then the `strftime` function to turn it into a good format for a CSV file (YYYYMMDD HH:mm:ss TZ). The final part of the loop puts the date/time data into a nested list:

```
def rpztempcsvexport():
        from time import strptime, strftime
        import csv
        csvdata = [[]]
        for row in open(templog):
                data = row.replace("RPZ Temperature at ","").split(": ")
                humandate = data[0]
                pydate = strptime(humandate,'%a %d %b %H:%M:%S %Z %Y')
                tempcelcius = float(data[1].split("'")[0])
                csvdateformat = strftime('%Y%m%d %H:%M:%S %Z',pydate)
                csvdata.append([csvdateformat,tempcelcius])
```

4. After the loop completes, the `csvdata` list is written out to a CSV file and a message is provided to the user.

```
        csvout = csv.writer(open(csvfile,"w"))
        csvout.writerows(csvdata)
        print "File written to %s" % csvfile
        return 0

if __name__ == '__main__':
    main()
```

5. Executing the program will generate the file and return a message. You can take a peek at your output CSV file with the `tail` command.

```
pi@rpz14101:~/share/ch4 $ python rpz_log_analysis_csvexport.py
File written to /home/pi/share/ch4/rpz_temps.csv
pi@rpz14101:~/share/ch4 $ tail -n5 /home/pi/share/ch4/rpz_temps.csv
20160821 09:35:01 PDT,36.9
20160821 09:36:01 PDT,35.8
20160821 09:37:01 PDT,39.5
20160821 09:38:01 PDT,41.2
20160821 09:39:01 PDT,36.9
```

Using a Python script to upload data online to a Google spreadsheet interface

Creating CSV is great; you can pretty much import that into any spreadsheet or database. What if you just want to skip that step and push your Raspberry Pi Zero data directly to Google spreadsheets? With Google's API and Python libraries, you can securely send your data to a spreadsheet in your Google account.

Getting ready

If you don't have a Google account, you will definitely need one for this recipe. The Google Developer documentation for **Getting Started** will have the most up-to-date instructions on setting up your application for authentication, but we will skip through it here. You can always refer to `https://developers.google.com/api-client-library/python/start/get_started` if you hit an issue.

1. First, go to the Google API Console located at `https://console.developers.google.com/apis`. When you click on **Credentials**, you will see a screen like this one:

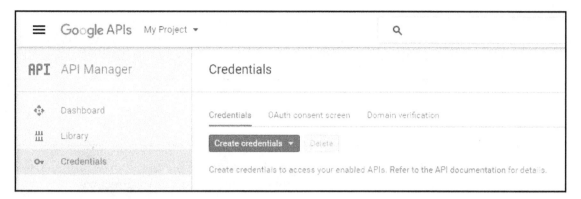

2. Click on **Credentials** and the **Create credentials** dropdown. Select **OAuth Client ID**. Select **Other** for the application type, give it a name, and click on **Create**.

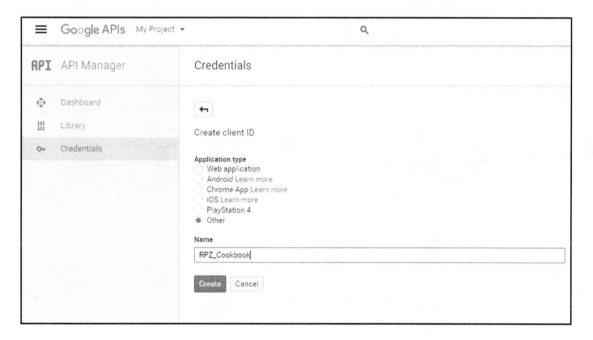

3. The next window will be a pop-up window where you can copy your client ID and Secret to you clipboard. You can save these to a file and also download them from the Credentials screen afterward.

4. Click on the Download icon to the right and save the file as `client_secrets.json`. Copy or move this into your /ch4/ directory.

5. If you want to pull the code for this recipe, it is available in the /ch4/ directory as `rpz_log_analysis_spreadsheets.py`. You will still need to set up your own Google account and client secrets for this recipe to work. You'll also need to have loaded the Google API and Spreadsheets libraries; if you haven't yet, you can find the instructions in the second recipe in this chapter.

How to do it

1. Like the previous recipe, we are just going to focus on the Google spreadsheet export and comment out (using #) the other functions to keep them from running. We're going to have this function export all log data to a new spreadsheet.

```
#!/usr/bin/env python
# COMMENTS BLOCK
from pylab import *
import smtplib
startuplog = "/var/log/rpz_startup.log"
templog = "/var/log/rpz_temp.log"
graphfile = "/home/pi/share/ch4/rpz_temp_plot.png"
csvfile = "/home/pi/share/ch4/rpz_temps.csv"

def main():
        #summary()
        #rpztempstats()
        #rpzplottemp(1440,0)
        #rpzemailgraph(1440)
        #rpztempcsvexport()
        rpztempgoogleexport()
        return 0
```

2. We're going to import several libraries for authentication, string manipulation, and Google's API.

```
def rpztempgoogleexport():
    from apiclient.discovery import build
    from time import strptime, strftime
    import oauth2client
    from oauth2client import client, file, tools
    from httplib2 import Http
```

3. Here, we use a time function to identify the date and time in a human-friendly format. We use this to name our new spreadsheet.

```
    nowtime = datetime.datetime.now()
    sheetname = "RPZ Templog as of " + str(nowtime)
```

4. The next chunk of code is directly from the Google API documentation. Here you identify the location of your `client_secrets.json` file and the API you will be authenticating to.

```
    SCOPES = "https://www.googleapis.com/auth/spreadsheets"
    CLIENT_SECRET_FILE = "/home/pi/client_secrets.json"
    APPLICATION_NAME = "RPZ"
    store = file.Storage('storage.json')
    creds = store.get()
    if not creds or creds.invalid:
        flow = client.flow_from_clientsecrets(CLIENT_SECRET_FILE,
        SCOPES)
        creds = tools.run_flow(flow, store)
```

5. In the following bit of code, we leverage the Google API to manipulate the spreadsheet. The documentation is extensive, and this is only the tip of the iceberg as far as what you can do with a spreadsheet and the API. First, we authenticate ourselves. Next, with the DATA variable, we name a new spreadsheet with the title we previously generated in `sheetname`. The fields of date and temperature are labeled, and then we run through our usual file-reading loop, stripping out the text and converting to spreadsheet-friendly data.

```
    NEWSHEET = build('sheets','v4', http=creds.authorize(Http()))
    DATA = {"properties": {"title": sheetname}}
    sheet = NEWSHEET.spreadsheets().create(body=DATA).execute()
    SHEET_ID = sheet['spreadsheetId']
    FIELDS = ["LogDate","TempC"]
    sheetdata = [FIELDS]
    for row in open(templog):
            data = row.replace("RPZ Temperature at ","").split(": ")
```

```
humandate = data[0]
pydate = strptime(humandate,'%a %d %b %H:%M:%S %Z %Y')
sheetdate = strftime('%Y/%m/%d %H:%M:%S %Z',pydate)
tempcelcius = float(data[1].split("'")[0])
sheetdata.append([sheetdate,tempcelcius])
```

6. After the loop completes, we execute the write operation and inform the user.

```
NEWSHEET.spreadsheets().values().update(spreadsheetId=SHEET_ID,range="A1",
body={"values":sheetdata},valueInputOption="RAW").execute()
        print "Your new spreadsheet is available or your account named %s"
% sheetname
        return 0

if __name__ == '__main__':
        main()
```

7. At least the first time, you will want to execute in a GUI. For this, you'll need to log in and authenticate your program to use your Spreadsheets account.

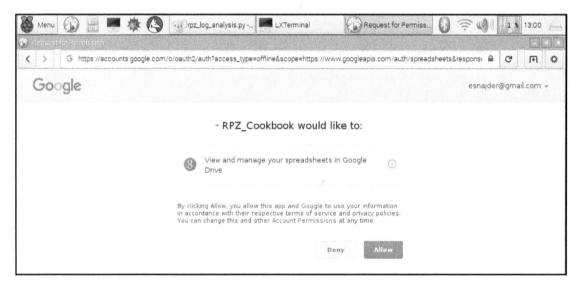

Be careful not to share your `client_secrets.json` file or upload it to a public repository. Any time you think you may have compromised your secrets, just go back to your Google account, delete them, and create new ones. This way you can ensure your account is secure, and you aren't letting other people use your API credentials to do things in your account.

8. Go back to the Google Developer Console, and enable the Google Sheets API.
9. Once you've worked through the authentication process, your program will work without having to go through the browser. Your program will finish executing, and soon you will find a new spreadsheet in your Docs collection.

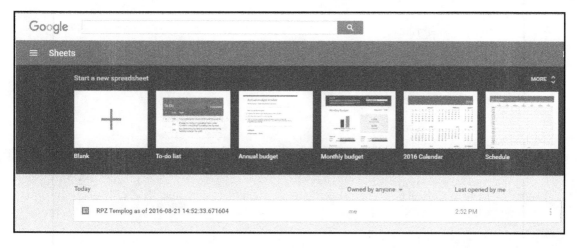

10. Opening the document shows our temperature readings. From here, we can leverage any spreadsheet feature to calculate or graph our data.

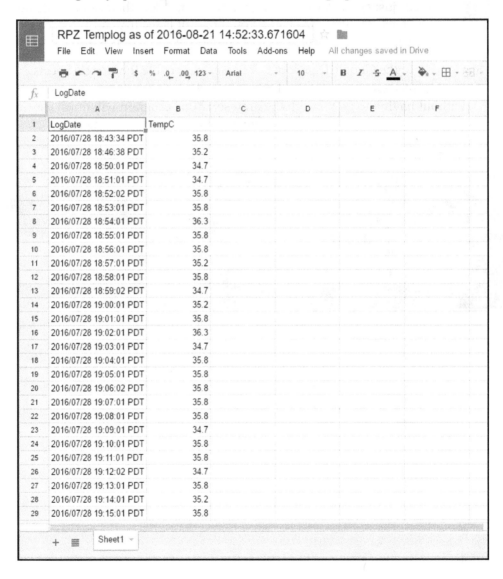

Now we have our Raspberry Pi Zero sending its temperature information to Google. Not bad for a $5 computer!

There's more...

The Google API lets you write to pretty much anywhere in Docs or Google Drive, and you can access a ton of useful services and data within Google's platform. If you want to write a document, create slides, or save a file to Google Drive, it is all possible with the API, and more features become available with each version. Look at the Google Developer's Documentation to learn about all of the great things you can leverage.

Adding help and parameters to your Python Program

In this chapter, we have taken a single Python program and given it the ability to:

- Scan logs to count the number of measurements and RPZ restarts
- Manipulate log strings to summarize RPZ temperature data
- Plot a graph of a range of RPZ temperature readings
- E-mail someone a graph of RPZ temperature readings
- Generate a CSV file of date/temperature readings
- Push date/temperature readings to Google spreadsheets

Up until now, I have just been adding functions to the main function and executing everything or commenting out the functions I don't want to execute for that recipe. With a little code polishing, this little collection of functions can be turned into a more useful utility, giving the user a choice of which functions will actually execute, and providing information on what each function will do. Python makes it very easy to add user interactivity, so we can create just the CSV, or we can provide the summary and display a graph–or even do everything.

Getting ready

If you have been adding to your `rpz_log_analysis.py` program, this is where we will finish it up. If you want to see the completed code for this chapter, you'll find it as `rpz_log_analysis.py` in `/ch4/`.

How to do it...

We only need to import one Python library and add some code to our `main()` function to make this little utility flexible and easy to use. The `argparse` library is the Python standard for processing input parameters and flags as well as producing useful help output. We will take each of the functions we've applied in previous recipes and make them options when we run the program.

1. The code starts the same, with an added import of `argparse`. Since we are going to make this program execute any of the functions, we will want all of our variables defined.

```
from pylab import *
import smtplib
import argparse
startuplog = "/var/log/rpz_startup.log"
templog = "/var/log/rpz_temp.log"
graphfile = "/home/pi/share/ch4/rpz_temp_plot.png"
csvfile = "/home/pi/share/ch4/rpz_temps.csv"
```

2. We are going to initialize the argument parser first and include a description and epilog value. These will be the headers and footers of your help output.

```
def main():
        parser = argparse.ArgumentParser(description="Raspberry Pi Zero Log
Analysis Utility",epilog="Select any function or
combination of functions.")
```

3. Next, we add the arguments we will want the user to be able to execute. We don't have to add a `-help` option; `argparse` already takes care of that for you. We include some information in each argument definition:

   - The first argument is the flag name. This is what the user will pass when they want to execute that part of the program. The `help` string will be what is sent to the user when passing `-h` or `-help` for help.
   - The final part of the first two arguments, `action="store_true"`, means that the argument doesn't require any additional information, such as a parameter.

   ```
   parser.add_argument("--summary",help="Show RPZ Logs
   Summary",action="store_true")
   parser.add_argument("--stats",help="Show RPZ Temperature Log
   Statistics", action="store_true")
   ```

4. When a parameter is required, such as the number of readings to plot, we add the type description, and can use the `metavar` field for the help output to make sense to the reader. The last two arguments are similar to the first two, in that they do not require additional parameters.

```
parser.add_argument("--plot",metavar="READINGS",help="Show RPZ Plot
for X measurements",type=int)
parser.add_argument("--email",metavar="READINGS",help="Email RPZ
Plot
for X measnurements",type=int)
parser.add_argument("--csv",help="Export CSV File of Temperature
Data",action="store_true")
parser.add_argument("--spreadsheet",help="Upload RPZ
Temperature Data to Google Spreadsheets",action="store_true")
```

5. Finally, we tell Python to parse the received arguments and use if conditions to decide which functions we want to execute. If two flags are passed, two functions will execute. If all flags are passed, it will provide the summary and statistics, draw a plot, send an e-mail, export a CSV, and upload to the Google spreadsheet all in one shot.

```
args = parser.parse_args()
if args.summary:
        summary()
if args.stats:
        rpztempstats()
if args.plot:
        rpzplottemp(args.plot,0)
if args.email:
        rpzemailgraph(args.email)
if args.csv:
        rpztempcsvexport()
if args.spreadsheet
        rpztempgoogleexport()
return 0
```

6. If you have all of your functions in your program, you should be all set. Run the program from the command line, starting with the help option, and then see what else you can do!

```
pi@rpz14101:~/share/ch4 $ python rpz_log_analysis.py --help
usage: rpz_log_analysis.py [-h] [--summary] [--stats] [--plot READINGS]
                           [--email READINGS] [--csv] [--spreadsheet]

Raspberry Pi Zero Log Analysis Utility

optional arguments:
  -h, --help       show this help message and exit
  --summary        Show RPZ Logs Summary
  --stats          Show RPZ Temperature Log Statistics
  --plot READINGS  Show RPZ Plot for X measurements
  --email READINGS Email RPZ Plot for X measnurements
  --csv            Export CSV File of Temperature Data
  --spreadsheet    Upload RPZ Temperature Data to Google Spreadsheets

Select any function or combination of functions.
pi@rpz14101:~/share/ch4 $ python rpz_log_analysis.py --summary
There are 34006 measurements in the file /var/log/rpz_temp.log
There are 8 RPZ Startups logged in file /var/log/rpz_startup.log
pi@rpz14101:~/share/ch4 $ python rpz_log_analysis.py --summary --stats --spreadsheet
There are 34006 measurements in the file /var/log/rpz_temp.log
There are 8 RPZ Startups logged in file /var/log/rpz_startup.log
Max Temperature of 45.5C on Sat 20 Aug 17:00:01 PDT 2016
Average Temp: 34.53C
Your new spreadsheet is available or your account named RPZ Templog as of 2016-08-28 11:55:05.176669
pi@rpz14101:~/share/ch4 $ python rpz_log_analysis.py --email 6580 --stats
Max Temperature of 45.5C on Sat 20 Aug 17:00:01 PDT 2016
Average Temp: 34.53C
pi@rpz14101:~/share/ch4 $
```

Now your Python program is a fully functional utility that anyone can use. All they need is a Raspberry Pi Zero!

5
Getting Your Hands Dirty Using the GPIO Header

Here, we will start diving into the more physical side of cooking with the Raspberry Pi Zero:

- Pin configurations and precautions for using the GPIO pins
- Using the GPIOs with the WiringPi library
- Connecting an LED with RPZ and controlling it using C, Python, and a shell
- Basics of the UART port and getting data from the desktop on the serial port using Minicom
- Writing a Python/C program to get UART data in your code
- Basics of I2C and checking the I2C devices present on a port
- Basics of SPI and setting up an SPI module
- Converting a 5V signal into a 3.3V signal and slew rates
- Running RPZ on a battery
- Controlling GPIOs using a web interface
- Making RPZ a radio transmitter and sharing music
- Using a Node.js library to control the GPIOs
- Interfacing the ESP8266 WiFi module with RPZ

Introduction

The General Purpose Input Output Header, known as the GPIO, is one of the things that stands out compared to "normal" computers. The pins of the GPIO give you the ability to have your Raspberry Pi talk communicate with just about anything. Here are just a few things that can be leveraged with the GPIO Header:

- Turning on and off LEDs, Motors and Speakers
- Receiving digital inputs from sensors and monitors
- Communicating with other computers over a serial port
- Chaining multiple devices or sensors using different interface protocols

This is just a short list of what is possible, and once you get comfortable using the Raspberry Pi Zero GPIO, you'll be able to have it control or communicate with just about anything!

Pin configurations and precautions for using the GPIO pins

The general-purpose input/output, or GPIO, on the Raspberry Pi Zero is the port for interacting with the physical world. Not only can you control things such as motors and lights, but you can also read data from things such as thermometers or light sensors. The GPIO can read information or send commands, and you can use programs such as C or Python to handle the logic for what to do.

Getting ready

This is the point where we will start integrating other devices over the GPIO pins. While you don't have to do anything for this recipe except have your Raspberry Pi Zero up and running, you will probably want to attach a header and, ideally, a breadboard cobbler to prepare for the upcoming recipes.

How to do it…

The most important thing to remember when using your Raspberry Pi Zero is that the GPIO has no voltage regulation. If you push too much power over GPIO, you could end up with **BSOD**, or **Blue Smoke of Death (also commonly referred to as "Magic Smoke")**.

Even when doing something as simple as a single LED demo, you want to make sure to have enough resistance to limit your power draw from a 3.3V pin to 16mA. We will cover how to do this when we actually start connecting things, and in the end, you will find that if you need that much power, your circuit may need a separate power source instead of drawing over the GPIO, but we can cross that bridge later.

The GPIO is extremely flexible and can be configured for infinite different configurations. There are several different libraries you can use to communicate with the GPIO, but the most basic identification methods are GPIO.BOARD and GPIO.BCM. When you set your project to use GPIO.BOARD, you will use the physical pin numbers, from 1 to 40, to work with the pins you need. If using GPIO.BCM, you'll use a different numbering system, based on a standard Raspberry Pi library. There are pros and cons to either, but for certain solutions, you will need to use GPIO.BCM.

Let's take a closer look at the Raspberry Pi Zero pins and their uses:

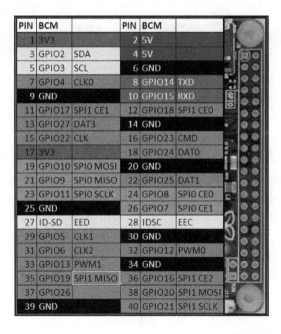

PIN	BCM		PIN	BCM	
1	3V3		2	5V	
3	GPIO2	SDA	4	5V	
5	GPIO3	SCL	6	GND	
7	GPIO4	CLK0	8	GPIO14	TXD
9	GND		10	GPIO15	RXD
11	GPIO17	SPI1 CE1	12	GPIO18	SPI1 CE0
13	GPIO27	DAT3	14	GND	
15	GPIO22	CLK	16	GPIO23	CMD
17	3V3		18	GPIO24	DAT0
19	GPIO10	SPI0 MOSI	20	GND	
21	GPIO9	SPI0 MISO	22	GPIO25	DAT1
23	GPIO11	SPI0 SCLK	24	GPIO8	SPI0 CE0
25	GND		26	GPIO7	SPI0 CE1
27	ID-SD	EED	28	IDSC	EEC
29	GPIO5	CLK1	30	GND	
31	GPIO6	CLK2	32	GPIO12	PWM0
33	GPIO13	PWM1	34	GND	
35	GPIO19	SPI1 MISO	36	GPIO16	SPI1 CE2
37	GPIO26		38	GPIO20	SPI1 MOSI
39	GND		40	GPIO21	SPI1 SCLK

The table on the left corresponds to the pin configuration of the Raspberry Pi Zero on the right. It is easy to identify pin 1; it is the pin surrounded by a square. The column named PIN corresponds to the identification you would use when in GPIO.BOARD mode. The BCM column is for GPIO.BCM. The bright and dark red rows are the Raspberry Pi power sources, 3.3V and 5V, respectively. The black rows are ground; these grounds are common to each other, so you can use whichever one is most convenient. The rows in green are the GPIO pins that can be configured to do whatever you want.

Pins 8 and 10 (in purple) are the serial communication pins. If you have been following along, you've been using this to talk to your RPZ already. Pins GPIO7 through GPIO11 (blue) are for the Serial Peripheral Interface, and finally, the yellow rows are for the Raspberry Pi Inter-Integrated Circuit, or I2C, typically used for communicating with external peripherals.

The third column is the standard function of the pin. You don't have to worry about this now, but it should be a useful reference when you get more familiar with manipulating the GPIO interface.

The WiringPi library that we will jump into in the next recipe uses GPIO numbering, as identified in the BCM column in the previous table.

Using the GPIOs with the WiringPi library

The **WiringPi** project is a library written in C that makes it easy to work with the GPIO. It has been actively updated with each board revision, includes command-line utilities, and has several wrappers available in higher-level languages such as Ruby and Python.

Getting ready

For this recipe, you will want to install the GPIO libraries for the Raspberry Pi. You might already have them installed, but it is easy enough to make sure it is installed and upgraded, with the following commands:

```
sudo apt-get install wiringpi
sudo apt-get upgrade wiringpi
```

You'll also want to get the Python wrapper installed, which you can do with this command:

```
sudo pip install wiringpi2
```

 If this command fails, first try `sudo apt-get install python-dev`.

How to do it...

1. Once you have the libraries installed, you will have a new command-line utility, `gpio`. Unplug anything you have connected to your GPIO pins and give it a test.

2. Let's start with `gpio -v`:

```
pi@rpz14101:~ $ gpio -v
gpio version: 2.32
Copyright (c) 2012-2015 Gordon Henderson
This is free software with ABSOLUTELY NO WARRANTY.
For details type: gpio -warranty
Raspberry Pi Details:
  Type: Pi Zero, Revision: 03, Memory: 512MB, Maker: Sony
  * Device tree is enabled.
  * This Raspberry Pi supports user-level GPIO access.
    -> See the man-page for more details
    -> ie. export WIRINGPI_GPIOMEM=1
```

3. The `gpio readall` command will show us the current configuration of all the pins. The output will be like the following:

```
pi@rpz14101:~ $ sudo gpio readall
+-----+-----+---------+------+---+-Pi Zero-+---+------+---------+-----+-----+
| BCM | wPi |   Name  | Mode | V | Physical | V | Mode |  Name   | wPi | BCM |
+-----+-----+---------+------+---+----++----+---+------+---------+-----+-----+
|     |     |    3.3v |      |   |  1 || 2  |   |      | 5v      |     |     |
|   2 |   8 |   SDA.1 | ALT0 | 1 |  3 || 4  |   |      | 5V      |     |     |
|   3 |   9 |   SCL.1 | ALT0 | 1 |  5 || 6  |   |      | 0v      |     |     |
|   4 |   7 | GPIO. 7 |   IN | 1 |  7 || 8  | 1 | ALT0 | TxD     | 15  | 14  |
|     |     |      0v |      |   |  9 || 10 | 1 | ALT0 | RxD     | 16  | 15  |
|  17 |   0 | GPIO. 0 |   IN | 0 | 11 || 12 | 0 | IN   | GPIO. 1 | 1   | 18  |
|  27 |   2 | GPIO. 2 |   IN | 0 | 13 || 14 |   |      | 0v      |     |     |
|  22 |   3 | GPIO. 3 |   IN | 0 | 15 || 16 | 0 | IN   | GPIO. 4 | 4   | 23  |
|     |     |    3.3v |      |   | 17 || 18 | 0 | IN   | GPIO. 5 | 5   | 24  |
|  10 |  12 |    MOSI | ALT0 | 0 | 19 || 20 |   |      | 0v      |     |     |
|   9 |  13 |    MISO | ALT0 | 0 | 21 || 22 | 0 | IN   | GPIO. 6 | 6   | 25  |
|  11 |  14 |    SCLK | ALT0 | 0 | 23 || 24 | 1 | OUT  | CE0     | 10  | 8   |
|     |     |      0v |      |   | 25 || 26 | 1 | OUT  | CE1     | 11  | 7   |
|   0 |  30 |   SDA.0 |   IN | 1 | 27 || 28 | 1 | IN   | SCL.0   | 31  | 1   |
|   5 |  21 | GPIO.21 |   IN | 1 | 29 || 30 |   |      | 0v      |     |     |
|   6 |  22 | GPIO.22 |   IN | 1 | 31 || 32 | 0 | IN   | GPIO.26 | 26  | 12  |
|  13 |  23 | GPIO.23 |   IN | 0 | 33 || 34 |   |      | 0v      |     |     |
|  19 |  24 | GPIO.24 |   IN | 0 | 35 || 36 | 0 | IN   | GPIO.27 | 27  | 16  |
|  26 |  25 | GPIO.25 |   IN | 0 | 37 || 38 | 0 | IN   | GPIO.28 | 28  | 20  |
|     |     |      0v |      |   | 39 || 40 | 0 | IN   | GPIO.29 | 29  | 21  |
+-----+-----+---------+------+---+----++----+---+------+---------+-----+-----+
| BCM | wPi |   Name  | Mode | V | Physical | V | Mode |  Name   | wPi | BCM |
+-----+-----+---------+------+---+-Pi Zero-+---+------+---------+-----+-----+
```

WirtingPi gpio readall output

Here, we can see the physical pin number and BCM and WiringPi identification as well as what the port is currently doing.

4. Now, let's try adjusting a pin's value and mode with the utility. We will read the wPi pin 25, BCM 26, pin 37 value, which, as we can see from the screenshot, should be 0.

```
pi@rpz14101:~ $ gpio read 25
0
```

5. With `gpio write`, you can change the value of the pin; in this case, we want to go from 0 to 1:

```
pi@rpz14101:~ $ gpio write 25 1
```

6. If we read it again, however, we don't get the results we want:

```
pi@rpz14101:~ $ gpio read 25
0
```

7. If you look at the `readall` output from step 3, you'll see that the mode is set to `IN`. This is why it didn't take our write command. We can fix that by changing that pin's mode and attempting the write and read again:

```
pi@rpz14101:~ $ gpio mode 25 output
pi@rpz14101:~ $ gpio write 25 1
pi@rpz14101:~ $ gpio read 25
1
```

8. Success! If you run `gpio readall` again, you'll see that your updated values are shown:

```
pi@rpz14101:~ $ sudo gpio readall
```

BCM	wPi	Name	Mode	V	Physical	V	Mode	Name	wPi	BCM
		3.3v			1 || 2			5v		
2	8	SDA.1	ALT0	1	3 || 4			5V		
3	9	SCL.1	ALT0	1	5 || 6			0v		
4	7	GPIO. 7	IN	1	7 || 8	1	ALT0	TxD	15	14
		0v			9 || 10	1	ALT0	RxD	16	15
17	0	GPIO. 0	IN	0	11 || 12	0	IN	GPIO. 1	1	18
27	2	GPIO. 2	IN	0	13 || 14			0v		
22	3	GPIO. 3	IN	0	15 || 16	0	IN	GPIO. 4	4	23
		3.3v			17 || 18	0	IN	GPIO. 5	5	24
10	12	MOSI	ALT0	0	19 || 20			0v		
9	13	MISO	ALT0	0	21 || 22	0	IN	GPIO. 6	6	25
11	14	SCLK	ALT0	0	23 || 24	1	OUT	CE0	10	8
		0v			25 || 26	1	OUT	CE1	11	7
0	30	SDA.0	IN	1	27 || 28	1	IN	SCL.0	31	1
5	21	GPIO.21	IN	1	29 || 30			0v		
6	22	GPIO.22	IN	1	31 || 32	0	IN	GPIO.26	26	12
13	23	GPIO.23	IN	0	33 || 34			0v		
19	24	GPIO.24	IN	0	35 || 36	0	IN	GPIO.27	27	16
26	25	GPIO.25	OUT	1	37 || 38	0	IN	GPIO.28	28	20
		0v			39 || 40	0	IN	GPIO.29	29	21
BCM	wPi	Name	Mode	V	Physical	V	Mode	Name	wPi	BCM

Pi Zero

WiringPi Pin 25 is now set to output, ON

9. What about Python? If you installed the wiringpi2 library with pip, it should be very easy! Jump into Python with sudo python, and with the following commands, see how we set the pin back to its original value:

```
>>> import wiringpi
>>> wiringpi.wiringPiSetup()
0
>>> wiringpi.digitalRead(25)
1
>>> wiringpi.digitalWrite(25,0)
>>> wiringpi.pinMode(25,0)
>>> wiringpi.digitalRead(25)
0
```

10. If you exit the interface and run gpio readall again, you'll find that Physical pin 37 is set back to what it once was.

This is just the start of what we will get into with the GPIO in this chapter.

Connecting an LED with RPZ and controlling it using C, Python, and a shell

Finally, some real hardware! This is truly the **Hello World** of the Internet of Things, but it is a great place to get started if you've never worked with circuits and sensors. Some basic electronics knowledge is quite helpful here. For resistor color codes, there is a great chart and calculator available on Digi-Key (http://www.digikey.com/en/resources/conversion-calculators/conversion-calculator-resistor-color-code-4-band). To understand polarity, which is important for working with diodes and capacitors, Sparkfun has a great tutorial, available here: https://learn.sparkfun.com/tutorials/polarity

Getting ready

Here is where you will need some real hardware. I recommend using a breadboard and Raspberry Pi Cobbler to make prototyping fast and easy; soldering each recipe will definitely take a long time.

There are a ton of great starter kits available from places such as Adafruit that give you a nice variety of things to get started with. I've also found some great deals on Amazon, with kits containing almost every device we will use in this book. For this one, the requirements are pretty simple:

- 1 LED
- One 330 Ohm resistor

How to do it...

We will use the same port: WiringPi 25, BCM 26, physical pin 37. Connect your LED and resistor as follows:

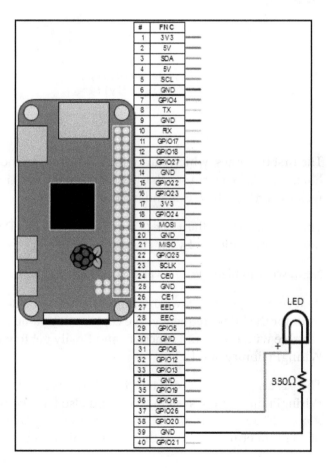

#	FNC
1	3V3
2	5V
3	SDA
4	5V
5	SCL
6	GND
7	GPIO4
8	TX
9	GND
10	RX
11	GPIO17
12	GPIO18
13	GPIO27
14	GND
15	GPIO22
16	GPIO23
17	3V3
18	GPIO24
19	MOSI
20	GND
21	MISO
22	GPIO25
23	SCLK
24	CE0
25	GND
26	CE1
27	EED
28	EEC
29	GPIO5
30	GND
31	GPIO6
32	GPIO12
33	GPIO13
34	GND
35	GPIO19
36	GPIO16
37	GPIO26
38	GPIO20
39	GND
40	GPIO21

LED

330Ω

Part 1 – blinking the LED using C

While we won't be using the C programming language a lot in this cookbook, it is good to see how relatively easy it is to leverage the WiringPi library:

1. Create a directory in your Pi home for chapter 5 and create a new file, blink.c. You can also pull down the completed blink.c code from the Git repository. If you are starting from scratch, enter the following code:

```c
#include <wiringPi.h>
#include <stdio.h>
int main() {
    int dly;
    printf("Enter blink delay in milliseconds: ");
    scanf("%d",&dly);
    wiringPiSetup();
    pinMode(25,OUTPUT);
    for (;;)
        {
        digitalWrite(25, HIGH); delay(dly);
        digitalWrite(25, LOW); delay(dly);
        }
    return 0;
}
```

The first two lines, which start with #include, are how you identify libraries in C. You can see that we mention the WiringPi package as well as stdio, which is Standard Input/Output.

The next line starts the main() function; much like Python, this is where the main operations of your program will live.

Next, we initialize the dly variable, which will be our blink delay.

By leveraging stdio, we can prompt the user to enter the value they want for the blink frequency. We capture this value into our dly variable with the scanf function, and finally get to working on the WiringPi library and LED.

The wiringPiSetup() call tells the library we will be using the WiringPi numbering system. We could also have chosen wiringPiSetupGpio or wiringPiSetiupPhys to use the Broadcom BCM numbering system or the physical pin numbers, respectively.

2. Next, we set our pin to output mode, and finally run it through a loop, using `digitalWrite(25,HIGH)` to turn on the LED, delay to hold the state, and `digitalWrite(25,LOW)` to turn the LED off again.

3. Once you've entered the code, save it, and then use the following command to compile:

```
gcc -Wall -o blink blink.c -lwiringPi
```

This will compile your C program and make the LED blink.

4. All you have to do now is run your compiled program (use `sudo` to operate the GPIO ports), and you are ready to blink!

```
pi@rpz14101:~/share/ch5 $ sudo ./blink
Enter blink delay in milliseconds: 200
```

Part 2 – blinking the LED using Python

While C is perfectly capable of handling your GPIO functions, writing more complex programs in it can be quite challenging. It is usually easier to work in a higher-level language such as Python or Ruby for many solutions: the development and debugging time will be shorter, and overall, it is easier to make out what the programs are doing just by looking at them.

Let's make the same blink application in Python, using the Python wrapper for the WiringPi library. You can make a new file from scratch or in the Genie IDE, whichever you prefer.

Create the `blink.py` file and enter the following code:

```python
#!/usr/bin/env python
# Chapter 5 - blink.py
# Blink LED with wiringpi Library
import wiringpi
import argparse
from time import sleep
def main():
        parser = argparse.ArgumentParser(description="RPZ LED
Blink",epilog="Enter WiringPi Pin Number and blink delay in milliseconds")
        parser.add_argument("pin", metavar="P",type=int,help="WiringPi GPIO
Pin Number", choices=xrange(0,31))
        parser.add_argument("dly", metavar="D",type=int, help="Blink delay
in milliseconds")
        args = parser.parse_args()
        blink_led(args.pin,args.dly)
```

```
        return 0

def blink_led(pin,dly):
        try:
                #Choose the Pin Numbering Configuraiton
                wiringpi.wiringPiSetup()
                #Set port to write mode
                wiringpi.pinMode(pin,1)
                while True:
                        wiringpi.digitalWrite(pin,1)
                        sleep(dly/1000.0)
                        wiringpi.digitalWrite(pin,0)
                        sleep(dly/1000.0)
        except KeyboardInterrupt:
                print "Terminated by user."
        finally:
                #Turn off LED at end of program
                wiringpi.digitalWrite(pin,0)

if __name__ == '__main__':
        main()
```

With Python libraries we've already worked with, we have made our program a little more robust and flexible. Using the `argparse` library, we will take arguments for both the WiringPi pin number and the blink delay:

```
parser.add_argument("pin", metavar="P",type=int,help="WiringPi GPIO Pin
Number", choices=xrange(0,31))
        parser.add_argument("dly", metavar="D",type=int, help="Blink delay
in milliseconds")
```

Note how the `choices` option is used for the `pin` argument to limit the choices between 0 and 30, which is the range for the WiringPi number system. We add our help text to make the -h flag useful to our users. After capturing the pin and delay time, they are passed to the `blink_led` function, which will use the `wiringPi` and `time` libraries to light the LED and hold it for a specified time. We can now use our Python program to light an LED from any available port.

We've also taken advantage of Python's `try...catch` system in this program. By wrapping our on/off events into `try`, not only can we report back when the user stops execution, but with the `finally` block, we can ensure that the LED is turned back off before the program completes. Let's take a look at how it functions:

```
pi@rpz14101:~/share/ch5 $ sudo ./blink.py -h
usage: blink.py [-h] P D
RPZ LED Blink
```

```
positional arguments:
  P                WiringPi GPIO Pin Number
  D                Blink delay in milliseconds
optional arguments:
  -h, --help  show this help message and exit
Enter WiringPi Pin Number and blink delay in milliseconds
pi@rpz14101:~/share/ch5 $ sudo ./blink.py 50 1000
usage: blink.py [-h] P D
blink.py: error: argument P: invalid choice: 50 (choose from 0, 1, 2,
3, 4, 5, 6, 7, 8, 9, 10, 11, 12, 13, 14, 15, 16, 17, 18, 19, 20, 21, 22,
23, 24, 25, 26, 27, 28, 29, 30)
pi@rpz14101:~/share/ch5 $ sudo ./blink.py 25 500
^CTerminated by user.
```

Now we have a program that checks the range of our pin number, allows you to choose any pin to work with, and makes sure everything is off before the program exits.

Part 3 – blinking the LED from the shell

With the WiringPi library installed, you've already tried out the gpio command-line utility. This same utility can be used to control your LED. We can do so with just a few lines, as shown here:

```bash
#!/bin/bash
#Chapter 5 LED Blink with Bash
#Parameters wiringPi Pin # and delay time in SECONDS (e.g. blink.sh 25 .5)
PIN=$1
DLY=$2
gpio mode ${PIN} output
while true; do
        gpio write ${PIN} 1;
        sleep ${DLY};
        gpio write ${PIN} 0;
        sleep ${DLY};
done
```

Save this code as blink.sh, and give the file execution permissions with sudo chmod +x blink.sh. When you execute this script, use seconds, such as 0.25, 1, or 2.5. All we do in this script is collect our parameters for pin and delay and pass them on to the gpio utility. Running this script will give you the same results, with the same flexibility as our Python script where we can choose the pin number and delay.

Now that we've seen how easy and flexible using the GPIO interface is, no matter what kind of coding you prefer, you should be able to start imagining the possibilities of the things you can do with your Raspberry Pi Zero.

Basics of the UART port and getting data from the desktop on the serial port using Minicom

We used the GPIO pins for the serial port to contact the Raspberry Pi from a desktop computer in an earlier chapter. Physical pins 8 and 10 (BCM GPIO 14 and 15) for transmit (TX) and receive (RX), respectively, can also be used to talk from your Raspberry Pi Zero out to other devices. Let's explore the Universal Asynchronous Receiver/Transmitter (UART) a bit further.

Getting ready

For this recipe, all you'll need is your Raspberry Pi Zero and a jumper wire to connect your TX and RX pins.

How to do it...

This is about as simple a setup you can have, but it is a typical way to verify you've set up your Raspberry Pi Zero to communicate outbound over serial. By default, the Raspbian OS has configured your GPIO's TX and RX to expect and handle incoming serial communication. If you connected from a desktop to your RPZ with a USB-to-serial adapter in Chapter 2, *Setting Up Physical and Wireless Connections* then you've already done this:

1. Enable UART on startup
2. Take a look at the `config.txt` file using your favorite editor.

Manually disabling the serial port

For communicating out, you will need to make some changes to how Raspbian starts up:

1. First, take a look at `/boot/cmdline.txt`:

```
pi@rpz14101:~/share/ch5 $ cat /boot/cmdline.txt
dwc_otg.lpm_enable=0 console=serial0,115200
console=tty1 root=/dev/mmcblk0p2 rootfstype=ext4
elevator=deadline fsck.repair=yes rootwait
modules-load=dwc2,g_ether
```

The section in bold is the one that tells Raspbian to have a console login available on `serial0`, which are your TX\RX pins on the GPIO.

2. Make a backup of your `cmdline.txt` file first:

   ```
   sudo cp /boot/cmdline.txt /boot/cmdline.txt.bak
   ```

3. Then, using your favourite editor, remove the serial console connection. . If your cmdline.txt looked like the example above it would now look like this:

   ```
   dwc_otg.lpm_enable=0 console=tty1 root=/dev/mmcblk0p2 rootfstype=ext4
   elevator=deadline fsck.repair=yes rootwait modules-load=dwc2,g_ether
   ```

4. The second piece that needs to be changed is the `getty` service. This is the service that manages your terminals. If we take a look at the status with `systemctl`, we can see whether it is running and enabled:

   ```
   pi@rpz14101:~/share/ch5 $ sudo systemctl status serial-
   getty@ttyAMA0.service
   ● serial-getty@ttyAMA0.service – Serial Getty on ttyAMA0
     Loaded: loaded (/lib/systemd/system/serial-getty@.service; enabled)
     Active: active (running) since Sun 2016-09-04 06:17:15 PDT;
     2 weeks 0 days ago
       Docs: man:agetty(8)
             man:systemd-getty-generator(8)
             http://0pointer.de/blog/projects/serial-console.html
   Main PID: 539 (agetty)
     CGroup: /system.slice/system-serial\x2dgetty.slice/
     serial-getty@ttyAMA0.service
             └─539 /sbin/agetty --keep-baud 115200 38400      9600
   ttyAMA0 vt102
   ```

5. We can stop the service with this command:

   ```
   sudo systemctl stop serial-getty@ttyAMA0.service
   ```

6. We can also disable the service from starting on boot:

   ```
   sudo systemctl disable serial-getty@ttyAMA0.service
   ```

With the changes to `cmdline.txt` and after disabling the service, your serial port will be free for you to use.

Disabling the serial port the easy way

Using the `raspi-config` utility, this is just a two-click process.

1. Start with this:

```
sudo raspi-config
```

> Pick **5**, **Interfacing Options**
>
> Pick **P6**, **Serial**

 Latest versions of Raspbian follow these menu choices, earlier versions had serial interface options under **Advanced Options**.

2. Finally, you are asked whether you want the login shell accessible.

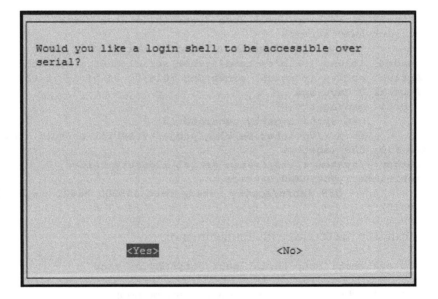

> Select **<No>** to both change the console configuration and disable the `getty` service. Upon exiting the utility, you may be prompted to reboot. Select **<Yes>** or reboot manually with this command:

```
sudo reboot now
```

3. After you start up and log back in, install the `minicom` utility. Minicom is a simple serial communication terminal.

```
sudo apt-get install minicom
```

4. After installing it, you can connect to your serial port using the following parameters:

```
minicom -b 115200 -o -D /dev/ttyAMA0
```

5. Connect the TX and RX pins, GPIO 14 and GPIO 15, or physical pins 8 and 10, as follows:

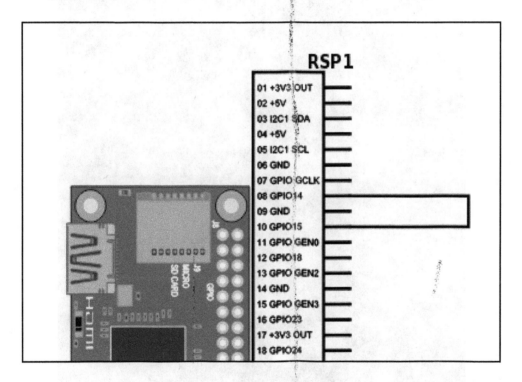

6. When you enter `minicom`, you will see a blank welcome screen. Type something in, such as `hello`. You'll see your text returned. While this isn't particularly interesting, what is happening behind the scenes is that Minicom is sending your characters out over the TX port on the GPIO. It is also reading in the RX port, which is receiving the data over the wire you connected. If you turn on echo on Minicom, where it echoes the text you entered and reads in your RX port, it should make more sense. To switch to echo, hit *Ctrl-A,* followed by Z and E. Here is a sample of what you will see:

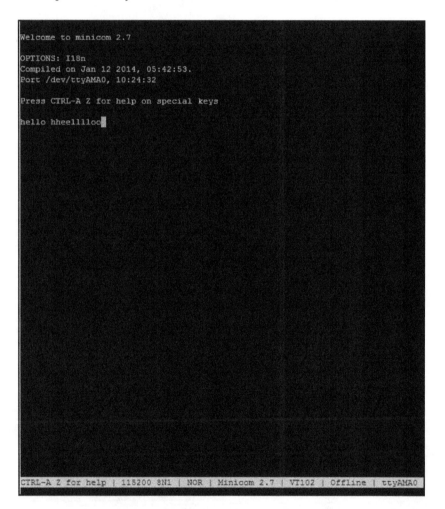

```
Welcome to minicom 2.7

OPTIONS: I18n
Compiled on Jan 12 2014, 05:42:53.
Port /dev/ttyAMA0, 10:24:32

Press CTRL-A Z for help on special keys

hello hheelllloo
```

```
CTRL-A Z for help | 115200 8N1 | NOR | Minicom 2.7 | VT102 | Offline | ttyAMA0
```

Sending hello over Minicom with echo off and on.

Now, you are set up for your Raspberry Pi Zero to talk out over serial and communicate with other devices that support UART. These could be other Raspberry Pis, Arduinos, and plenty of other gadgets you'll run into in your explorations of the Internet of Things.

Writing a Python/C program to get UART data in your code

While Minicom might be fine for real-time communication with a device, if you need something to continuously talk to your device or react when a certain message is received, you'll want to put together an application for that. Python of course has great libraries for serial communication, which makes it a good choice for managing or automating communication between two devices.

Getting ready

The previous recipe gets you set up for serial communication by freeing up the serial port bindings and virtual console for incoming serial communication. If you have finished the first recipe, you can use the same configuration to try out communication with serial.

How to do it...

Python can work with serial connections with a library named-you guessed it-serial! For this recipe, we will just perform a simple test to open and close the connection via serial.

Here, we will run a few commands to initialize, open, and view the status of the serial connection:

```
pi@rpz14101:~ $ sudo python
Python 2.7.9 (default, Sep 17 2016, 20:26:04)
[GCC 4.9.2] on linux2
Type "help", "copyright", "credits" or "license" for more information.
>>> import serial
>>> ser = serial.Serial()
>>> ser.baudrate = 115200
>>> ser.port = '/dev/ttyAMA0'
>>> ser
Serial<id=0xb6a12030, open=False>(port='/dev/ttyAMA0', baudrate=115200,
bytesize=8, parity='N', stopbits=1, timeout=None, xonxoff=False,
rtscts=False, dsrdtr=False)
```

```
>>> ser.open()
>>> ser
Serial<id=0xb6a12030, open=True>(port='/dev/ttyAMA0', baudrate=115200,
bytesize=8, parity='N', stopbits=1, timeout=None, xonxoff=False,
rtscts=False, dsrdtr=False)
>>> ser.close()
>>> ser
Serial<id=0xb6a12030, open=False>(port='/dev/ttyAMA0', baudrate=115200,
bytesize=8, parity='N', stopbits=1, timeout=None, xonxoff=False,
rtscts=False, dsrdtr=False)
```

There is a lot more we can do when we are talking to other devices that understand serial communication, such as GPS receivers. We will visit that again later in the book.

Basics of I2C and checking the I2C devices present on a port

I2C is an interface mode on the Raspberry Pi's GPIO that allows communication with all kinds of peripherals. We will be using one of these later on in this chapter when we transmit radio signals. This recipe will show you how to set it up and test it.

Getting ready

The easiest way to configure the use of the I2C interface is with `raspi-config`. Enter `sudo raspi-config` and select **Interfacing Options**. Option P5 will set up I2C communication. Select **Enable**, reboot, and you are ready to begin. Older versions of Raspbian have I2C in the Advanced Options Menu, as shown below:

```
┤ Raspberry Pi Software Configuration Tool (raspi-config) ├
A1 Overscan      You may need to configure overscan if black bars are present on display
A2 Hostname      Set the visible name for this Pi on a network
A3 Memory Split  Change the amount of memory made available to the GPU
A4 SSH           Enable/Disable remote command line access to your Pi using SSH
A5 SPI           Enable/Disable automatic loading of SPI kernel module (needed for e.g. PiFace)
A6 I2C           Enable/Disable automatic loading of I2C kernel module
A7 Serial        Enable/Disable shell and kernel messages on the serial connection
A8 Audio         Force audio out through HDMI or 3.5mm jack
A9 1-Wire        Enable/Disable one-wire interface
AA GPIO Server   Enable/Disable remote access to GPIO pins




        <Select>                                              <Back>
```

Finding I2C in older Raspbian versions

The newer releases of Raspbian have an Interface Menu, where you will find the I2C settings:

```
┤ Raspberry Pi Software Configuration Tool (raspi-config) ├
P1 Camera      Enable/Disable connection to the Raspberry Pi Camera
P2 SSH         Enable/Disable remote command line access to your Pi using SSH
P3 VNC         Enable/Disable graphical remote access to your Pi using RealVNC
P4 SPI         Enable/Disable automatic loading of SPI kernel module
P5 I2C         Enable/Disable automatic loading of I2C kernel module
P6 Serial      Enable/Disable shell and kernel messages on the serial connection
P7 1-Wire      Enable/Disable one-wire interface
P8 Remote GPIO Enable/Disable remote access to GPIO pins




        <Select>                                              <Back>
```

How to do it...

After enabling I2C and rebooting your Raspberry Pi, take a look at the device list:

```
pi@rpz14101:~ $ sudo ls /dev/*i2c*
/dev/i2c-1
```

Installing i2ctools will give you a few more options when working with the I2C interface:

```
sudo apt-get install i2c-tools
```

If we want to look at what is on the I2C bus, we can use i2cdetect. From the previous device listing, we see that we only have one activated, i2c-1.

```
pi@rpz14101:~ $ i2cdetect -y 1
     0  1  2  3  4  5  6  7  8  9  a  b  c  d  e  f
00:          -- -- -- -- -- -- -- -- -- -- -- -- --
10: -- -- -- -- -- -- -- -- -- -- -- -- -- -- -- --
20: -- -- -- -- -- -- -- -- -- -- -- -- -- -- -- --
30: -- -- -- -- -- -- -- -- -- -- -- -- -- -- -- --
40: -- -- -- -- -- -- -- -- -- -- -- -- -- -- -- --
50: -- -- -- -- -- -- -- -- -- -- -- -- -- -- -- --
60: -- -- -- -- -- -- -- -- -- -- -- -- -- -- -- --
70: -- -- -- -- -- -- -- --
```

Aside from the Power and Ground Pins, for I2C, the only pins you need to work with are, at most, the following:

PIN	BCM	Func	Desc
3	GPIO2	SDA	Data
5	GPIO3	SCL	Clock
27	ID-SD	EED	EEPROM Data
28	IDSC	EEC	EEPROM Clock

When we start connecting devices, we will be able to see values in this table. Since we will be trying it out with a radio transmitter, this is the perfect time to say "stay tuned!"

Basics of SPI and setting up an SPI module

The SPI, or Serial Peripheral Interface, is similar to the I2C bus, but has a few advantages for a few more wires. Generally, you'd choose I2C or SPI based on the peripheral you are trying to talk to and what protocol it supports. For this recipe, we will look at configuring SPI for upcoming recipes.

Getting ready

Just like setting up I2C in the previous recipe, the easiest way to get going is with raspi-config. Run with sudo, and select **Interfacing Options**. Select **P4** to enable **SPI**, and reboot.

```
┤ Raspberry Pi Software Configuration Tool (raspi-config) ├
P1 Camera      Enable/Disable connection to the Raspberry Pi Camera
P2 SSH         Enable/Disable remote command line access to your Pi using SSH
P3 VNC         Enable/Disable graphical remote access to your Pi using RealVNC
P4 SPI         Enable/Disable automatic loading of SPI kernel module
P5 I2C         Enable/Disable automatic loading of I2C kernel module
P6 Serial      Enable/Disable shell and kernel messages on the serial connection
P7 1-Wire      Enable/Disable one-wire interface
P8 Remote GPIO Enable/Disable remote access to GPIO pins




            <Select>                                        <Back>
```

How to do it...

Once you've enabled SPI and rebooted, you should find your bus on the device list:

```
[21:02:29] pi@rpz14103:~$ ls /dev/sp*
/dev/spidev0.0   /dev/spidev0.1
```

Working with the SPI module is a little bit more complex than I2C, but it gives you more flexibility as well as expandability to run multiple peripherals over the same bus. This will be a lot of fun later, but for now, let's look at the pins you will be using. Just like any connection to your Raspberry Pi Zero, the Power and Ground pins will be the same, but the pins reserved for SPI will be the following:

Pin	BCM	Func	Description
11	GPIO17	SPI1 CE1	Chip Enable\Chip Select (Secondary)
12	GPIO18	SPI1 CE0	Chip Enable\Chip Select (Secondary)
19	GPIO10	SPI0 MOSI	Master Out Slave In (Primary)
21	GPIO9	SPI0 MISO	Master In Slave Out (Primary)
23	GPIO11	SPI0 SCLK	Serial Clock (Primary)
24	GPIO8	SPI0 CE0	Chip Enable\Chip Select (Primary)
26	GPIO7	SPI0 CE1	Chip Enable\Chip Select (Primary)

35	GPIO19	SPI1 MISO	Master In Slave Out (Secondary)
36	GPIO16	SPI1 CE2	Chip Enable\Chip Select (Secondary)
38	GPIO20	SPI1 MOSI	Master Out Slave In (Secondary)
40	GPIO21	SPI1 SCLK	Serial Clock (Secondary)

With the 40-pin GPIO bus, SPI will support two separate channels for communication. Without those channels, you can connect multiple peripherals, thanks to the separation of the data ports (compared to I2C). This sets the stage for faster communication: over your serial bus, the separate clock and data lines ensure that both the master and the peripheral are synced, and an additional controller wire allows the interface to choose which device it wants to talk to on a particular channel.

Converting a 5V signal into a 3.3V signal and slew rates

Microcontrollers such as Arduinos have become extremely popular over the years and are great to have if getting involved in the Internet of Things. It would be completely natural to have an Arduino collecting measurements and sending that data to a Raspberry Pi for processing. A big issue between the two, however, is what they understand the HIGH signal to be. For a Raspberry Pi, the HIGH signal is 3.3V. For an Arduino, HIGH is 5V. Before your data is sent from a 5V high system to a 3.3V HIGH system, you need to convert it. That's what we will cover in this recipe. Technically the Raspberry PI will interpret any voltage under 0.8V as LOW and any voltage above 1.3V as HIGH. In between, depends on the input logic.

When unconnected, CMOS inputs will oscillate rapidly and may draw a dangerous amount of power. This is why the RPi has weak 50KΩ pull up resistors enabled by default on all GPIOs on startup. Inputs can also be configured to use Schmitt trigger input filtering can be enabled on most pins which will retain their previous state in this voltage region.

Getting ready

For this recipe, you'll need the following equipment:

- 1 1000 Ohm resistor
- 1 2000 Ohm resistor
- A breadboard

How to do it...

The schematic is quite simple:

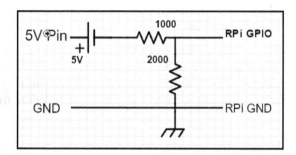

With this circuit, you can connect a device with a 5V output, such as an Arduino, to the 3.3V Raspberry Pi input, without any issues. The 5V side will connect to the output of the Arduino, and the 3v3 side will connect to your GPIO pin. It's as easy as that!

Running RPZ on a battery

For prototyping, using a regular AC power source or desktop computer is the way to go. Once you've come up with some ideas for projects, perhaps outdoor temperature monitors or humidity sensors in your attic, you might find that there isn't AC power available.

Now that you know how to run your Raspberry Pi Zero wirelessly, with a battery source, you could run it as a low-profile, remote system. There are dozens of different things you can do with a wireless, battery-powered computer and a few sensors-your only limitation is how long your batteries can run.

Getting ready

Depending on how simple, long-lasting, or low-profile your solution is, there are a few different options.

USB battery pack

USB battery packs have become common, small, and inexpensive over the years. This is the easiest and most advisable way to go: you just connect the battery pack to the micro-USB power input on the Raspberry Pi Zero. This way, you have all of the voltage regulation and protection of the Pi's power system.

Prebuilt power convertor

Plenty of online stores offer battery power convertors that will provide a stable 5V to run your Raspberry Pi Zero. The Elegoo UNO R3 Complete Starter Kit includes a small board and a connector to a 9V battery. This is an easy way to wire up your Raspberry Pi Zero to battery power, and it also has features such as a power switch, light, and multiple input and output sources.

DIY power convertor

If you like to live dangerously and want make your own circuit from scratch, you will need the following items:

- 7805 voltage regulator
- 1 10uF electrolytic capacitor
- 1 0.1uF capacitor (these capacitors are sometimes marked "104")
- Small 9V battery and connector
- Connecting wires

How to do it...

USB battery packs

USB power is really the easiest way to go and gives you additional options, such as having your battery pack recharge with solar panels or some other kind of renewable energy source. You could potentially create a forever-running system! It will run faithfully as long as it has enough power, and typically, the power consumption is extremely low, unless it is thinking or running other devices that require their own power. They are easy to disconnect and recharge and even easier to replace. Finally, it uses the "normal" power system, which includes safeguards that aren't available over the GPIO pins.

Prebuilt power convertor

Prebuilt inexpensive little power converter boards will provide a stable 5V source for your Raspberry Pi Zero from USB or a battery source. The Elego MBV2 in the kit also has a power switch and light, which is a nice plus, since the RPZ doesn't have its own on/off button.

1. Using the 9V battery, barrel jack connector, and the power convertor, test the 5V out port on the board before wiring it up to your Raspberry Pi Zero. When you turn it on, you should see a steady 5 volts on your multimeter. Some parts can be faulty, so if the voltage is higher than 5V, do not connect it to your Raspberry Pi. Pretty much any time you are using a new power source, or one you've made yourself, the most important thing to do to protect your Raspberry Pi Zero is to test the voltage.
2. If everything looks good so far, turn the power board off with the switch (or disconnect the battery) and connect the Ground wire on the power supply to any ground pin on your Raspberry Pi Zero.
3. Next, connect 5V power out on the power supply to pin 2 5V on the GPIO bus. Powering it on should start it up just like if you were plugged into a wall. Now you can really get small and portable!

DIY voltage regulator

Batteries don't provide a consistent voltage: as they drain, their voltage drops, which means the output on the voltage divider will drop. New batteries might be a little over their stated voltage, which could be too much for your Raspberry Pi Zero. When working with a power source, you want something that will either give you a steady, consistent voltage, or nothing at all. The inexpensive, popular 7805 linear voltage regulator is a great solution. You can find this regulator online or in your local electronics store, and it should not cost more than a couple dollars. This regulator will take an input voltage as low as 7 volts, and for some models up to 35 volts, and convert it to a consistent 5-volt output.

The circuit you'll build also needs a 10uF and 0.1uF capacitor. For the 10uF capacitor, the longer leg is the positive side, and that's important. Here's what the whole circuit will look like:

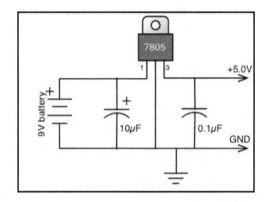

The function of the voltage regulator is to make sure that the RPZ always gets 5 volts, whether you're sucking lots of power to drive motors or you saving power in sleep mode. Since the power required can change very quickly, we use capacitors to help the battery and regulator react to those changes. The 10µF capacitor helps the battery handle the big changes, while the 0.1µF capacitor helps the 7805 deal with the really fast ones.

After you've put it together, but before wiring it to your Raspberry Pi Zero, follow these steps

1. Connect a 9V battery and test your output voltage. It should be a near-perfect 5 volts.
2. Now, connect your circuit ground to the Raspberry Pi Zero GPIO ground, and the output power of the circuit to the 5V pin on the GPIO, and you should be running yet again!

Controlling GPIOs using a web interface

You've been writing programs and running command-line tools and utilities to get things done, because you are the Raspberry Pi Zero expert! While it isn't too hard, you don't necessarily want to write and run a program each time you want to turn on a motor or light or take a sensor reading. For this recipe, we are going to see how we can control the GPIO bus from a web page, being served by a web server on your Raspberry Pi Zero.

Getting ready

For this recipe, we will continue using Python, but with a new library called Flask. Flask is a micro-framework for rendering Python programs into web pages, and it will work perfectly for creating a web-based GPIO controller. If you already have `python` and `pip` updated and configured, the command should be as simple as the following:

```
sudo pip install flask
```

After that, we jump right into coding!

How to do it...

1. In your `ch5` directory, create a new directory called templates with the `mkdir` command:

    ```
    mkdir /home/pi/share/ch5/templates
    ```

2. This is where we will store the HTML template file that Flask uses to create our web page.

3. Now, create a new file named `gpioweb.py` and enter the following code:

```python
#! /usr/bin/env python
# Chapter 5
# GPIO Web Control

#import libraries for WiringPi, flask and strings
from flask import Flask, render_template, redirect,      url_for,
request
import wiringpi
from string import split
#Set Pin Numbering Mode to Wiring Pi
wiringpi.wiringPiSetup()
```

```
app = Flask(__name__)
#Turn on Debugging in Flask
app.debug=1
#Set our web application root
@app.route("/")
def gpioread():
#This function reads the GPIO pin states and values
        pinlist = []
        #Iterate through wriringPi numbers 0 through
        31
        for pinid in range(0,31):
                #Get GPIO Pin Value
                gpiopin = wiringpi.wpiPinToGpio(pinid)
                pinout = {}
                #Determine if Pin is IN or OUT
                if wiringpi.getAlt(pinid) == 1:
                        pinmode = "OUT"
                else:
                        pinmode = "IN"
                #Determine if Pin is ON or OFF
                if wiringpi.digitalRead(pinid) == 1:
                        pinval = "ON"
                else:
                        pinval = "OFF"
                #Create dictionary entry for pin
                pinout["pinid"] = pinid
                pinout["gpiopin"] = gpiopin
                pinout["pinmode"] = pinmode
                pinout["pinval"] = pinval
                pinlist.append(pinout)
        #once pinlist is generated, send to HTML
        Template
        return
render_template('gpioweb.html',pinlist=pinlist)
#Updating Pins and Modes
@app.route('/update_pin', methods=['POST'])
def update_pin():
        #Read in form entry. Since they are all
        buttons, you should only get one
        actions = request.form
        #The Key Name contains the action to be
        performed (change mode or set value) and the
        Pin #.
        #We parse it into the action and the pin
        number
        for key in actions:
            ops = split(key,":")
            action = ops[0]
```

```
                pinid = int(ops[1])
                #If action is to change the IN\OUT mode,
                read current value and switch it
                if action == "changemode":
                        currmode = wiringpi.getAlt(pinid)
                        if currmode == 0:
                                newmode = 1
                        else:
                                newmode = 0
                        wiringpi.pinMode(pinid,newmode)
                #If action is to change the value, read
                current value and switch it
                #This will only work if pin mode is set to OUT
                elif action == "changeval":
                        curval = wiringpi.digitalRead(pinid)
                        print curval
                        if curval == 0:
                                newval = 1
                        else:
                                newval = 0
                        wiringpi.digitalWrite(pinid,newval)
                #print action, pinid
        #After updating pin, re-read GPIO
        return redirect(url_for('gpioread'))
    if __name__=="__main__":
            app.run()
```

4. Next create the HTML template file, named `gpioweb.html`, in your `templates` directory, and enter the following code:

```
<!doctype html>
<head>
<title>Rapsberry Pi Zero GPIO Configuration</title>
</head>
<body>
<h1>Raspberry Pi Zero GPIO Configuration</h1>
<table border="1">
<tr><th>WPi Pin<th>GPIO<th>Mode<th>Value</tr></b>
<form action="{{ url_for('update_pin') }}"
method=post>
{% for pin in pinlist %}
{% macro modebutton(name,value) -%}
        <input type="submit" name="changemode:{{
        pin.pinid }}" value="{{ pin.pinmode }}">
{%- endmacro %}
{% macro valbutton(name,value) -%}
        <input type="submit" name="changeval:{{
        pin.pinid }}" value="{{ pin.pinval }}">
```

```
{%- endmacro %}
        <tr><td>{{ pin.pinid }}<td>{{ pin.gpiopin }}
<td>{{ modebutton(pin.pinid,pin.pinmode) }}<td>{{
valbutton(pin.pinid,pin.pinval) }}</tr>
{% endfor %}
</form>
</table>
```

You can give it a try by running the Python program. You should see the following response if everything went well:

```
pi@rpz14101:~/share/ch5 $ sudo python gpioweb.py
 * Running on http://127.0.0.1:5000/ (Press CTRL+C to quit)
 * Restarting with stat
 * Debugger is active!
 * Debugger pin code: 101-213-364
```

If you connect to a local browser on your Raspberry Pi Zero and go to
`http://127.0.0.1:5000`, you'll get the current state of your GPIO interface:

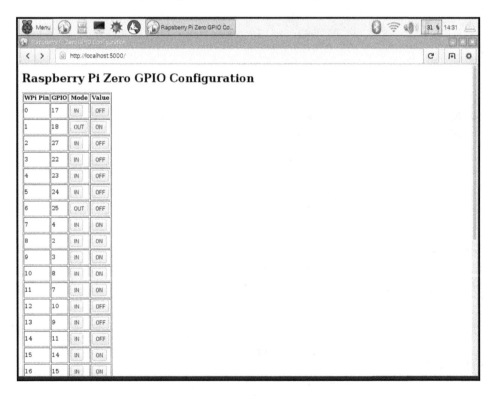

How it works...

Let's take a look at the code in a little more detail. The Python program should look pretty familiar if you've been working with the wiringPi Library. First, we set up our Python program with the libraries it will need. We also set the wiringPi library to read the wiringPi pin configuration:

```
from flask import Flask, render_template, redirect, url_for, request
import wiringpi
from string import split
#Set Pin Numbering Mode to Wiring Pi
wiringpi.wiringPiSetup()
app = Flask(__name__)
#Turn on Debugging in Flask
app.debug=1
```

This is a great configuration to use for this interface as the configurable pins are all number sequentially and easy to throw into a loop. We also make some calls to configure Flask for our application. Setting app.debug=1 will display any errors we have in our code on the web page. The rest of the program consists of only two functions; the first function reads the mode and value of each pin, and the second function updates a selected pin's mode or function.

Flask will serve web pages to the location identified by @app.route("/location"). For the root of our web page, we just want to see the current readings of the GPIO pin on our Raspberry Pi Zero. We set up a list to contain the values for each pin.

```
@app.route("/")
def gpioread():
#This function reads the GPIO pin states and values
        pinlist = []
        #Iterate through wriringPi numbers 0 through 31
```

Then we simply loop through each pin to determine its mode and value. The getAlt() function will return the mode (1 for OUT, 0 for IN), and digitalRead() returns the output. Before rendering, we store each value in pinlist[] for rendering:

```
        for pinid in range(0,31):
                #Get GPIO Pin Value
                gpiopin = wiringpi.wpiPinToGpio(pinid)
                pinout = {}
                #Determine if Pin is IN or OUT
                if wiringpi.getAlt(pinid) == 1:
                        pinmode = "OUT"
                else:
                        pinmode = "IN"
```

```
                #Determine if Pin is ON or OFF
                if wiringpi.digitalRead(pinid) == 1:
                        pinval = "ON"
                else:
                        pinval = "OFF"
                #Create dictionary entry for pin
                pinout["pinid"] = pinid
                pinout["gpiopin"] = gpiopin
                pinout["pinmode"] = pinmode
                pinout["pinval"] = pinval
                pinlist.append(pinout)

        #once pinlist is generated, send to HTML Template
```

The last part of the `gpioread` function references our HTML template (stored in the templates/ directory) and includes the list as part of the rendering:

```
    return render_template('gpioweb.html',pinlist=pinlist)
```

This is where our `gpioeb.html` file comes in. Most of the file is static HTML, setting up the page title and headings for our GPIO table. The more substantial part of the template is as follows:

```
<form action="{{ url_for('update_pin') }}" method=post>
{% for pin in pinlist %}
{% macro modebutton(name,value) -%}
        <input type="submit" name="changemode:{{ pin.pinid }}" value="{{
pin.pinmode }}">
{%- endmacro %}
{% macro valbutton(name,value) -%}
        <input type="submit" name="changeval:{{ pin.pinid }}" value="{{
pin.pinval }}">
{%- endmacro %}
        <tr><td>{{ pin.pinid }}<td>{{ pin.gpiopin }}<td>{{
modebutton(pin.pinid,pin.pinmode) }}<td>{{ valbutton(pin.pinid,pin.pinval)
}}</tr>
{% endfor %}
```

The `<form>` tag identifies the page as a form that references `update_pin`. This is routed in the Python program for the second function, which changes the pin values. Because clicking any button on the page will trigger a pin mode or value toggle, every button can be associated with the form. Flask allows loops in a web page with the following syntax:

```
{%  for x in range %}
...
{% endloop %}
```

In our loop, we iterate through each pin and populate the wiringPi pin number and GPIO number as table cells. The mode and value are also put into cells, but as buttons. Clicking on any button will call `update_pin` on the Python side, with the button name containing the pin number and what type of change is needed (mode or value). This value is parsed in the `update_pin` function, shown in the next code block. The function is preceded by another `@app.route`, which tells Flask that this function will be executed when that URL is accessed. This is the URL we defined in the HTML template as our form's POST location:

```
@app.route('/update_pin', methods=['POST'])
def update_pin():
        #Read in form entry. Since they are all buttons, you should only
get
```

We request all of the values provided in the form. In our case, this will only be the value of the clicked button:

```
        actions = request.form
        #The Key Name contains the action to be performed (change mode or
set value) and the Pin #.
        #We parse it into the action and the pin number
```

Here, we take the key name we pulled in from `request.form` and parse it into an action (changemode or changeval) and a wiringPi pin (0 through 31). When we know what we want to change, we can read the current value and set it to the opposite, using an if-then-else structure:

```
for key in actions:
                ops = split(key,":")
                action = ops[0]
                pinid = int(ops[1])
                #If action is to change the IN\OUT mode, read current
value...
                if action == "changemode":
                        currmode = wiringpi.getAlt(pinid)
                        if currmode == 0:
                                newmode = 1
                        else:
                                newmode = 0
                        wiringpi.pinMode(pinid,newmode)
                #If action is to change the value, read current value and
...
                #This will only work if pin mode is set to OUT
                elif action == "changeval":
                        curval = wiringpi.digitalRead(pinid)
                        print curval
                        if curval == 0:
```

```
                              newval = 1
                else:
                              newval = 0
                wiringpi.digitalWrite(pinid,newval)
          #print action, pinid
     #After updating pin, re-read GPIO
```

Finally, after updating the pin mode or value, we call the `gpioread` function again to update the page. We do this by telling flask to redirect back to the `root` (`/`):

```
return redirect(url_for('gpioread'))
```

With not too much code, we've put together a Python-driven GPIO controller in a web interface. From here, you can add any Python library or wiringPi function, which gives you the ability to have Python trigger events based on what it is reading or setting. If you want to really test out your new interface, attach an LED circuit to one of your GPIO pins like you did in an earlier recipe. You should be able to control on/off directly from the interface. This is only the beginning!

Making RPZ a radio transmitter and sharing music

For this recipe, we are going to really apply all we've learned, reconfigure our Pi for audio output, and send that out to a radio transmitter. You'll have your own Raspberry Pi radio station!

Getting ready

For this recipe, I used the Adafruit Si4713 FM radio transmitter; it's inexpensive and works great. If you want to run audio directly from your RPZ's audio out, you'll also need the following parts:

- 2 100 Ohm resistors
- 2 300 Ohm resistors
- 2 10uF capacitors
- 2 22pF capacitors
- Jumper wires

If using only the Si4713 and the built-in audio jack, you just need to have I2C enabled, which we covered in the I2C Basics recipe earlier in this chapter. If you are wiring the audio directly from the Pi, you will also need to make some changes to the pin configuration. By default, the Raspberry Pi Zero's audio output is not associated with any physical GPIO pin. We can reassign them easily with a reboot so that the PWM0 and PWN1 alternate pins serve audio. With this, we can connect our Raspberry Pi Zero's audio out directly to the transmitter's audio in. I prefer the `pigpio` and `python-pigpio` libraries (for C and Python, respectively), which can be installed with the following:

```
sudo apt-get update
sudo apt-get install pigpio python-pigpio
```

How to do it...

Connecting the transmitter to the Raspberry Pi is quite simple; it uses the I2C interface we looked at in a previous recipe:

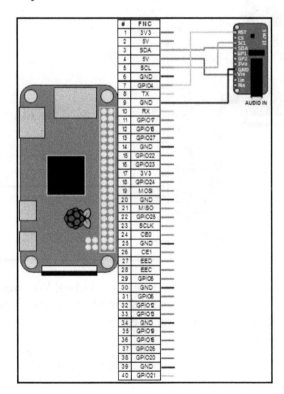

This will allow you to control your transmitter over your Raspberry Pi Zero, and you can input audio using the 3.5 mm jack on the transmitter. If you want to redirect your Raspberry Pi's audio, there are a few additional steps involved. First, you need to configure an audio filter and connect the components to GPIO13 and GPIO18, as shown here:

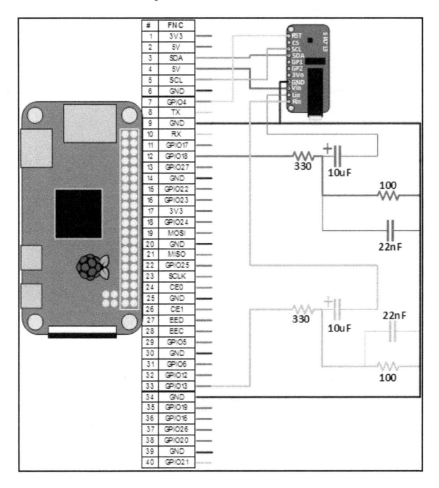

Once you have your circuit connected, it is time to configure! We need to make some changes so that GPIO13 and GPIO18 are using their alternate functions and acting as PWM0 and PWM1. First, we will need to add a line to the bottom of the `/boot/config.txt` file that sets the pins to audio out:

```
dtoverlay=pwm-2chan,pin=18,func=2,pin2=13,func2=4
```

If you have a setting for `dtoverlay` in your `config.txt` file from a previous recipe or hacking project, replace it with this setting. Save the file and reboot your RPZ. You can verify that your settings were committed by running the `gpio readall` command. You will see that physical pins 12 and 33 have had their modes changed to ALT5 and ALT0, respectively:

```
pi@rpz14101:~ $ gpio readall
+-----+-----+---------+------+---+-Pi Zero-+---+------+---------+-----+-----+
| BCM | wPi |   Name  | Mode | V | Physical | V | Mode |  Name   | wPi | BCM |
+-----+-----+---------+------+---+----++----+---+------+---------+-----+-----+
|     |     |    3.3v |      |   |  1 || 2  |   |      | 5v      |     |     |
|   2 |   8 |   SDA.1 | ALT0 | 1 |  3 || 4  |   |      | 5V      |     |     |
|   3 |   9 |   SCL.1 | ALT0 | 1 |  5 || 6  |   |      | 0v      |     |     |
|   4 |   7 |  GPIO. 7 |  IN | 1 |  7 || 8  | 1 | ALT0 | TxD     | 15  | 14  |
|     |     |      0v |      |   |  9 || 10 | 1 | ALT0 | RxD     | 16  | 15  |
|  17 |   0 |  GPIO. 0 |  IN | 0 | 11 || 12 | 1 | ALT5 | GPIO. 1 | 1   | 18  |
|  27 |   2 |  GPIO. 2 |  IN | 0 | 13 || 14 |   |      | 0v      |     |     |
|  22 |   3 |  GPIO. 3 |  IN | 0 | 15 || 16 | 0 | IN   | GPIO. 4 | 4   | 23  |
|     |     |    3.3v |      |   | 17 || 18 | 0 | IN   | GPIO. 5 | 5   | 24  |
|  10 |  12 |    MOSI | ALT0 | 0 | 19 || 20 |   |      | 0v      |     |     |
|   9 |  13 |    MISO | ALT0 | 0 | 21 || 22 | 0 | IN   | GPIO. 6 | 6   | 25  |
|  11 |  14 |    SCLK | ALT0 | 0 | 23 || 24 | 1 | OUT  | CE0     | 10  | 8   |
|     |     |      0v |      |   | 25 || 26 | 1 | OUT  | CE1     | 11  | 7   |
|   0 |  30 |   SDA.0 |  IN | 1 | 27 || 28 | 1 | IN   | SCL.0   | 31  | 1   |
|   5 |  21 | GPIO.21 |  IN | 1 | 29 || 30 |   |      | 0v      |     |     |
|   6 |  22 | GPIO.22 |  IN | 1 | 31 || 32 | 0 | IN   | GPIO.26 | 26  | 12  |
|  13 |  23 | GPIO.23 | ALT0 | 1 | 33 || 34 |   |      | 0v      |     |     |
|  19 |  24 | GPIO.24 |  IN | 0 | 35 || 36 | 0 | IN   | GPIO.27 | 27  | 16  |
|  26 |  25 | GPIO.25 |  IN | 0 | 37 || 38 | 0 | IN   | GPIO.28 | 28  | 20  |
|     |     |      0v |      |   | 39 || 40 | 0 | IN   | GPIO.29 | 29  | 21  |
+-----+-----+---------+------+---+----++----+---+------+---------+-----+-----+
| BCM | wPi |   Name  | Mode | V | Physical | V | Mode |  Name   | wPi | BCM |
+-----+-----+---------+------+---+-Pi Zero-+---+------+---------+-----+-----+
```

Finally, you need to force your audio through the 3.5 mm jack instead of HDMI. This is a simple change we can make with raspi-config. Run `sudo raspi-config`, select option 9, `Advanced Options`, and then select option A8, `Audio Output`. Select the 3.5 mm jack, as shown here:

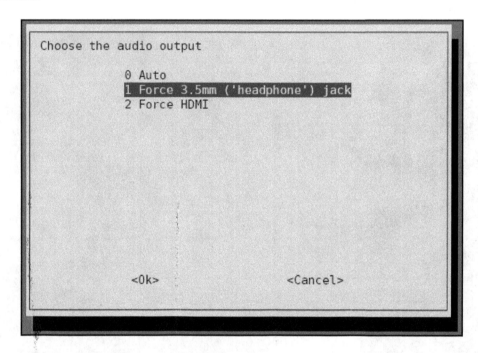

Now your audio output will be directed to the radio transmitter-all you need to do is start broadcasting!

The Si4713 library is written in C, but I prefer Python, and there is a great Python wrapper on GitHub that handles everything for you. Go to your `ch5` directory, and download the files from GitHub with the `git clone` command:

```
git clone https://github.com/daniel-j/Adafruit-Si4713-RPi.git
```

The file will create a directory and download the required files:

```
pi@raspberrypi:~/rpz $ git clone
https://github.com/daniel-j/Adafruit-Si4713-RPi.git
Cloning into 'Adafruit-Si4713-RPi'...
remote: Counting objects: 6, done.
remote: Total 6 (delta 0), reused 0 (delta 0), pack-reused 6
Unpacking objects: 100% (6/6), done.
Checking connectivity... done.
```

Finally, run `radio.py` as root:

```
sudo python radio.py
```

Once things get started, you should see feedback indicating things are running well, similar to the following output:

```
pi@rpz14101:~/share/ch5/Adafruit-Si4713-RPi $ sudo python radio.py
ASQ: 0x5 - InLevel: -7 dBfs - Power: 0 dBuV - ANTcap: 175 - Noise level: 41
ASQ: 0x5 - InLevel: -15 dBfs - Power: 90 dBuV - ANTcap: 7 - Noise level: 41
ASQ: 0x1 - InLevel: -47 dBfs - Power: 90 dBuV - ANTcap: 7 - Noise level: 41
ASQ: 0x1 - InLevel: -43 dBfs - Power: 90 dBuV - ANTcap: 7 - Noise level: 41
ASQ: 0x1 - InLevel: -40 dBfs - Power: 90 dBuV - ANTcap: 7 - Noise level: 41
ASQ: 0x1 - InLevel: -48 dBfs - Power: 90 dBuV - ANTcap: 7 - Noise level: 41
```

You should now be broadcasting on 101.1 MHz! Now all you need to do is send some audio out; you can play a WAV file, open a video, or find your favorite streaming station. If you tune in using an FM radio or SDR device, your audio output will be broadcast over the set frequency.

Using a Node.js library to control the GPIOs

When you are controlling the GPIO on your Raspberry Pi Zero, you aren't just limited to Python for building web pages. Node.js is a popular, portable JavaScript server that includes its own package manager and GPIO libraries. Generally speaking, it is also a little more common than serving web pages from Python.

Getting ready

For this, we will be using the popular Node.js and Node Package Manager, or npm. We'll also be using node-red, which is a node-based graphical GPIO configuration tool. This should all be installed with a default Raspbian build, but in case it isn't, you can install the packages individually with `apt-get`:

```
sudo apt-get update
sudo apt-get upgrade
sudo apt-get install nodejs
sudo apt-get install npm
```

Next, you will want to install the `rpi-gpio` package. I had some trouble with this, and had to install `node-gyp` before I could get the rpio-gpio package to install. Running the following worked great:

```
sudo npm install node-gyp
sudo npm install rpi-gpio
```

How to do it...

One of the coolest things you can do with Node.js, which isn't as practical with something like Python, is setting up a web port that can toggle GPIO changes. Create a file named `gpiocontrol.js` and enter the following code:

```
var http = require('http');
var url = require('url');
var path = require('path');
var gpio = require('rpi-gpio');
ledpin = 40;
blinkcycle = 1000;
gpio.setup(ledpin, gpio.DIR_OUT);
http.createServer(function (req, res) {
var requrl=url.parse(req.url, true);
if (requrl.pathname === '/') {
gpio.read(ledpin, function(err, value) {
res.writeHead(200, {'Content-Type': 'text/html'});
res.end('Current pin value: ' + value);
});
} else if (requrl.pathname === '/on') {
gpio.write(ledpin, true, function(err) {
if (err) throw err; });
res.writeHead(200, {'Content-Type': 'text/html'});
res.end('GPIO ON');
} else if (requrl.pathname === '/off') {
gpio.write(ledpin, false, function(err) {
if (err) throw err; });
res.writeHead(200, {'Content-Type': 'text/html'});
res.end('GPIO OFF');
} else if (requrl.pathname === '/cycle') {
ledstate = 0;
setInterval(function() {
ledstate = !ledstate;
gpio.write(ledpin, ledstate) }, blinkcycle);
res.writeHead(200, {'Content-Type': 'text/html'});
res.end('1s GPIO CYCLE');
} else {
res.writeHead(404, {'Content-Type': 'text/plain'});
```

```
res.end("GPIO Page Not Found");
}
}).listen(8080);
console.log('Server running on 8080');
```

When you run the code, it won't have much to say except for where the output is available:

```
pi@rpz14101:~/share/ch5 $ sudo node gpiocontrol.js
Server running on 8080
```

To control the LEDs, you simply need to go to the server started by the running node. There are four locations you can go to:

`localhost:8080/` shows the current LED status

`localhost:8080/on` turns the LED on

`localhost:8080/off` turns the LED off

`localhost:8080/cycle` will blink the LED every second

This is just the tip of the iceberg for what you can do with the Raspberry Pi Zero GPIO and Node.js; we will visit a variant of this code in a later chapter when we listen for events.

Interfacing the ESP8266 WiFi module with RPZ

Earlier in the book, we covered a hack for taking a USB Wi-Fi adapter and hard-wiring it to the Raspberry Pi Zero board. This works just fine, but you can also configure Wi-Fi communication over the GPIO port! Truly, the Raspberry Pi's flexibility in configuration is astounding. In this hack, we will connect and play around with the inexpensive and popular ESP8266 to get our RPZ talking over Wi-Fi. We will also use some of the skills we picked up in earlier recipes talking over the GPIO serial bus to open the door to even cooler hacks!

Getting ready

You don't need much for this except your Raspberry Pi Zero and the ESP8266. The one I used was from Adafruit, called the ESP-12-E, but there several options available. I would go with anyone that is already mounted to a board for prototyping, unless you are planning to solder it to a custom-made circuit board to attach to your Raspberry Pi Zero. If not, you'll need some jumper cables and a breadboard.

Here's the low-down on the ESP-8266: This is a high-performance microcontroller (80MHz) with an integrated WiFi module. It is often sold with a variety of different firmware. Be attentive when choosing the module, as some firmware will not understand the same protocol.

How to do it...

Wire the ESP8266 to the Raspberry Pi Zero like this:

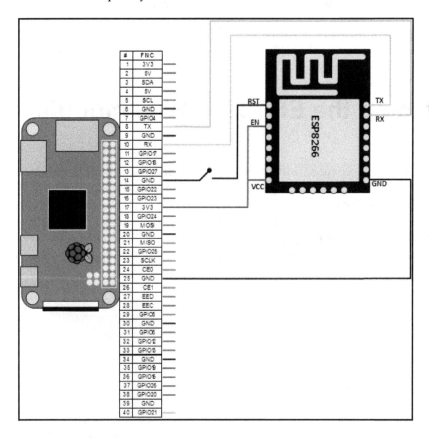

If you followed the earlier recipe, you will see that this is running on our Raspberry Pi Zero's serial port. There is a great Python wrapper on GitHub for testing and using the ESP8266. Go to your `/home/pi/share/ch5` folder and run the following command:

```
git clone https://github.com/guyz/pyesp8266.git
```

Once it has downloaded, go into the `pyesp` directory and run the test program on your home Wi-Fi network:

```
sudo python pyesp_test.py /dev/ttyAMA0 115200 <SSID> <SSIDPASSWORD>
```

If everything is wired up properly, you'll see the tool test connectivity, connect to the Wi-Fi network, and obtain an IP address. Now, you can relieve your Raspberry Pi Zero's USB port for another device, or reduce the overall size.

There's more...

This is just the start of what you can do with the ESP8266 chip. The wiki on GitHub (`https://github.com/esp8266/esp8266-wiki`) contains great examples for configuration and use, including operation using the RPZ SPI interface.

6
Controlling the LEDs and Displays

In this chapter, we will cook up some magic with LEDs!

- Setting up brightness using PWM
- Monitoring Twitter/e-mails to blink an LED
- Connecting a seven-segment number display module to the RPZ
- Connecting an LED matrix display to the RPZ
- Connecting an RGB LED and generating different colors
- Interfacing the 16×2 LCD display with RPZ
- Connecting the 74HC595N shift register to control many LEDs

Introduction

Output comes in many different varieties. It can be words printing to paper or a monitor, or it can be information sent to LCD panels. LEDs are outputs too, and can be easily configured to notify you of an event, with some simple programming and work with the GPIO Header. Let's explore how the Raspberry Pi Zero's GPIO interface can be used to run all sorts of different LEDs and Displays.

Setting up brightness using PWM

Pulse wave modulation, or **PWM** is a technique where the power is oscillated between on and off at a certain frequency. There are several applications for this. In this recipe, we will start off easy and see how it can control the perceived brightness of an LED. By changing the oscillation frequency using PWM, we can flicker an LED to give the effect of changing brightness. Let's try it out!

Getting ready

1. Check the current board and mode configuration.

 If you have SPI or I2C enabled, make sure not to use the pins that are reserved for that mode.

2. The following example uses pins still available while in SPI mode, and it should work for just about any configuration that you have for your GPIO as long as you aren't using GPIO 22, 23, and 24.

3. We're going to be using Python and the RPi.GPIO library. If you haven't set that up, you'll find all of the information you need in Chapter 5, *Getting Your Hands Dirty Using GPIO Header*.

How to do it...

1. Here is the circuit to set up; you'll see it is just three LED circuits like the ones we set up in the *Connecting an LED with RPZ controlling it using C, Python and Shell* recipe in the previous chapter:

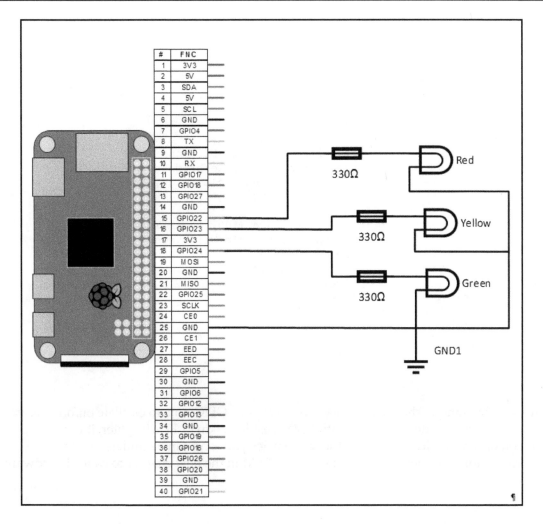

2. Once you have the circuit set up, it's time to control it with Python! Here is a little bit of code that will cycle the brightness up and down until you stop it:

```
import time
import RPi.GPIO as GPIO
GPIO.setmode(GPIO.BCM)
#Set up GPIO 22,23,24 as our LED outputs
GPIO.setup(22, GPIO.OUT)
GPIO.setup(23, GPIO.OUT)
GPIO.setup(24, GPIO.OUT)

red = GPIO.PWM(22,50)
green = GPIO.PWM(23,50)
```

```
yellow = GPIO.PWM(24,50)

red.start(0)
green.start(0)
yellow.start(0)
while True:
    try:
            print "up!"
            for brightness in range(0, 101):
                    red.ChangeDutyCycle(brightness)
                    green.ChangeDutyCycle(brightness)
                    yellow.ChangeDutyCycle(brightness)
                    time.sleep(0.07)
            print "down!"
            for brightness in range (100, 0, -1):
                    red.ChangeDutyCycle(brightness)
                    green.ChangeDutyCycle(brightness)
                    yellow.ChangeDutyCycle(brightness)
                    time.sleep(0.07)
    except KeyboardInterrupt:
            print "Finished!"
    finally:
            red.stop()
            green.stop()
            yellow.stop()
            break
```

This simple example shows how easy it is to set your GPIO pins to oscillate on/off at any frequency. You can do a lot more with PWM beside making LEDs brighter; it is also a method of communication, where the frequencies you send can be understood by controllers for other devices. We'll cook with PWM in the next chapter to control hardware.

Monitoring Twitter/e-mails to blink an LED

The Internet of Things concept is all about connecting the Web with the physical world. This goes in both directions: the data collection of physical devices goes up, and information from the Internet can be communicated out to physical devices. We can build on our previous example and have our LED circuits notify us when we receive an e-mail or tweet!

Getting ready

For hardware, you can use the same circuit as the previous recipe's circuit. Instead of a yellow LED, I used a blue one to notify me of Twitter messages.

If you followed the recipe in Chapter 4, *Sending an e-mail from a Python Script*, you should already have an app password for your Gmail account. If not, you can find out how in the *Getting Ready* section of the recipe.

I also used the Python library tweepy to manage incoming tweets. You can install this using pip:

```
sudo pip install tweepy
```

Lastly, you will need a Twitter account and authorization keys.

1. Log in to your Twitter account, and go to https://apps.twitter.com.
2. Click on the **Create New App**, as seen here:

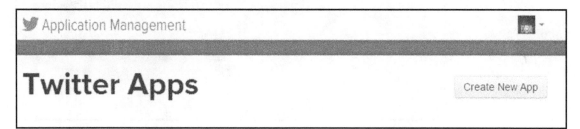

3. Next, fill in the application information in the form. You don't have to have a public URL; you can put in a placeholder:

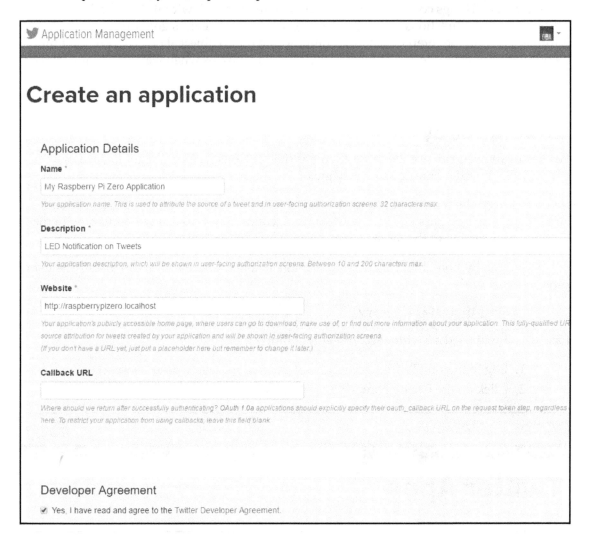

4. You are almost done! After clicking on **Create Application**, you'll be taken to your application window, which will look something like this:

5. Finally, click on **manage keys and access tokens** and then on the **Create my access token** button:

My Raspberry Pi Zero Application

Details   Settings   Keys and Access Tokens   Permissions

Application Settings

Keep the "Consumer Secret" a secret. This key should never be human-readable in your application.

Consumer Key (API Key)   xYOj1UVGqdPmQSeHDnnS2Iwmn

Consumer Secret (API Secret)   j7z5rOlz68gQ3X9SaafVtfScw4yRlybP7CqMygBRh01HO1kPUh

Access Level   Read and write (modify app permissions)

Owner   EdThaDBA

Owner ID   1929310489

Application Actions

Regenerate Consumer Key and Secret   Change App Permissions

Your Access Token

This access token can be used to make API requests on your own account's behalf. Do not share your access token secret with anyone.

Access Token   1929310489-E1yVI4r0ZSq2dXEOCfpy3l7Va8bs2g4Ri8uwOj8

Access Token Secret   B4dYOElemRRRXMMelkFueJ3l7eXDLkjR3XeHusOAIU967

Access Level   Read and write

Owner   EdThaDBA

Owner ID   1929310489

6. This will generate all of the keys you need to access Twitter from your Raspberry Pi Zero.

The keys you will need are the Consumer Key, Consumer Secret, Access Token, and Access Token Secret. Keep these handy as we move into the recipe.

Once you are done testing, or if you think your credentials were compromised in any way, go back to the key-management page and regenerate your access token and secret. The previous ones will be discarded and unusable. If you have decided to make a new application or aren't using the one you set up, you can delete the entire application, which permanently removes both the consumer key and the access key.

How to do it...

1. Use the same circuit as the previous recipe, but instead of a yellow LED, use a blue one for new tweets. Create the `led_notifier.py` file in the `ch6` directory, and enter the following code:

```python
#!/usr/bin/env python
# Raspberry Pi Zero Cookbook
# Chapter 6
# New Email and Tweet LED Notifier
from tweepy.streaming import StreamListener
from tweepy import OAuthHandler
from tweepy import Stream
import time
import imaplib
import RPi.GPIO as GPIO
GPIO.setmode(GPIO.BCM)
#Set up GPIO 22,23,24 as our LED outputs
GPIO.setup(22, GPIO.OUT)
GPIO.setup(23, GPIO.OUT)
GPIO.setup(24, GPIO.OUT)

red = GPIO.PWM(22,50)
green = GPIO.PWM(23,50)
blue = GPIO.PWM(24,50)

#Twitter API Key Information
consumer_token = "*************************************"
consumer_secret = "*************************************"
access_token = "**********-****************************************"
access_secret = "************************************"

#String to Search on Twitter
```

```
searchstring = "python"

#Set up Listener for Twitter
class RPZStreamListener(StreamListener):
    def on_data(self, data):
            blinkblue()
            return True
    def on_error(self, status):
            print(status)

def main():
    red.start(0)
    green.start(0)
    blue.start(0)
    print "online"
    green.ChangeDutyCycle(100)
    auth = OAuthHandler(consumer_token, consumer_secret)
    auth.set_access_token(access_token, access_secret)
    sl = RPZStreamListener()
    stream = Stream(auth, sl)
    #Start Stream to Check for New Tweets
    stream.filter(track=[searchstring],async=True)
    #Run Loop to check for new email every 10 seconds
    while True:
            try:
                    emailcheck()
                    time.sleep(10)
            except KeyboardInterrupt:
                    print "Finished!"
                    red.stop()
                    green.stop()
                    blue.stop()
                    break
            except:
                    print "Error: ", sys.exc_info()[0]
def blinkred():
    for x in range(0,5):
            red.ChangeDutyCycle(100)
            time.sleep(0.1)
            red.ChangeDutyCycle(0)
            time.sleep(0.1)
def blinkblue():
    for x in range(0,5):
            blue.ChangeDutyCycle(100)
            time.sleep(0.1)
            blue.ChangeDutyCycle(0)
            time.sleep(0.1)
def emailcheck():
```

```
mailin = imaplib.IMAP4_SSL('imap.gmail.com')
mailin.login('MYEMAIL@gmail.com','**** **** **** ****')
mailin.list()
mailin.select('inbox')
(retcode, messages) = mailin.search(None, 'UNSEEN')
if retcode == 'OK':
        if messages[0] != "":
                blinkred()
if __name__ == "__main__":
    main()
```

2. Running this program will do a few things:

    1. First, it will turn the green light on to tell you it is running.

    2. Second, it will connect to Twitter and listen for new Tweets with whatever I have set in the `searchstring` variable and then light the blue LED five times quickly.

    3. Finally, it will check my e-mail account every 10 seconds (or whatever value I provide to `time.sleep()`) and blink the red LED if there are unread messages.

A lot of this code should look familiar, but let's take a closer look at some of the new code, starting with what we need for checking Tweets:

1. In *Getting Started*, you should have created your Twitter API credentials and application. Here is where you put the values of your consumer and access tokens and secrets:

```
#Twitter API Key Information
consumer_token = "***********************************"
consumer_secret = "***********************************"
access_token = "**********-***************************************"
access_secret = "***********************************"
```

2. You can search for any term you want, though `python` seems to be a good one that doesn't tweet continuously (like `"sports"`) but isn't sporadic enough that you aren't sure whether you program is working.

```
#String to Search on Twitter
searchstring = "python"
```

3. In the next section, we'll create a Python class so that we can initialize a listener to Twitter. A class is really just a collection of commands that you can create several instances of. If we wanted to, we could create several of these classes to listen for different search strings. This class doesn't do a ton; it leverages Tweepy's `StreamListener` and will call the `blinkblue` function if data is received or an error code if there is a problem.

```
#Set up Listener for Twitter
class RPZStreamListener(StreamListener):
        def on_data(self, data):
                blinkblue()
                return True
        def on_error(self, status):
                print(status)
```

4. The most common problem and error code you'll see is 420, the rate limit error. This means you have hit the Twitter API too quickly and they want you to take a break. Rate limit information is available in the Twitter developer documentation; although when debugging, it is pretty easy to hit the limit fast. When you do, don't keep retrying–your timeout penalty will be increased. The only thing you can really do is wait about 15 minutes and then try again–good time to add comments to your code, stretch your legs, or read the next recipe.

5. Skipping over the `main()` function for now, you'll see that the `blinkred` and `blinkblue` functions shouldn't need much explanation: they turn their respective LEDs off and on again five times.

```
def blinkblue():
        for x in range(0,5):
                blue.ChangeDutyCycle(100)
                time.sleep(0.1)
                blue.ChangeDutyCycle(0)
                time.sleep(0.1)
```

6. The `emailcheck` function, the opposite of the send e-mail function we created in Chapter 4, *Programming with Python*, uses Python's `imaplib` to check for any e-mails that are marked as unread. If we find any, we call the `blinkred` function. You can really pull any information you want from your e-mail, but since we are only making a notifier, we only need to know whether any new e-mails exist:

```
def emailcheck():
        mailin = imaplib.IMAP4_SSL('imap.gmail.com')
        mailin.login('MYEMAIL@gmail.com','**** **** **** ****')
        mailin.list()
        mailin.select('inbox')
```

```
(retcode, messages) = mailin.search(None, 'UNSEEN')
if retcode == 'OK':
        if messages[0] != "":
                blinkred()
```

7. Looking finally at the main function, we initialize our LEDs and turn the green one on. That's our "service running" LED.

8. Next, we pass on our authorization information to log on to the Twitter API and create an object checking for our search string. We use the `aysnc=True` value in `stream.filter` to run as a separate thread and allow the program execution to continue. Without it, Python would hold there and just wait for new Tweets. We also want to check for e-mails:

```
def main():
        red.start(0)
        green.start(0)
        blue.start(0)
        print "online"
        green.ChangeDutyCycle(100)
        auth = OAuthHandler(consumer_token, consumer_secret)
        auth.set_access_token(access_token, access_secret)
        sl = RPZStreamListener()
        stream = Stream(auth, sl)
        #Start Stream to Check for New Tweets
        stream.filter(track=[searchstring],async=True)
```

9. We don't have a push method for e-mail checks, so we will just go ask every 10 seconds. We'll add in a try/except so that we can break the loop:

```
        #Run Loop to check for new email every 10 seconds
        while True:
                try:
                        emailcheck()
                        time.sleep(10)
                except KeyboardInterrupt:
                        print "Finished!"
                        red.stop()
                        green.stop()
                        blue.stop()
                        break
                except:
                        print "Error: ", sys.exc_info()[0]
```

10. With a connection to the Internet and a GPIO, there is virtually nothing you can't check online and send a physical notification to somewhere through your Raspberry Pi. Add a few more LEDs, and have different search strings or e-mail accounts light different LEDs in your array. This is a pretty simple notification method.

Let's move on and improve our Raspberry Pi Zero's ability to communicate!

Connecting a seven-segment number display module to the RPZ

The seven-segment number display is a great way to test out different kinds of communication. With a little bit of circuitry, we can get our Raspberry Pi Zero to operate a display with ease.

Getting ready

For this recipe, you'll need the following

- A common-cathode seven-segment number display
- Two 330 Ohm resistors
- Jumper wires

How to do it...

1. The schematic for running a seven-segment number display isn't hard at all. Here is how you'll connect it:

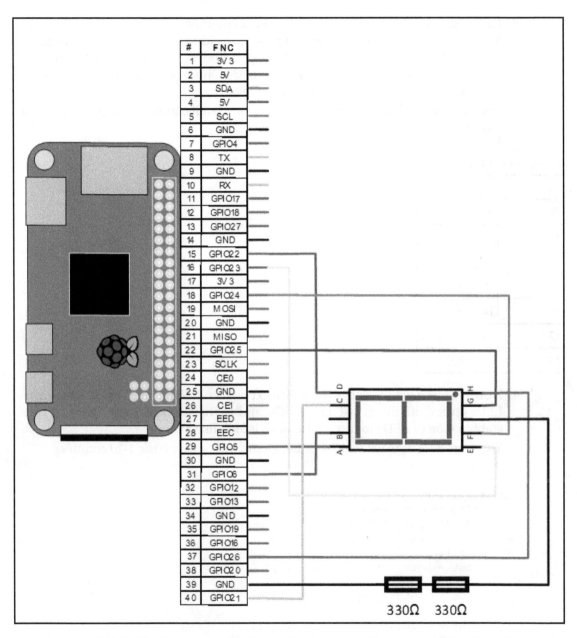

#	FNC
1	3V3
2	5V
3	SDA
4	5V
5	SCL
6	GND
7	GPIO4
8	TX
9	GND
10	RX
11	GPIO17
12	GPIO18
13	GPIO27
14	GND
15	GPIO22
16	GPIO23
17	3V3
18	GPIO24
19	MOSI
20	GND
21	MISO
22	GPIO25
23	SCLK
24	CE0
25	GND
26	CE1
27	EED
28	EEC
29	GPIO5
30	GND
31	GPIO6
32	GPIO12
33	GPIO13
34	GND
35	GPIO19
36	GPIO16
37	GPIO26
38	GPIO20
39	GND
40	GPIO21

330Ω   330Ω

While the 7 segment displays often have similar pin configurations, there is no guarantee they are identical. Always check your manufacturer's datasheet for the correct pin configuration for any microcontroller or complex device.

2. Each segment A-H is an LED, and there is a common ground connector, located at the top and bottom center pins (you can use either one). For the other pins, use the eight free GPIO pins for each of the eight diodes, representing each number segment and the decimal. I went with two 330 Ohm resistors as they are pretty common and enough to keep the current low.

3. Check the manufacturer's data sheet for more details, but most displays are set as follows:

Letter/pin	LED
A	Top left
B	Middle
C	Top
D	Top right
E	Bottom left
F	Bottom
G	Bottom right
H	Decimal

4. Now we just need to control it. We are experienced with using the GPIO to turn LEDs on and off; this is just more LEDs, and we have to know the right combination of LEDs to turn on to make it look like a number.

5. There are a lot of ways to do this. Let's start with a very basic 1-10 counter program:

```
import wiringpi
from time import sleep
#Define LED pins to letters
wiringpi.wiringPiSetupGpio()
def main():
        one = setdisplay(0,0,0,1,0,0,1,0)
        sleep(1)
        two   = setdisplay(0,1,1,1,1,1,0,0)
        sleep(1)
        three = setdisplay(0,1,1,1,0,1,1,0)
        sleep(1)
        four = setdisplay(1,1,0,1,0,0,1,0)
        sleep(1)
        five = setdisplay(1,1,1,0,0,1,1,0)
        sleep(1)
```

```
        six = setdisplay(1,1,0,0,1,1,1,0)
        sleep(1)
        seven = setdisplay(0,0,1,1,0,0,1,0)
        sleep(1)
        eight = setdisplay(1,1,1,1,1,1,1,0)
        sleep(1)
        nine = setdisplay(1,1,1,1,0,0,1,0)
        sleep(1)
        zero = setdisplay(1,0,1,1,1,1,1,0)
        sleep(1)
        off = setdisplay(0,0,0,0,0,0,0,0)
def setdisplay(b1,b2,b3,b4,b5,b6,b7,b8):
        a = 5     #Top Left
        b = 6     #Middle
        c = 21    #Top
        d = 22    #TopRight
        e = 23    #BottomLeft
        f = 24    #Bottom
        g = 25    #BottomRight
        h = 26    #Decimal
            wiringpi.pinMode(a,1)
wiringpi.pinMode(b,1)
wiringpi.pinMode(c,1)
wiringpi.pinMode(d,1)
wiringpi.pinMode(e,1)
wiringpi.pinMode(f,1)
wiringpi.pinMode(g,1)
wiringpi.pinMode(h,1)
        wiringpi.digitalWrite(a,b1)
        wiringpi.digitalWrite(b,b2)
        wiringpi.digitalWrite(c,b3)
        wiringpi.digitalWrite(d,b4)
        wiringpi.digitalWrite(e,b5)
        wiringpi.digitalWrite(f,b6)
        wiringpi.digitalWrite(g,b7)
        wiringpi.digitalWrite(h,b8)
if __name__ == "__main__":
        main()
```

6. Displaying numbers is a matter of activating the right LEDs, so we create a function that controls the on/off function for the panel. By setting the proper connections to on or off, we can render any number. Running the program will cycle the numbers 1 through 10 and then turn off the display.

7. Here we are at number 5!

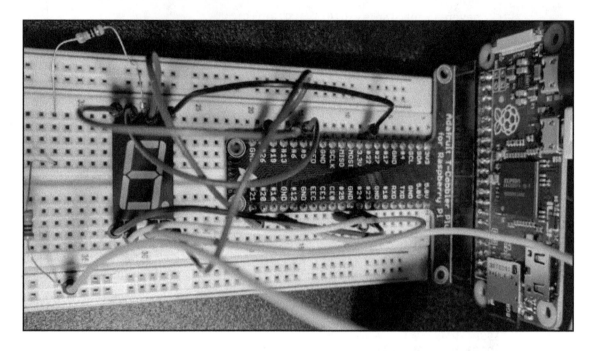

Connecting an LED matrix display to the RPZ

Operating one LED is fun for about a minute, but what if you want to do some really interesting things, or operate a matrix of LEDs?

Getting ready

You'd need some kind of LED matrix. There were two different matrices I tried out. The first was Adafruits's 8×8 LED display, but there was also an 8×8 LED display included in my Elego Complete Starter Kit.

Aside from that, you really only need jumper wires and Python. The 8×8 matrix commonly uses a max7219 driver. Install the Python driver library with pip:

```
sudo pip install max7219
```

How to do it...

1. There are five pins on the LED matrix, which use your Raspberry Pi Zero's SPI interface. Connect the matrix to the RPZ as shown here:

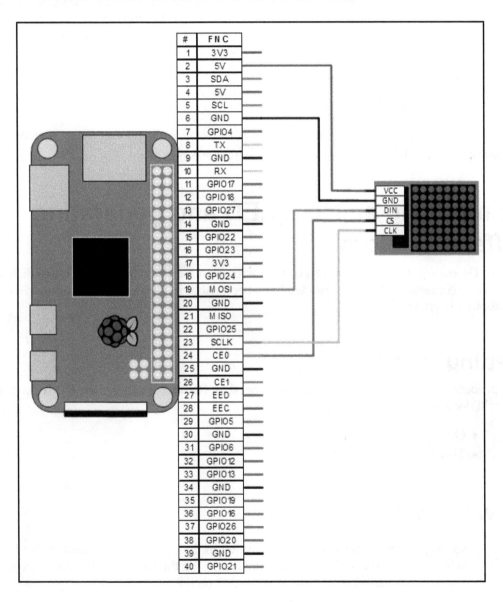

#	FNC
1	3V3
2	5V
3	SDA
4	5V
5	SCL
6	GND
7	GPIO4
8	TX
9	GND
10	RX
11	GPIO17
12	GPIO18
13	GPIO27
14	GND
15	GPIO22
16	GPIO23
17	3V3
18	GPIO24
19	MOSI
20	GND
21	MISO
22	GPIO25
23	SCLK
24	CE0
25	GND
26	CE1
27	EED
28	EEC
29	GPIO5
30	GND
31	GPIO6
32	GPIO12
33	GPIO13
34	GND
35	GPIO19
36	GPIO16
37	GPIO26
38	GPIO20
39	GND
40	GPIO21

2. There is a great library for interfacing an 8×8 matrix using a `max7219` driver in Python, appropriately named `max7219`. With this, it is easy to write messages or light any LED in the matrix.

3. You can make a messaging program in just a few lines! Create a program named `maxtix8x8.py` in the `ch6` folder and enter the following code:

```
import max7219.led as led

device = led.matrix()
message = raw_input('Enter message: ')
device.show_message(message)
```

That's it! Run the program with `sudo pythonmatrix8x8.py`, and enter your message. Congratulations, your Raspberry Pi Zero is talking back to you!

Connecting an RGB LED and generating different colors

RGB LEDs are another thing you can control with your Raspberry Pi Zero. These LEDs have a few more connectors than the ones we have been using in previous recipes, but will emit just about any color.

Getting ready

You probably know from the title that you'll need an RGB LED. Here is the entire parts list you will need for this recipe:

- One common-cathode RGB LED
- Three 330 Ohm resistors

How to do it...

1. Configure the RGB LED circuit as shown in the diagram. The common lead, which goes to the RPZ ground, is the longest of the LED legs. We'll use the same ports that we used for the first PWM LED recipe:

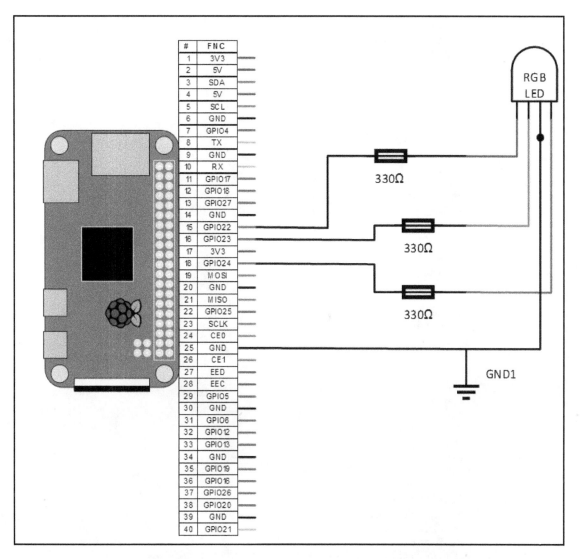

2. Our RGB LED program will use the same concepts as the PWM LED program. An RGB LED is really three LEDs in a single container. By lighting each of the internal LEDs at a different intensity (with PWM adjustments), the LED will render the combination of the colors, to the human eye appearing to be a completely different color. Create a new file in the ch6 directory named rgbled.py, and enter the following code:

```
import time
import RPi.GPIO as GPIO
```

```
GPIO.setmode(GPIO.BCM)
#Set up GPIO 22,23,24 as our LED outputs
GPIO.setup(22, GPIO.OUT)
GPIO.setup(23, GPIO.OUT)
GPIO.setup(24, GPIO.OUT)

red = GPIO.PWM(24,120)
green = GPIO.PWM(23,120)
blue = GPIO.PWM(22,120)

#RGB Values
redbr=50
greenbr=50
bluebr=50

red.start(0)
green.start(0)
blue.start(0)

def main():
      rgblight(0,0,0)
      print "Blue"
      rgblight(0,0,100)
      time.sleep(2)
      print "Red"
      rgblight(100,0,0)
      time.sleep(2)
      print "Green"
      rgblight(0,100,0)
      time.sleep(2)
      print "Cyan"
      rgblight(0,100,100)
      time.sleep(2)
      print "Magenta"
      rgblight(100,0,100)
      time.sleep(2)
      print "Yellow"
      rgblight(100,100,0)
      time.sleep(2)
      rgblight(0,0,0)
def rgblight(rpwm,gpwm,bpwm):
      red.ChangeDutyCycle(rpwm)
      green.ChangeDutyCycle(gpwm)
      blue.ChangeDutyCycle(bpwm)
if __name__== '__main__':
      main()
```

The start of this code should look identical to the PWM LED recipe. Where it changes is in the use of a function named `rgblight`, which sets the intensity of each of the LEDs accordingly:

```
def rgblight(rpwm,gpwm,bpwm):
        red.ChangeDutyCycle(rpwm)
        green.ChangeDutyCycle(gpwm)
        blue.ChangeDutyCycle(bpwm)
```

The main part of the code executes through different basic colors. Red, green, and blue are simply single LED nodes lit with the other two off; yellow, magenta, and cyan are a combination of two; and white is all three LEDs lit. What other colors can you make with PWM brightness adjustment? Give it a try!

Interfacing the 16×2 LCD display with RPZ

As we progress along on our mastery of output control with our Raspberry Pi Zero, we are ready to get a little higher resolution. With this, you'll be able to produce whatever text output you can fill on a higher-resolution 16×2 (16 characters wide by 2 rows high) LCD screen. With the gaining popularity of the Internet of Things, LCD displays have become quite inexpensive and are a great way to output any information your Raspberry Pi Zero has a hold of.

Getting ready

There are a lot of different 16×2 LCD displays available. Adafruit has a great one, Product ID 181xxxxx, and there was also one included in my Elego Kit. You'll also need a 10k potentiometer to control the brightness, which is included in Adafruit's LCD + extras kit. You'll definitely want a breadboard and Raspberry Pi cobbler of some sort.

The Python library I used is the easy-to-use `lcdscreen`. You can install it through the Python Package Index with pip:

```
sudo pip install lcdscreen
sudo pip install subprocess
```

This library will work with the Adafruit or Elegoo 16×2 LCD panels as well as a variety of others.

How to do it…

1. Attach the LCD display to a breadboard. Here is the full schematic, including the connections from the LCD to the potentiometer:

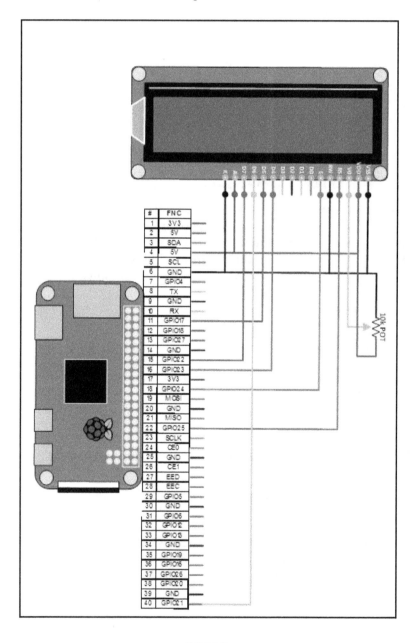

2. Here is a table of the connections between the LCD and the Raspberry Pi Zero. You can really use any available GPIO pin, as you can configure it when running `lcdscreen`:

Raspberry Pi Zero GPIO	LCD pin
GND	VSS
5V	VDD
<To potentiometer>	V0
GND	RW
GPIO 24	E
<Not used>	D0
<Not used>	D1
<Not used>	D2
<Not used>	D3
GPIO 23	D4
GPIO 17	D5
GPIO 21	D6
GPIO 22	D7
5V	A
GND	K

3. Once you have it all wired up, you should see both the backlight and the LCD pixels. Adjusting the potentiometer will adjust the LCD output so that it isn't too saturated or light.

4. Now we can get to the coding. Create the `lcd_info.py` file in the `ch6` directory and enter the following code:

```python
#!/usr/bin/env python
# Raspberry Pi Zero Cookbook
# Chapter 6
# Controlling a 16x2 LCD Display

import time
import subprocess
from lcdscreen import LCDScreen
```

```
def main():
    #Setup LCD Screen
    lcd =
    LCDScreen({'pin_rs':25,'pin_e':24,'pins_db':[23,17,21,22],'dimensio
ns':[16,2]})
    lcd.clear()
    while True:
        try:
            #Collect Information to Display
            dt =    subprocess.check_output(["date","+%F"])
            tm =    subprocess.check_output(["date","+%T"])
            tmp =
subprocess.check_output(["vcgencmd","measure_temp"])
            clk =
subprocess.check_output(["cat","/sys/devices/system/cpu/cpu0/cpufreq/scalin
g_cur_freq"])
            clock_mhz = str(float(clk)/1000000.00) + " MHz"
            #Push information on to LCD
            l1 = lcd.push_up(dt)
            lcd.delay(2)
            l2 = lcd.push_up(tm)
            lcd.delay(2)
            l3 = lcd.push_up(tmp)
            lcd.delay(2)
            l4 = lcd.push_up(clock_mhz)
            lcd.delay(2)
        finally:
            lcd.clear()
if __name__ == "__main__":
    main()
```

5. You can run the program with this command:

```
sudo python lcd_info.py
```

If you don't see anything, first double check your connections. If everything looks right, you may need to adjust the contrast using the potentiometer.

6. This should scroll the date, time, RPZ temperature, and clock speed until you break out from the program. We pull in information using Python's `subprocess` library. This lets us retrieve output from some of the command-line information tools and pull it into variables in Python. Then, the `lcdscreen` library makes pushing it to the panel very easy. First, we define the LCD's configuration:

```
lcd = LCDScreen(
{'pin_rs':25,'pin_e':24,'pins_db':[23,17,21,22],'dimensions':[16,2]})
```

7. The pins correspond to the Raspberry Pi's GPIO/BCM pins; you can match the pins to the table, with the `pins_db` value containing the D4-D7 GPIO connections.

8. With that, we can use `lcd.message('your message here')` to add a message to the screen, or `lcd.push_up('message')` and `lcd.push_down('message')` to bump the screen up a line and add what is provided in the message. Throwing it into a loop keeps the values updating every time they return.

Connecting the 74HC595N shift register to control many LEDs

So far, we've been controlling LEDs with individual GPIO pins. Not only is this a rather inefficient use of the Raspberry Pi Zero GPIO, but even if we used every single available pin for an LED, that would be a pretty boring light show. Instead, by adding in an LED driver such as the inexpensive 74HC595N, you easily get the ability to leverage several LEDs, or multiple 4×7-segment-number displays. In this recipe, we will use the SPI interface to control an eight-LED array. Let's get cooking!

Getting ready

Here is what you'll need for this recipe. At this point, you should be able to improvise with LED options. I used the 74HC595N, which is a commonly available chip online and also included in Elegoo's Super Complete Starter Kit.

- Eight 330 Ohm resistors
- One 74HC595N LED driver
- Eight LEDs, any color you want
- Jumper cables, breadboard, cobbler

- We will also be using the `PiShiftPy` library, available on pip:

```
sudo pip install PiShiftPy
```

How to do it…

1. Wiring the 74HC595N to the Raspberry Pi Zero is as easy as any SPI connection, with the outputs of the driver running your LED array. Here is the wiring schematic:

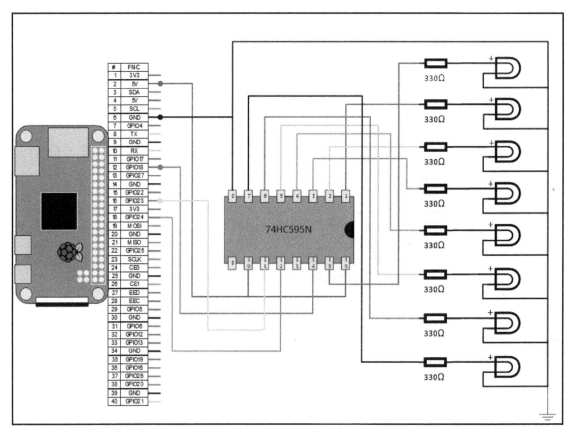

2. The code to test this out is quite simple. Create the `shiftregled.py` file in the `ch6` folder and enter the following code:

```
#!/usr/bin/env python
# Raspberry Pi Cookbook
```

```
# Chapter 6
# Multiple LEDs on Shift Register
import PiShiftPy as shift
import time
def main():
    shift.init()
    shift.write_all(0x00)
    while True:
            try:
                    ledseq(1,0,0,0,0,0,0,0)
                    ledseq(1,1,0,0,0,0,0,0)
                    ledseq(1,1,1,0,0,0,0,0)
                    ledseq(0,1,1,1,0,0,0,0)
                    ledseq(0,0,1,1,1,0,0,0)
                    ledseq(0,0,0,1,1,1,0,0)
                    ledseq(0,0,0,0,1,1,1,0)
                    ledseq(0,0,0,0,0,1,1,1)
                    ledseq(0,0,0,0,0,0,1,1)
                    ledseq(0,0,0,0,0,0,0,1)
                    ledseq(0,0,0,0,0,0,1,1)
                    ledseq(0,0,0,0,0,1,1,1)
                    ledseq(0,0,0,0,1,1,1,0)
                    ledseq(0,0,0,1,1,1,0,0)
                    ledseq(0,0,1,1,1,0,0,0)
                    ledseq(0,1,1,1,0,0,0,0)
                    ledseq(1,1,1,0,0,0,0,0)
                    ledseq(1,1,0,0,0,0,0,0)
            finally:
                    ledseq(0,0,0,0,0,0,0,0)

def ledseq(a,b,c,d,e,f,g,h):
    shift.push_bit(a)
    shift.push_bit(b)
    shift.push_bit(c)
    shift.push_bit(d)
    shift.push_bit(e)
    shift.push_bit(f)
    shift.push_bit(g)
    shift.push_bit(h)
    shift.write_latch()
    time.sleep(0.1)
if __name__ == "__main__":
    main()
```

3. The `PiShiftPy` library makes operating one or more shift registers a breeze. The default GPIO pins used are GPIO 18 for data, GPIO 23 for the clock, and GPIO 24 for the latch, which is why we didn't have to put anything into `init()`. If we want to use different pins or are using more than one shift register, we can explicitly define our configuration:

```
shift.init(data_pin=18, clock_pin=23, latch_pin=24, chain_number=1)
```

4. The pins correspond to the BCM GPIO numbers, and `chain_number` indicates how many shift registers are connected.

The `ledseq()` function simply identifies the eight bits associated with the eight LED connections, and sets them on or off. The `write_latch()` function latches the pushed bits to the output pins on the 74HC595N. This prevents the LEDs from flickering as we push the bits one at a time.

```
def ledseq(a,b,c,d,e,f,g,h):
    shift.push_bit(a)
    shift.push_bit(b)
    shift.push_bit(c)
    shift.push_bit(d)
    shift.push_bit(e)
    shift.push_bit(f)
    shift.push_bit(g)
    shift.push_bit(h)
    shift.write_latch()
    time.sleep(0.1)
```

5. In the `main()` function, we just call the `ledseq` function in a loop with the on/off configuration we're looking for. It is simple to trigger any LED configuration, having certain LEDs notify you of different events, or to run different patterns.

6. Furthermore, you can extend it to additional 74HC595N chips, and run even more LEDs using the same three GPIO pins on the Raspberry Pi. This is done by connecting pin 9 of this 74HC595N to pin 14 of the next one. Pins 11 & 12 are connected directly to each other. This saves your other pins for other sensors, lights, displays, or motors, some of which we've played with here and others we'll move on to in the next chapter

7
Controlling the Hardware

In this chapter, we will explore the following recipes:

- Integrating voltage translators with the RPZ
- Controlling a stepper motor using a RPZ and motor drivers
- Connecting a DC motor and controlling its speed and direction
- Controlling high power AC load using relays
- Controlling high power DC load using MOSFETs
- Controlling a buzzer with an RPZ
- Monitoring the physical health of the RPZ hardware
- Interfacing the PiFace with the RPZ

Introduction

In the previous chapter, we started getting into more advanced external device control, starting with the manipulation of different LEDs and LCD output peripherals. For the recipes in this chapter, we will utilize other microcontrollers as well as the Raspberry Pi Zero's own protocols to run more advanced peripherals and those that require independent or high-voltage power supplies.

Integrating voltage translators with the RPZ

With many peripherals understanding a 5V digital input and the Raspberry Pi Zero operating at 3.3V, you might require a voltage shift from the output of the Raspberry Pi GPIO to an external device. While there are a few ways to accomplish this, the use of a voltage translator will ensure the fastest and most error-free communication. While a voltage divider works great most of the time, the slew rate can cause dirty signal reads, and voltage dividers can only be used for inputs. By having a voltage translator in our toolkit, we expand our ability for the Raspberry Pi Zero to communicate with anything that uses 3.3V or 5V inputs or outputs.

Getting ready

For this recipe, I used a breakout board from Adafruit, the *4-channel I2C-safe Bi-directional Logic Level Converter* (`https://www.adafruit.com/products/757`). There are other logic translators available, but this one will work with 5V I2C devices, which are commonly used with microcontrollers such as the Arduino.

How to do it...

The voltage converter will take up to 4 pins and provide voltage translation for either direction. The A0, A1, A2, and A3 pins are the low-voltage side. These will connect to your Raspberry Pi Zero GPIO. The B0, B1, B2, and B3 pins will connect to your 5V devices or controllers.

Your grounds and power will connect to your grounds low and high voltages and low and high signals as follows:

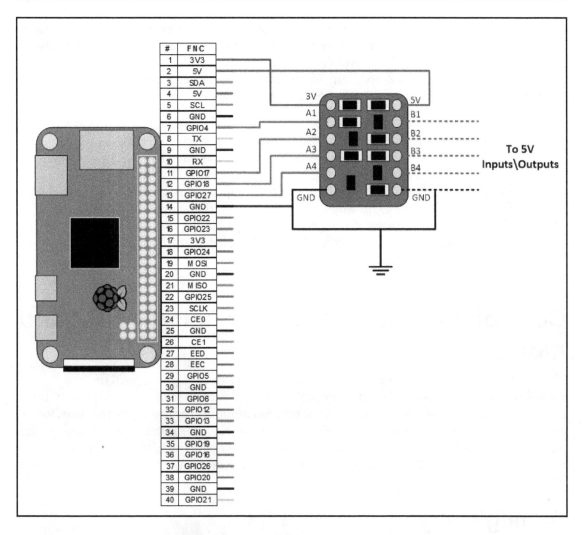

#	FNC
1	3V3
2	5V
3	SDA
4	5V
5	SCL
6	GND
7	GPIO4
8	TX
9	GND
10	RX
11	GPIO17
12	GPIO18
13	GPIO27
14	GND
15	GPIO22
16	GPIO23
17	3V3
18	GPIO24
19	MOSI
20	GND
21	MISO
22	GPIO25
23	SCLK
24	CE0
25	GND
26	CE1
27	EED
28	EEC
29	GPIO5
30	GND
31	GPIO6
32	GPIO12
33	GPIO13
34	GND
35	GPIO19
36	GPIO16
37	GPIO26
38	GPIO20
39	GND
40	GPIO21

Here, we have GPIO 4, 17, 18, and 27 connected to the low-power side of our translator. This is connected to a 5V microcontroller or device, such as an Arduino, on the opposite side. On the low-power side, anything outgoing will produce a 3V signal, and incoming signals will also be set to 3V. On the high-power side, you will produce and receive 5V signals. This board is ideal to have when you are working with different sensors, motors, and controllers, as some understand only a 5V signal, which the outputs on the Raspberry Pi Zero cannot provide. With the voltage translator available, you can make these connections through the boards with almost no effort.

This recipe will be helpful any time you want to use a sensor or motor that is expecting a 5V Volt signal. In later recipes, you may find you already have devices available which either send a 5V signal, or expect a 5V input. These bi-directional convertors are ideal for connecting the Raspberry Pi Zero to any 5V device, and works especially great for bi-directional devices that communicate over I2C (such as Digital Humidity Temperature Sensors).

One important thing to note is that this regulator is for changing signal voltage, not for transforming voltage for things such as LEDs or switching mechanical relays. Small LEDs require about 100 times the current (or amperage) needed for a digital signal. Small motors and relays will need over 10,000 times the amount of current! For that, you would want to use a level shifter or amplifier circuit. Level shifting was discussed in the previous chapter, and we will use a transistor to amplify a GPIO signal in the forthcoming recipe on relays.

Controlling a stepper motor using a RPZ and motor drivers

Now that we can handle any device that understands 3V or 5V signals, we'll use the Raspberry Pi Zero to controller a stepper motor. Stepper motors take digital inputs to turn the motor a single "step." A step is a specific rotation amount that the motor will turn for each input. Very precise motors may have hundreds of steps per rotation, which are great for things such as high-resolution 3D printers or CNC routers. The L293D motor driver makes it easy to control these motors with the Raspberry Pi Zero.

Getting ready

For this recipe, you will need an L293D chip and a stepper motor. There is a huge variety of stepper motors to choose from. I went with the 5V 28BYJ-48 motor included in the Elegoo starter kit, but any small 5V stepper motor (larger ones will need their own power supply) will work without additional power. Other than jumper cables, a breadboard, a 10uF capacitor, and your Raspberry Pi Zero, you should be ready to go!

How to do it...

1. The schematic for the circuit is as follows:

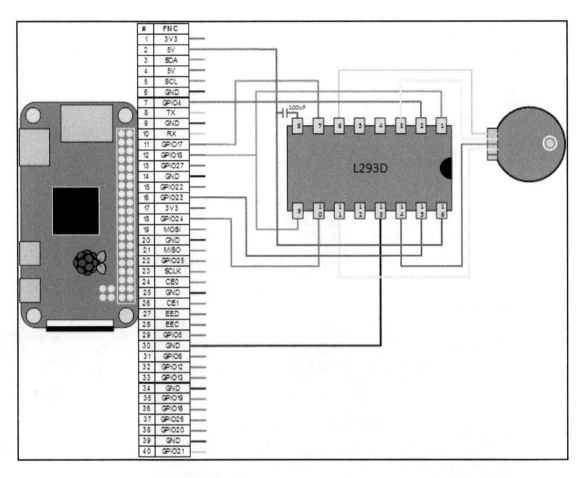

#	FNC
1	3V3
2	5V
3	SDA
4	5V
5	SCL
6	GND
7	GPIO4
8	TX
9	GND
10	RX
11	GPIO17
12	GPIO18
13	GPIO27
14	GND
15	GPIO22
16	GPIO23
17	3V3
18	GPIO24
19	MOSI
20	GND
21	MISO
22	GPIO25
23	SCLK
24	CE0
25	GND
26	CE1
27	EED
28	EEC
29	GPIO5
30	GND
31	GPIO6
32	GPIO12
33	GPIO13
34	GND
35	GPIO19
36	GPIO16
37	GPIO26
38	GPIO20
39	GND
40	GPIO21

L293D

You might have a pink or purple wire, but typically, you will have blue, orange, yellow, and red as stepper motor wires. You don't need to connect the red wire. Once you have it wired up, we will use the Rpi.GPIO library to control the motor.

2. Create the movestepper.py program in the ch7 directory of your Cookbook folder, and enter the following code:

```
#!/usr/bin/env python
# Raspberry Pi Zero Cookbook
```

```
# Stepper Motor Control
import RPi.GPIO as GPIO
import time
import argparse
GPIO.setmode(GPIO.BCM)

input1 = 4   #To A1 Coil
input2 = 17 #To A2 Coil
input3 = 24 #To B1 Coil
input4 = 23 #To B2 Coil
enable1 = 18
GPIO.setwarnings(False)
GPIO.setup(enable1, GPIO.OUT)
GPIO.setup(input1, GPIO.OUT)
GPIO.setup(input2, GPIO.OUT)
GPIO.setup(input3, GPIO.OUT)
GPIO.setup(input4, GPIO.OUT)

def main():
    parser = argparse.ArgumentParser()
    parser.add_argument("steps",type=int,help="Number
of steps to turn the motor")
        parser.add_argument("stepdelay",type=int,help="Delay
between steps, in milliseconds")
    parser.add_argument("direction",help="Direction to    turn the
motor",choices=['forward','back'])
    args = parser.parse_args()
    delay = args.stepdelay/1000.00
    if args.direction == "back":
            for x in range(1,args.steps):
                    step_4(delay)
                    step_3(delay)
                    step_2(delay)
                    step_1(delay)
    else:
            for x in range(1,args.steps):
                    step_1(delay)
                    step_2(delay)
                    step_3(delay)
                    step_4(delay)

def step_1(delay):
    set_step(1,0,1,0,delay)
def step_2(delay):
    set_step(0,1,1,0,delay)
def step_3(delay):
    set_step(0,1,0,1,delay)
def step_4(delay):
```

```
        set_step(1,0,0,1,delay)
    def set_step(a1,a2,b1,b2,delay):
        GPIO.output(input1,a1)
        GPIO.output(input2,a2)
        GPIO.output(input3,b1)
        GPIO.output(input4,b2)
        time.sleep(delay)

    if __name__ == "__main__":
        main()
```

3. Running with `sudo python movestepper.py <steps> <delay>` `<direction>` will move the motor forward or backward for as many steps provided. If you don't recall the parameters, our use of argparse makes it easy to recall:

```
pi@rpz14101:~/share/ch7 $ sudo python movestepper.py -h
usage: movestepper.py [-h] steps stepdelay {forward,back}
positional arguments:
  steps                Number of steps to turn the motor
  stepdelay            Delay between steps, in milliseconds
  {forward,back}       Direction to turn the motor
optional arguments:
  -h, --help           show this help message and exit
```

It is as simple as that! With a known number of steps per rotation, you can have very precise control of how far your stepper motor moves.

Connecting a DC motor and controlling its speed and direction

DC motors are not for precision movement like stepper motors are, but useful for things such as running fans or turning motors where you care more about the speed of the rotation than the accuracy. Using the same L293D chip and the same libraries as the previous chapter, we can control a DC motor's speed and direction.

Getting ready

Instead of a stepper motor, you will want a small DC motor. They are pretty easy to tell apart: a stepper motor has 4 or 5 wires (bipolar stepper motors only have 4, and lack the coil center-tap red wire), and a DC motor only has two. You'll also need an external power source for this one–a 4xAA battery pack is perfect. You can use the same L293D from the previous recipe.

How to do it...

This recipe's schematic is a bit simpler than the previous one, as there is less you have to control with a DC motor.

1. You'll also add in the AA battery pack:

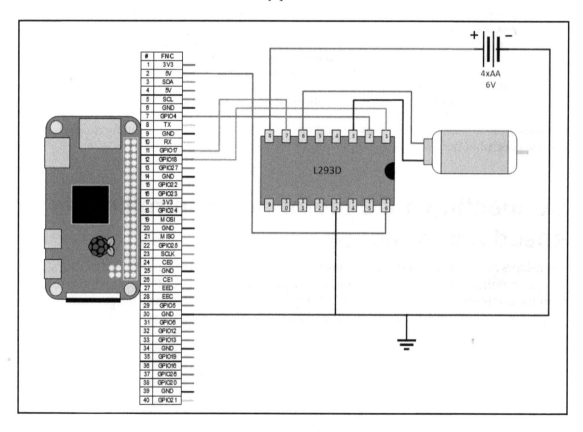

2. Controlling the DC motor is similar to controlling LED brightness with PWM. Create the movedc.py file and enter the following:

```python
#!/usr/bin/env python
# Raspberry Pi Zero Cookbook
# DC Motor Control
import RPi.GPIO as GPIO
import time
import argparse
GPIO.setmode(GPIO.BCM)

input1 = 4   #To Red DC Lead
input2 = 17 #To Black DC Lead
enable1 = 18
GPIO.setwarnings(False)
GPIO.setup(input1, GPIO.OUT)
GPIO.setup(input2, GPIO.OUT)
GPIO.setup(enable1, GPIO.OUT)
motor = GPIO.PWM(enable1, 100)
motor.start(0)
def main():
    parser = argparse.ArgumentParser()
    parser.add_argument("speed",type=int,help="Motor     Speed
0-99",choices=range(0,100))
    parser.add_argument("time",type=int,help="Time to     run motor, in
seconds")
    parser.add_argument("direction",help="Direction to     turn the
motor",choices=['forward','back'])
    args = parser.parse_args()
    if args.direction == "back":
            motor.start(args.speed)
            back()
            time.sleep(args.time)
    else:
            motor.start(args.speed)
            forward()
            time.sleep(args.time)
def forward():
    GPIO.output(input1, GPIO.HIGH)
    GPIO.output(input2, GPIO.LOW)
def back():
    GPIO.output(input1, GPIO.LOW)
    GPIO.output(input2, GPIO.HIGH)
if __name__ == "__main__":
    main()
```

3. As you will notice here, the only difference in the motor's direction is which lead is on and which one is off. Aside from that, you pass the PWM value to indicate a relative speed and the duration you'd like to run the motor for, like this, for example:

```
sudo python share/ch7/movedc.py 50 1 forward
```

This will run the DC motor at 50% speed for one second in the forward direction. . If the motor isn't turning, check your connections. You may also need to specify a larger value. Now that we can control fans, we can have them speed up when the temperature increases, or we could do something unique, such as turning on the fan when we get a new e-mail.

A word of caution: Do not run for more than 5 or 6 seconds at a time at high speeds! The L293D is designed to operate with a heat sink and will get hot enough to burn you! (Typically the heat sink is in the circuit board; this is why there are four ground pins in the middle of the chip. Breadboards do not offer any substantial thermal dissipation.)

Controlling high power AC load using relays

Control of high-power devices, such as 120V power outlets, is an objective of home automation. While a Raspberry Pi Zero cannot power devices on its own, it does can control relays that are designed to control power sources.

Working with AC power, such as 120V house power (also known as line voltage), is **extremely dangerous and potentially lethal**. Do not ever attempt to work with live circuits, and always work with experienced electricians when designing systems that control power. Mishandling high power can be deadly!

Getting ready

For this recipe, you will need a protective relay. The one included in the Elegoo Kit works perfectly for this recipe, but any relay that takes a 5V DC switching input should work. You'll also need the following components, along with the usual breadboard, jumper cables, and Raspberry Pi Zero:

- 1N4001 diode, though any small diode will work here, except for Zener diodes
- 2N2222 transistor

- 2kOhm resistor (2.2KOhms+/-5% resistors are common and will work for this circuit)

How to do it...

1. Each relay can control the operation of a different power source. The following figure is how you would connect a single 120V outlet. Typically, the power capabilities of a relay are displayed right on top of the relay, but you may need to look up a datasheet. Before jumping right into high-voltage AC things, you can generally test your circuit and capabilities with a simpler LED circuit, as shown here:

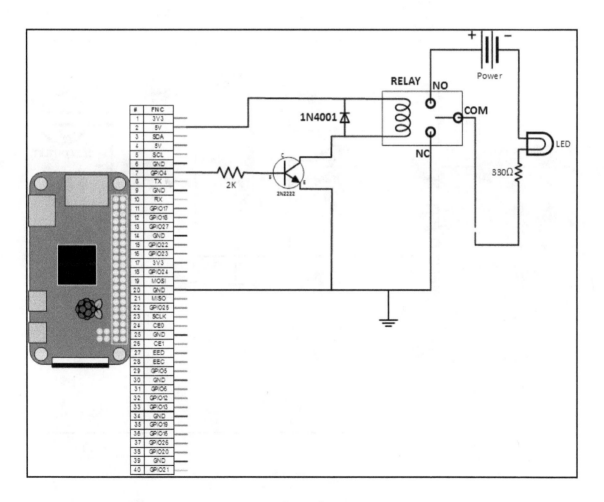

Let's look at this circuit a little more closely. Protective relays are used to trigger a switching operation (from Normally Closed to Normally Open) triggered by an independent coil. It is protective in the sense that the power to activate the relay switch is independent of the power used on the switching side. For the previous diagram, if we send a 5V signal to the relay, it will switch the other side from Normally Closed (NC) to Normally Open (NO). Typical design will have NC mean off and NO mean on; if there is a failure, power will be cut by default. In the previous figure, we have an independent LED circuit with its own power that will be turned on when activating the relay, but many protective relays are used for running much more powerful and/or AC circuits, such as house wiring. While an LED is good for a test, if I wanted to control something like a 120V AC outlet through my Raspberry Pi Zero, the wiring would be nearly identical:

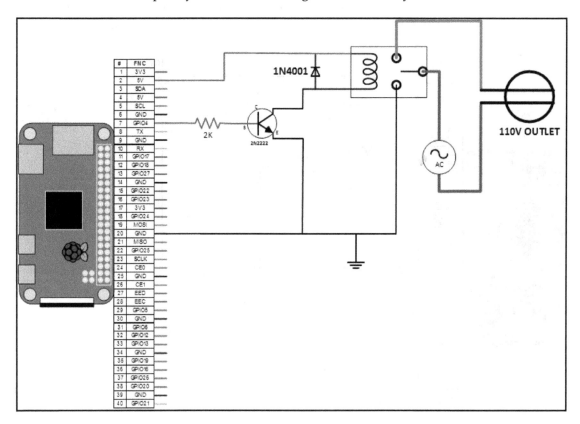

I can't stress enough how dangerous working with things like house voltage can be. It is very, very easy to end up severely injured or dead from mishandling high power. Test only systems like this with direct supervision from experienced people, work in a safe environment, and use test equipment to verify things are dead before touching anything. Devices such as capacitors can hold a deadly voltage after all direct power has been cut, so assume that everything is always alive and dangerous–this philosophy will keep you alive too.

2. In simpler terms, a relay is just a power-activated switch, which happens to also be what our transistor is! The big difference is that the 2N2222 transistor is "solid-state," so the switching operation happens without any mechanical movement. Transistors don't really protect your circuit the way mechanical relays do either: they are more ideal for logic switching and lower-power designs, though there certainly are transistors for high-power systems as well.

3. The transistor has three leads: a base, emitter, and collector (B, E, C, respectively). When we raise the voltage on the RPZ pin, a small amount of current flows from the emitter to the base, through the resistor, to the pin. This small amount of current permits a larger amount of current to flow from the emitter to the collector, through the relay's coil, activating it. The proportion of these two currents is called the gain and is represented with the symbol h_{FE}. The 2N2222 is an NPN transistor. The current flows the opposite direction in PNP transistors. The base receives our RPZ GPIO signal, and this works as the on/off mechanism for the collector's 5V circuit. When we send a signal to the base, this will "turn on" the 5V circuit from the Raspberry Pi to the relay, which in turn activates the relay. In circuitry and electronics, you will often find switches running other switches, just like we are doing here.

There are thousands of diodes, transistors, relays and capacitors, and in many cases, you can substitute one for another, depending on what you are trying to do. The 2N2222 is a very common transistor and serves many purposes in the lower-voltage world, and it has many variants, though most of them should work in a circuit like the previous one. For everything you use, the datasheet has the answer, and these days, just about every data sheet is available on the Internet.

4. To test this relay circuit, we can use the `blink.sh` script from Chapter 5, *Getting Your Hands Dirty Using the GPIO Header*. This is a simple on/off GPIO cycle, so it works for anything that you have connected, not just LEDs. In case you skipped that chapter, the code is listed here:

```
#!/bin/bash
#parameters wiringPi Pin # and delay time in SECONDS
(e.g. blink.sh 25 .5)
PIN=$1
DLY=$2
gpio mode ${PIN} output
while true; do
        gpio write ${PIN} 1;
        sleep ${DLY};
        gpio write ${PIN} 0;
        sleep ${DLY};
done
```

5. Now, with a simple run, we can test our relay circuit:

```
blink.sh 7 1
```

6. Even without an LED or other power source, you can hear most mechanical relays when activated; you should hear a little click every second if you used the aforementioned parameters.

Controlling high power DC load using MOSFETs

For scenarios where you need to handle a lot of DC power and current, MOSFETs are a great solid-state alternative to mechanical relays. With proper power and heat-sinking, many common power MOSFETs can power over 1000 LEDs!

 AC or DC power are both dangerous! Just like the previous recipe, use extreme caution when using high-power loads. In this case, we will be using a 9V DC load–not too dangerous, but many MOSFET circuits can handle high-voltage and amperage solutions.

Getting ready

For this recipe, we will need the following equipment:

- 3 N-channel power MOSFETs (the IRLB8721 MOSFETS are inexpensive and available from Adafruit (https://www.adafruit.com/product/355)
- 12V analog LED light strip; with a 2 A source, you can run about 3 meters of 60 LED/m lights.
- 9V-12V power source (1-2 A is perfect)

How to do it...

1. Wiring a MOSFET is quite simple. One side will be connected to the Raspberry Pi to control the MOSFET, while the other side will is for handling the high-power output. The wiring diagram is as follows:

Handling and connecting should be done with great care. MOSFETs contain a small diode that is quite sensitive. If too much current flows across this diode, the MOSFET will no longer "switch off." Worse yet, there is no magic smoke that escapes; the device just stops working. Static electricity can damage this small diode in much the same way.

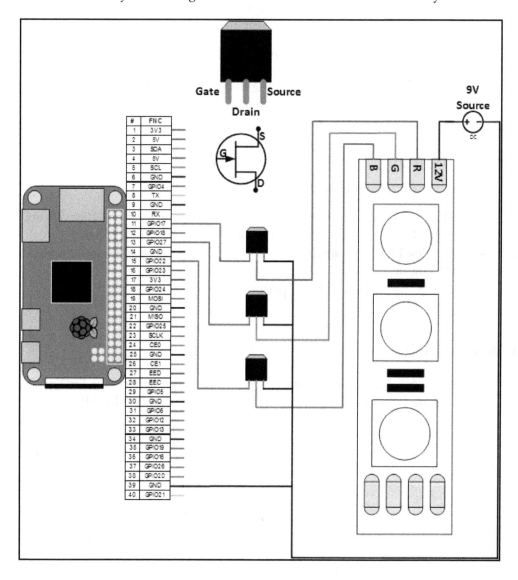

2. Each LED is in fact three LEDs (just like " Connecting RGB LED and generating different colors" in `Chapter 6`, *Controlling the LEDs and Displays*), and each GPIO pin handles one of the colors. The circuit for the light strip power is controlled by the MOSFETs. Although the analog strips say 12V on them, that's really the maximum, and your strip will be bright on 9V.

3. We can use the RGB LED demo from `Chapter 6`, *Controlling the LEDs and Displays* to test the circuit; all we need to do is change our pin numbers. In the `ch7` directory, enter the following code as `rgb_mostfet.py`:

```
import time
import RPi.GPIO as GPIO
GPIO.setmode(GPIO.BCM)
#Set up GPIO 17,27,22 as our LED outputs
GPIO.setup(17, GPIO.OUT)
GPIO.setup(27, GPIO.OUT)
GPIO.setup(22, GPIO.OUT)

red = GPIO.PWM(17,50)
green = GPIO.PWM(27,50)
yellow = GPIO.PWM(22,50)

red.start(0)
green.start(0)
yellow.start(0)
while True:
    try:
            print "up!"
            for brightness in range(0, 101):
                    red.ChangeDutyCycle(brightness)
                    green.ChangeDutyCycle(brightness)
                    yellow.ChangeDutyCycle(brightness)
                    time.sleep(0.07)
            print "down!"
            for brightness in range (100, 0, -1):
                    red.ChangeDutyCycle(brightness)
                    green.ChangeDutyCycle(brightness)
                    yellow.ChangeDutyCycle(brightness)
                    time.sleep(0.07)
    except KeyboardInterrupt:
            print "Finished!"
    finally:
            red.stop()
            green.stop()
            yellow.stop()
            break
```

4. This is just a simple example, but you aren't limited to 9 volts or 2 A, even with this MOSFET. The datasheet has all the answers, though if you approach the maximums, be sure to have a heat sink or other cooling solution, or the semiconductor will get very hot.

Controlling a buzzer with an RPZ

We've done a lot with light, but what about sound? The RPZ can run a simple buzzer with ease.

Getting ready

All you will need here is a piezo buzzer, which is a commonly available electronic component.

How to do it...

1. The piezo buzzer circuit is about as simple as it gets. There are only two leads: one is assigned to a GPIO port, and the other to ground. We can use PWM to adjust the frequency.

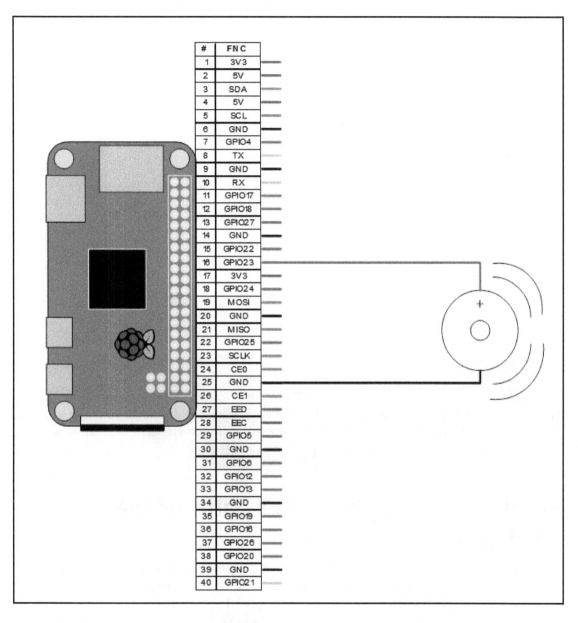

#	FN C
1	3V3
2	5V
3	SDA
4	5V
5	SCL
6	GND
7	GPIO4
8	TX
9	GND
10	RX
11	GPIO17
12	GPIO18
13	GPIO27
14	GND
15	GPIO22
16	GPIO23
17	3V3
18	GPIO24
19	MOSI
20	GND
21	MISO
22	GPIO25
23	SCLK
24	CE0
25	GND
26	CE1
27	EED
28	EEC
29	GPIO5
30	GND
31	GPIO6
32	GPIO12
33	GPIO13
34	GND
35	GPIO19
36	GPIO16
37	GPIO26
38	GPIO20
39	GND
40	GPIO21

2. The code is simple too. The following is the code to run a buzzer test from 0 to 1 MHz and back down. Enter the code and run it as `piezo.py`:

```
#!/usr/bin/env python
# Raspberry Pi Zero Cookbook
# Chapter 6 – Piezo Buzzer Operation
```

```
import time
import RPi.GPIO as GPIO
GPIO.setmode(GPIO.BCM)
GPIO.setwarnings(False)
#Set up GPIO 21 as buzzer output
GPIO.setup(21, GPIO.OUT)

# No freq to start
buzzer1 = GPIO.PWM(21,0.5)
# Set Volume
buzzer1.start(50)
while True:
    try:
            print "up!"
            for freq in range(1, 1001):
                    buzzer1.ChangeFrequency(freq)
                    time.sleep(0.02)
            print "down!"
            for freq in range (1000, 1, -1):
                    buzzer1.ChangeFrequency(freq)
                    time.sleep(0.02)
    except KeyboardInterrupt:
            print "Finished!"
    finally:
            buzzer1.stop()
            break
```

That's all there is to it! The Internet has a lot of great libraries to do things with piezo buzzers. You can have different frequencies represent different alerts, or even make simple, very lo-fi music.

Monitoring the physical health of the RPZ hardware

We took a look earlier on in the look at some of the measurements. In this recipe, we will dive a little bit deeper and use our new knowledge of outputs to regulate and alert on changes in the Raspberry Pi's health.

Getting ready

For this recipe, we will need the buzzer from the previous recipe, an RGB 4-lead LED, and three 330-Ohm resistors. If you don't have an RGB LED, you can alternatively make the same circuit using individual LEDs.

How to do it...

1. Configure the following circuit:

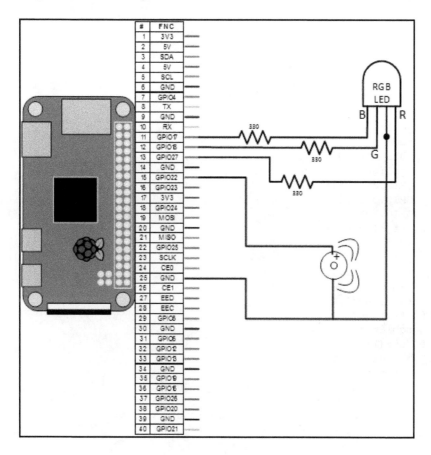

2. The following Python code will monitor the Raspberry Pi's health and change the values if there is a problem. Create a file named `rpz_alert.py` and enter the following code:

```python
#!/bin/env python
# Chapter 7 Hardware Control
# RPZ Health Monitoring and Alerting
import time
import os
import RPi.GPIO as GPIO
GPIO.setmode(GPIO.BCM)
redpin=18
greenpin=17
bluepin=27
buzzerpin=22
GPIO.setup(redpin, GPIO.OUT)
GPIO.setup(bluepin, GPIO.OUT)
GPIO.setup(greenpin, GPIO.OUT)
GPIO.setup(buzzerpin, GPIO.OUT)
buzzer = GPIO.PWM(buzzerpin, 0.5)
tempyellow = 35.0
tempred= 40.0
tempbuzz = 42.0
def rgblight(r,g,b):
    GPIO.output(redpin,r)
    GPIO.output(greenpin,g)
    GPIO.output(bluepin,b)
def greenlight():
    rgblight(0,1,0)
def yellowlight():
    rgblight(1,1,0)
def redlight():
    rgblight(1,0,0)
def offlight():
    rgblight(0,0,0)
def buzz():
    buzzer.start(50)
    for x in range(0,10):
            buzzer.ChangeFrequency(500)
            time.sleep(.4)
            buzzer.ChangeFrequency(750)
            time.sleep(.4)
    buzzer.stop()
def checkrpz():
    loadavg=os.getloadavg()
    rpztemp=os.popen('vcgencmd measure_temp').readline()
    rpztemp=float(rpztemp.replace("temp=","").replace("'C\n",""))
```

```
            print rpztemp
            if loadavg[0] >= 0.99 or rpztemp>=tempyellow:
                    yellowlight()
            if loadavg[1] >= 0.99 or rpztemp>=tempred:
                    redlight()
            if loadavg[2] >= 0.99 or rpztemp>=tempbuzz:
                    redlight()
                    buzz()
            if loadavg[0]<0.99 and loadavg[1]<0.99 and loadavg[2]<0.99 and
    rpztemp<tempyellow:
                    greenlight()
        def main():
            print "Monitoring System Health"
            while True:
                    try:
                            checkrpz()
                            time.sleep(5)
                    except KeyboardInterrupt:
                            offlight()
                            break
        if __name__ == '__main__':
            main()
```

3. This script does a few things. First, it initializes the pins in use for the LED and the buzzer. It sets the buzzer for PWM so we can adjust the frequency, but since we will only be after green/yellow/red for the LED, we can just set those to off and on. From there, every 5 seconds, it checks the Raspberry Pi Zero's load and temperature. If the load is greater than or equal to 0.99 (which is 99% of a single core's capacity) in the 1-minute sample, it will turn the LED yellow. If the 5-minute average is above 0.99, it will turn red. Finally, if the 15-minute average exceeds 0.99 (meaning the RPZ has been sustaining a 99% average load for 15 minutes), the buzzer will sound. If no high load is reported, the LED stays green.

4. It also checks the temperate and alerts using the vcgencmd utility. After converting the string to a float, it checks the threshold values for tempyellow, tempred, and tempbuzz. If the tempyellow temperature is exceeded, the RGB turns yellow. It will turn red and buzz if those temperature thresholds are exceeded.

5. Opening a few windows at once is an easy way to change the state from green to yellow to red to red+buzz for CPU load. Temperature is pretty easy to increase as well, but be careful not to burn your Raspberry Pi Zero–or yourself!

Interfacing the PiFace with the RPZ

The PiFace module is a board for any Raspberry Pi, and it provides eight outputs, two protective relays, eight inputs, and all of the circuitry–you need to use only your SPI channel on your Raspberry Pi. With high-voltage terminals, this is an ideal board for running several motors, lights, and sensors simultaneously.

Getting ready

For this, you'll need the PiFace Digital Revision 2 Board. This is available online through Element 14 (`https://www.element14.com/community/docs/DOC-69001`) and other resellers. It attaches directly to your Raspberry Pi Zero if the RPZ has a male header; otherwise, you'll need a ribbon cable. You also want a couple of LEDs and 330 Ohm resistors.

Here' what the top of the PiFace Digital 2 looks like:

The top of the PiFace Digital 2

Here's the PiFace and Raspberry Pi Zero footprint:

The PiFace adds a bit to the overall Raspberry Pi Zero footprint

How to do it...

1. You'll need to have SPI enabled, which is covered in in Chapter 5, *Getting Your Hands Dirty Using the GPIO Header*. The PiFace Emulator uses Python 3, and it can be installed with `apt-get`:

   ```
   sudo apt-get install python3-pifacedigital-emulator
   ```

2. For the Python used at the end of this recipe, you'll want the Python 2 adapter:

   ```
   sudo apt-get install python-pifacedigitalio
   ```

3. While I use Python 2 in this book and this recipe, the PiFace Emulator is written in Python 3, and libraries for the Python 3 are more comprehensive and up to date than its predecessor. If you really get deep into using the PiFace board, you'll probably want to start working with Python 3 to get the most out of it. The PiFace is a digital companion board that provides the following components:

   - Two mechanical relays
   - Eight input terminals (four with push-button switches)
   - Eight LEDs connected
   - Eight output terminals

4. All of the components are configurable, and there is a Python wrapper that makes it very easy to use. The following diagram shows the connectors and jumpers on the PiFace:

5. Here's the description of every component of the PiFace:

Component	Description
JP1/JP2	Address jumpers if you are using multiple boards over your SPI channel. If the jumper is set to pins 1 and 2 (top to bottom in previous diagram), the pin's address is 0. If set to 2 and 3, it is 1. The combination of JP1 and JP2 settings allows addresses 00, 01, 10, and 11 to be used.

JP3	Connect RPZ 5V to PiFace 5V. If you want to run your PiFace power from a separate source, disconnect this jumper and connect your power source to the PiFace's 5V and GND terminals.
JP4	Activate 5V snubber diodes. Remove this jumper if you are using voltages on your outputs that are greater than 5 volts.
JP5\JP6	Enable Relay 0/1. Remove these jumpers if you just want the outputs and aren't using the relays for anything.
JP7	5V power enabled for LEDs and relay coils
S0-S3	Push-button switches connected to INPUT 0-3
INPUT 0-7	Input ports. If connected to ground, input will be true. Inputs 0-3 run through switches S0-S3
OUTPUT 0-1	Output ports for relays 0 and 1. A signal of HIGH on output 0 will trigger relay 0 and light LED 0.
OUTPUT 2-7	Output ports to send signals to. These would be used to control your components, light meters, and LEDs. They only close the circuit; you have to have a power source.
LED0-LED7	Indicates the state of OUTPUT 0-7. If the state is HIGH, the LED will be lit.
RELAY0\RELAY1	Electromechanical relays. Their Common, Normal Open, and Normal Closed terminals are below the relays.

6. If you've install the PiFace Digital Emulator, you should have an icon on the desktop you can double-click to open. The interface very easy to use:

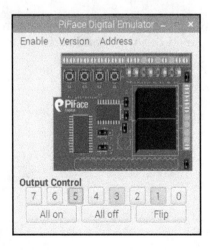

7. Using the menu, you can go to Enable | Outputs to control the outputs using the buttons on the screen. Try clicking on 0. You should see LED0 light up, and if your JP5 jumper is in, you should have heard the relay click as well. Buttons 2-7 will light the LED, but without the click. If you press any of the buttons, the emulator will indicate you've pressed the button and which terminal was activated. This is an easy way to test, and now we can move on to a simple external circuit. Add a couple of LEDs and resistors, like this:

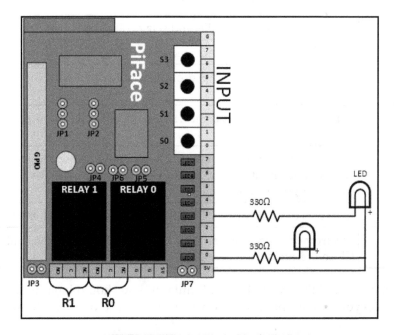

8. We will have the switches control a few different functions with the following code. Create a file named `pface.py` and enter the following:

```
#!/bin/env python
# Chapter 7 Hardware Control
# Working with the PiFace Controller
import pifacedigitalio
pf = pifacedigitalio.PiFaceDigital()
import time
def lightseq(o0,o1,o2,o3,o4,o5,o6,o7):
    pf.output_pins[0].value=o0
    pf.output_pins[1].value=o1
    pf.output_pins[2].value=o2
    pf.output_pins[3].value=o3
    pf.output_pins[4].value=o4
    pf.output_pins[5].value=o5
```

```
        pf.output_pins[6].value=o6
        pf.output_pins[7].value=o7

def dothecylon():
    dly=0.2
    lightseq(1,0,0,0,0,0,0,0)
    time.sleep(dly)
    lightseq(1,1,0,0,0,0,0,0)
    time.sleep(dly)
    lightseq(1,1,1,0,0,0,0,0)
    time.sleep(dly)
    lightseq(0,1,1,1,0,0,0,0)
    time.sleep(dly)
    lightseq(0,0,1,1,1,0,0,0)
    time.sleep(dly)
    lightseq(0,0,0,1,1,1,0,0)
    time.sleep(dly)
    lightseq(0,0,0,0,1,1,1,0)
    time.sleep(dly)
    lightseq(0,0,0,0,0,1,1,1)
    time.sleep(dly)
    lightseq(0,0,0,0,0,0,1,1)
    time.sleep(dly)
    lightseq(0,0,0,0,0,0,0,1)
    time.sleep(dly)
    lightseq(0,0,0,0,0,0,1,1)
    time.sleep(dly)
    lightseq(0,0,0,0,0,1,1,1)
    time.sleep(dly)
    lightseq(0,0,0,0,1,1,1,0)
    time.sleep(dly)
    lightseq(0,0,0,1,1,1,0,0)
    time.sleep(dly)
    lightseq(0,0,1,1,1,0,0,0)
    time.sleep(dly)
    lightseq(0,1,1,1,0,0,0,0)
    time.sleep(dly)
    lightseq(1,1,1,0,0,0,0,0)
    time.sleep(dly)
    lightseq(1,1,0,0,0,0,0,0)
    time.sleep(dly)

def main():
    print "Press S0 to click on relay and LED"
    print "Press S1 to toggle LED"
    print "Press S2 to activate Cylon"
    print "Press S3 to exit"
    while True:
```

```
                    if pf.input_pins[0].value==1:
                            time.sleep(.2)
                            pf.output_pins[0].value=1
                            time.sleep(1)
                            pf.output_pins[0].value=0
                    elif pf.input_pins[1].value==1:
                            time.sleep(.2)
                            state=pf.output_pins[3].value
                            print "Value: ", state
                            time.sleep(.2)
                            if state==1:
                                    pf.output_pins[3].value=0
                            else:
                                    pf.output_pins[3].value=1
                    elif pf.input_pins[2].value==1:
                            time.sleep(.1)
                            print "Do the Cylon! Ctrl-C to Stop"
                            while True:
                                    try:
                                            dothecylon()
                                    except KeyboardInterrupt:
                                            lightseq(0,0,0,0,0,0,0,0)
                                            break
                    elif pf.input_pins[3].value==1:
                            break
    if __name__ == "__main__":
        main()
```

9. The `pifacedigitalio` library makes it easy to work with the board through Python. The PiFace Digital object uses the `input_pins[x]` and `output_pins[x]` variables to let you control their values. Note that when you turn on output pins 0 and 1, you'll also activate the relay, unless you've pulled the jumper. Input pins 0, 1, 2, and 3 are also activated by the switches, so we can use these to control our activities. Running the program gives you this simple menu:

```
pi@raspberrypi:~ $ sudo python pface.py
Press S0 to click on relay and LED
Press S1 to toggle LED
Press S2 to activate Cylon
Press S3 to exit
```

10. Pressing S0 runs a simple 1-second on/off toggle for the first LED. You'll also hear the relay click. S1 checks the current state of the non-relay terminal (O3) and toggles it. S2 runs an LED sequence on the board (the `dothecylon` function in the code) until you send a keyboard interrupt, and the last switch, S3, exits the program. With just a little bit of code, you have the versatility of several variable-power outputs, internal and external inputs, and relays for things such as AC power. For everything that comes already built and ready to go, the PiFace Digital 2 is a cost-effective addition to your home hacking toolbox.

8
Taking Digital Inputs to the Raspberry Pi Zero

Here's what we will cover in this chapter:

- Interfacing push switches
- Interfacing toggle switches and setting debouncing
- Avoiding the floating states of the input line
- Interfacing a keypad with the RPZ
- Interfacing RTC to get accurate time
- Setting up interrupts on a toggle switch through GPIO
- Interfacing RFID tags with the RPZ
- Interfacing a GPS module with the RPZ

Introduction

In this chapter, we move from controlling external devices, such as motors and LEDs, to reading input from devices. The flexibility of the GPIO allows both, and the libraries we used previously to drive outputs work just as well for understanding device inputs.

Interfacing push switches

As we move on to capturing input from the Raspberry Pi Zero, let's start with a simple push switch. Like most of what we've done in the cookbook, the simple circuits show how easy it is to move on to more complex solutions.

Getting ready

You'll need the following for this recipe:

- RGB LED (or three LEDs)
- Three 330-Ohm resistors
- One four-leg pushbutton switch

If you still have the circuit wired from the previous chapter's Raspberry Pi Health Check, you can keep the circuit intact with the piezo buzzer and there won't be any conflicts when adding the pushbutton.

How to do it...

1. Configure the following circuit with your Raspberry Pi:

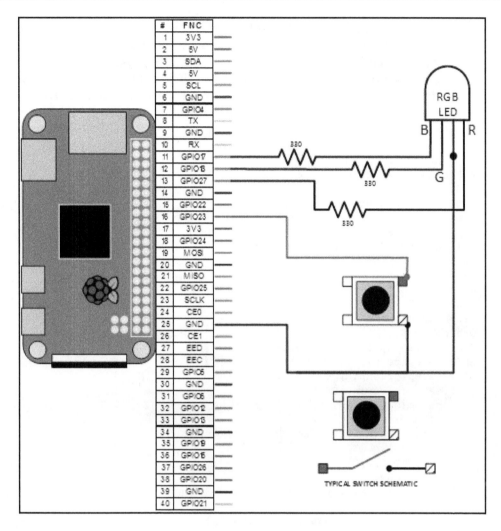

#	FNC
1	3V3
2	5V
3	SDA
4	5V
5	SCL
6	GND
7	GPIO4
8	TX
9	GND
10	RX
11	GPIO17
12	GPIO18
13	GPIO27
14	GND
15	GPIO22
16	GPIO23
17	3V3
18	GPIO24
19	MOSI
20	GND
21	MISO
22	GPIO25
23	SCLK
24	CE0
25	GND
26	CE1
27	EED
28	EEC
29	GPIO5
30	GND
31	GPIO6
32	GPIO12
33	GPIO13
34	GND
35	GPIO19
36	GPIO16
37	GPIO26
38	GPIO20
39	GND
40	GPIO21

TYPICAL SWITCH SCHEMATIC

A four-leg-switch doesn't have an up or a down, or a "pin 1". Simply orient the switch so that is looks like the diagram and it will work, even if it "upside-down"

2. In the previous chapters, we focused mostly on what to output from the GPIO, to control things such as LEDs and motors. Now we will start looking at accepting inputs on the GPIO. The pushbutton switch basically closes the circuit to ground when pressed down. This will read as input HIGH (or 1) on the Raspberry Pi (if the pin is set to INPUT mode). When not pressed, it will read the LOW, or 0, state. Create the `button.py` file in the `ch8` directory and enter the following code:

```python
#!/usr/bin/env python
# Raspberry Pi Zero Cookbook
# Chapter 8
# Detecting Pushbutton Inputs
import time
import RPi.GPIO as GPIO
GPIO.setmode(GPIO.BCM)
#LED output pins
redpin=17
greenpin=18
bluepin=27
#Pushbutton input pin
buttonpin=23
#Configure inputs and outputs
GPIO.setup(redpin, GPIO.OUT)
GPIO.setup(greenpin, GPIO.OUT)
GPIO.setup(bluepin, GPIO.OUT)
GPIO.setup(buttonpin, GPIO.IN, pull_up_down=GPIO.PUD_UP)
def main():
    print "Press Button to Change Color"
    counter=1
    rgblight(1,0,0)
    while True:
        if GPIO.input(buttonpin)==False:
            counter+=1
            colorcycle(counter%9)
def colorcycle(bincolor):
    print bincolor
    rgb=list(bin(bincolor).replace("0b",""))
    if (len(rgb)==1):
        rgblight(0,0,1)
    if (len(rgb)==2):
        rgblight(0,int(rgb[0]),int(rgb[1]))
    if (len(rgb)==3):
        rgblight(int(rgb[0]),int(rgb[1]),int(rgb[2]))
def rgblight(r,g,b):
    GPIO.output(redpin,r)
    GPIO.output(greenpin,g)
    GPIO.output(bluepin,b)
```

```
if __name__ == '__main__':
    main()
```

3. We used a similar function in the previous chapter's recipe on health monitoring, but we added the `colorcycle` function to provide some more color variety from the LED. Activating the pushbutton runs a counter through a cycle and sends the modulus 9 value to `colorcycle`, returning values 1 through 8. When the input pin is open, the value is HIGH (1, True). Pressing the button and shorting the pin to ground changes it to a LOW (0, False) value, which triggers the `if` condition that changes the light's color.

4. The `colorcycle` function takes the input and converts it to a binary value (001 through 111 are the binary values of 1 through 8). It sends the binary digits to `rgblight` to change the LED's color.

5. Running the program will prompt you to press the button and indicate the value it is sending to light. You should have a color-changing LED!

Interfacing toggle switches and setting debouncing

If you tried the previous recipe, you probably noticed that the color cycling switched quickly while the button was pressed. This was because the input behavior would loop as fast as the Raspberry Pi Zero could process the input, which is pretty fast! A simple software method to allow for a more human-speed signal recognition is called debouncing.

Getting ready

You'll want the following equipment in addition to your Raspberry Pi Zero, a breadboard, and jumper wires:

- Two 330-Ohm resistors
- Two LEDs, any color
- Three-way toggle switch (A\off\B)
- Tactile pushbutton

How to do it...

1. For this recipe, configure the circuit as follows:

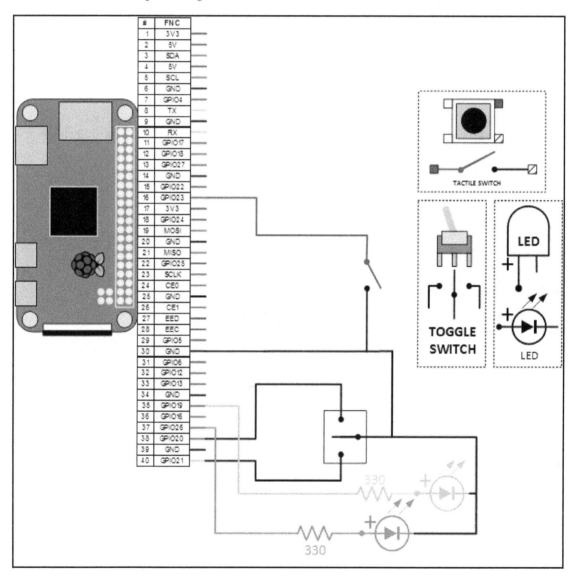

2. Next, create the `toggle.py` file, and put in the following code to test it out:

```
#!/usr/bin/env python
# Raspberry Pi Zero Cookbook
```

```
# Chapter 8
# Toggle Switch and Debouncing
import time
import RPi.GPIO as GPIO
GPIO.setmode(GPIO.BCM)
GPIO.setwarnings(False)
#LED output pins
led1=19
led2=26
#Pushbutton input pin
buttonpin=23
togglea=20
toggleb=21
#Set debounce time
debounce=0.2
#Configure inputs and outputs
GPIO.setup(led1, GPIO.OUT)
GPIO.setup(led2, GPIO.OUT)
GPIO.output(led1, GPIO.LOW)
GPIO.output(led2, GPIO.LOW)
GPIO.setup(buttonpin, GPIO.IN, pull_up_down=GPIO.PUD_UP)
GPIO.setup(togglea, GPIO.IN, pull_up_down=GPIO.PUD_UP)
GPIO.setup(toggleb, GPIO.IN, pull_up_down=GPIO.PUD_UP)
def main():
    lastexec=time.time()
    time.sleep(debounce)
    onoff=0
    print "Ready, Toggle Switch to light an LED, push button to turn
both LEDs on/off"

while True:
now=time.time()
if GPIO.input(buttonpin)==False:
desiredOnOff='both'
else:
desiredOnOff='none'
if GPIO.input(togglea)==False:
desiredToggle='a'
elif GPIO.input(toggleb)==False:
desiredToggle='b'
if onoff != desiredOnOff and now-lastexec>debounce:
onoff = desiredOnOff
GPIO.output(led1,desiredOnOff == 'both')
GPIO.output(led2,desiredOnOff == 'both')
lastexec=time.time()
if toggle != desiredToggle and now-lastexec>debounce:
toggle = desiredToggle
GPIO.output(led1,toggle == 'a')
```

```
GPIO.output(led2,toggle == 'b')
lastexec=time.time()
if __name__=="__main__":
    main()
```

3. The beginning of the code should look familiar if you've been going through the recipes. It sets up our pin configuration and GPIO port modes. A new variable, debounce, is the amount of time we will wait before accepting another input from the same input source. A setting of 0.2, or 200 milliseconds, is generally a good delay between receiving the first input and checking for a new one.

4. The toggle switch requires two input pins, one for the left switch and one for the right. The center pin of the toggle switch goes to ground. While the debouncing setting isn't completely necessary for these switches, they do eliminate the possibility of fast-switching states in the moment it takes to switch from one toggle side to the other; furthermore, there isn't usually a need to check a toggle state as fast as your CPU will allow.

5. Running the program with `sudo python interrupt_toggle.py` will initialize your GPIO, check the toggles, and set the LEDs on or off appropriately. With the toggle set to the off (center) position, try the pushbutton. Each press should turn both LEDs on or off. Now try holding the button down for a few seconds. Do you get about a 200 ms on/off cycle? Good! Now turn the LEDs off and try the toggles.

6. This isn't the only way to handle switch bouncing. We will explore another great technique using interrupts later in this chapter.

 An additional way to reduce or eliminate bouncing is to add a 0.01 uF (ceramic 104) across each switch terminal, as shown in this figure:

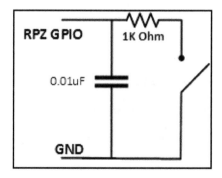

While this doesn't give you a delay, it does reduce the mechanical noise that comes from pressing a switch or toggle and the potential for shifting signals as a result. You can use both to ensure clean switch signals as well as include delays to reduce the frequency of the signal being handled.

Avoiding the floating states of the input line

When using the GPIO pins for input, the HIGH state is active when the pin is receiving 3V, and LOW when it is grounded. GPIO inputs, however, are quite sensitive and can receive unintended HIGH signals from external factors, even self-noise produced from a prototype circuit. When a GPIO input pin can jump between 0 and 1 from influences outside of its control, it is said to be in a floating state. Fortunately, we can use the Raspberry Pi Zero's built-in circuitry or make our own to ensure that our inputs remain in a consistent state, unless our circuit and programming logic wants it to change.

The actual voltages are given in the data sheet. Typically 2.5V (sometimes 1.8V) and above is consider logic HIGH, while below 0.8V is considered logic LOW. Voltages between this will cause input noise. This is because CMOS input circuitry typically does not employ hysteresis, unless the datasheet denotes the input buffer with a " $\square$ " symbol. When a pin is neither being driven HIGH nor LOW, it is said to be in a "floating" state. This allows multiple outputs to share a single wire without causing a short. Leaving an input unconnected can cause errors, noise, input oscillation and unintentional power draw.

Getting ready

For this recipe, you will need the following equipment in addition to your Raspberry Pi Zero, breadboard, and jumper cables:

- Two tactile push-button switches
- Two 1 KOhm resistors

How to do it...

1. To eliminate the occurrences of floating-state inputs, a pull-up or pull-down circuit is required. The schematic for a hardware pull-down circuit is shown here:

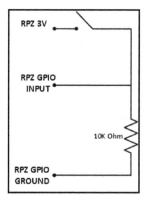

When the switch is open, the input goes to Ground, reading 0. When the button is pressed, it will read 3V.

2. When the button is not pressed, the RPZ GPIO input will have a circuit open to GROUND, in essence being "pulled down" to a LOW state. When the button is pressed, the circuit will take the path of least resistance, and the input will read from the 3V source, producing a HIGH input.

3. The pull-up circuit is quite similar, but as you might have guessed, the "normal" state will be HIGH:

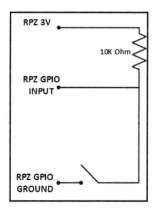

When the switch is open, the pin reads 3V. When the button closes, the path of least resistance is Ground, reading 0.

Here, with the pushbutton open, the input will read a 3V signal and read in a HIGH state. When the button is pressed, the path of least resistance is to ground, thus sending a LOW to our GPIO input.

4. These are simple enough circuits to set up, but you don't really need them with your Raspberry Pi Zero. You can set your GPIO inputs to work as a pull-up or pull-down circuit. Setting an input to pull-up or pull-down effectively adds these circuits to the board itself, so all you need to do is add the switch:

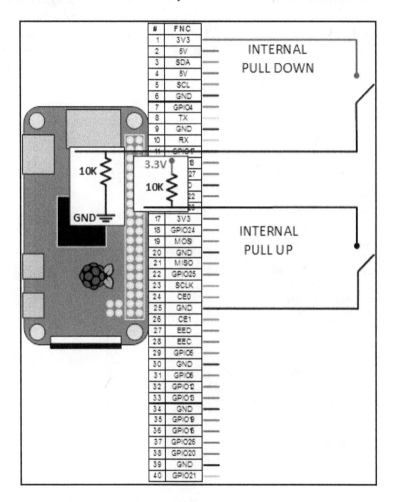

The Raspberry Pi contains Internals that will let you pull-up or pull-down a circuit

The 1 KOhm resistors aren't necessary–you can just have your switch go straight to ground or 3V–but throwing in a 1K resistor will reduce current draw and won't impact your circuit negatively at all. Too much current, on the other hand, can be bad for your Raspberry Pi, so if you are getting your 3V from another power source, add a resistor for protection.

5. To detect input on a switch that goes to ground, we "pull it up" to show a value of 1 (True) until the switch is closed, which then sends it to ground, a value of 0 (False). Conversely, if we have a switch connected to a voltage source, we "pull the circuit down" to 0, or False. When the circuit closes and voltage runs through, then the value of 1/True is read. You can use whichever you prefer, as long as you remember than the button press event is True/On/1 for a pull-down circuit and False/Off/0 for a pull-down one.

6. We can test the behavior of our pull-up and pull-down inputs with very little Python. Enter the following code in the ch8 directory and save it as pullupdown.py:

```
#!/usr/bin/env python
# Raspberry Pi Zero Cookbook
# Chapter 8
# Pull-up and Pull-down Cicuit GPIO Settings
import time
import RPi.GPIO as GPIO
GPIO.setmode(GPIO.BCM)
GPIO.setwarnings(False)
#LED output pins
#Pull-up circuit goes to ground
pullup=23
#Pull-down circuit goes to 3V
pulldown=17
#Set Up GPIO pins for buttons
#Enable this pin as a Pull Up
GPIO.setup(pullup, GPIO.IN, pull_up_down=GPIO.PUD_UP)
#Enable this pin as a Pull Down
GPIO.setup(pulldown, GPIO.IN, pull_up_down=GPIO.PUD_DOWN)
def main():
    print "Started. "
    print "Pull-up Circuit reads
",GPIO.input(pullup),"(",bool(GPIO.input(pullup)),")"
    print "Pull-down Circuit reads ",
GPIO.input(pulldown),"(",bool(GPIO.input(pulldown)),")"
    try:
            while True:
                    if GPIO.input(pulldown)==True:
                            print "Pull-down Pressed and now
```

```
reads",GPIO.input(pulldown),"(",bool(GPIO.input(pulldown)),")"
                            time.sleep(0.5)
                    elif GPIO.input(pullup)==False:
                        print "Pull-up Pressed and now
reads",GPIO.input(pullup),"(",bool(GPIO.input(pullup)),")"
                            time.sleep(0.5)
        except KeyboardInterrupt:
                print "Finished"
        finally:
                GPIO.cleanup()
    if __name__=="__main__":
        main()
```

7. Running the program with `sudo python pullupdown.py` will show the starting state of the pins we've set. If we left the pins without setting pull-up or pull-down, our script may have detected changes to the inputs without using the buttons–not the desired state. We'll set the inputs up or down in the `GPIO.setup` method:

```
GPIO.setup(pullup, GPIO.IN, pull_up_down=GPIO.PUD_UP)
```

8. When the button is pressed, the state of the input is reassessed. A pin that is pulled up will show False when pressed, while a pin that is pulled down will show True. Try to stay consistent within your programs (unless you require something more complex that both circuits are useful), and it will be less confusing when troubleshooting and debugging. We'll need our pull-up/down knowledge for the next recipe, where we integrate a numeric keypad with the Raspberry Pi Zero GPIO.

 You may have noticed that most of the pins on the RPZ remain unconnected during these recipes. If you look at the GPIO state by running "gpio readall" in the terminal, you will see that when the RPZ first boots up many of those pins are configured as inputs. Remember before that leaving an input unconnected can cause random problems? Why do you think all of our recipes seem to work just fine if all these GPIO pins are unconnected? That's right! The internal pull-up resistors are also enabled on those inputs so that it's safe for us to experiment with only a few pins at a time.

Interfacing a keypad with the RPZ

Now that we've looked at the Raspberry Pi Zero's pull-up and pull-down resistor options, we can apply our knowledge to operating a 12- or 16-digit keypad. Let's take a look!

Getting ready

All you'll need for this recipe is a 16-key numeric keypad. One is included in the Elegoo kit, and they are available from most online retailers. A typical keyboard input looks something like this:

How to do it…

1. There are eight pins on a 16-key numeric keypad. Here is how you wire them to your Raspberry Pi:

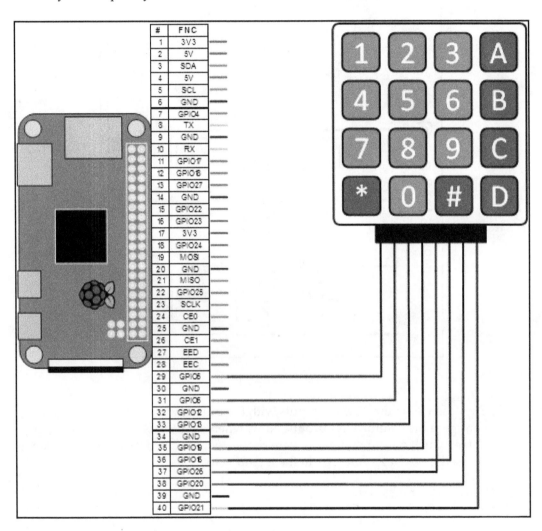

2. Understanding the internals of the keypad makes it easy to understand how to control it. Effectively, each number is a switch tied to a column and a row, as shown here:

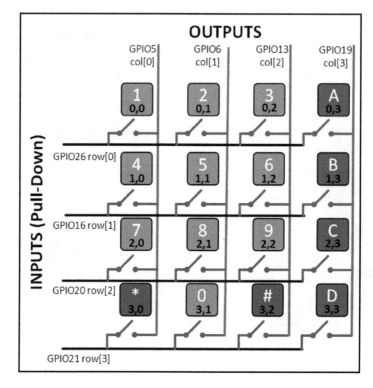

The Internals of a 16-key Input Pad

3. Suppose we set our rows as inputs with the pull-down circuit enabled and configure the columns as outputs. Now, when a button is pressed, if we can detect which output and input were connected, we can determine which key was pressed. Look at keypad.py in the ch8 directory, shown here:

```
#!/usr/bin/env python
# Raspberry Pi Zero Cookbook
# Chapter 8 - Keypad Input
import time
import RPi.GPIO as GPIO
GPIO.setwarnings(False)
GPIO.setmode(GPIO.BCM)
#Keypad Inputs
cols=[5,6,13,19]
```

```
rows=[26,16,20,21]
#4x4 Keypad matrix
keypad=[
[1,2,3,"A"],
[4,5,6,"B"],
[7,8,9,"C"],
["*",0,"#","D"]]
def main():
    #Set Pull-Up to Down on Row Pins
    for row in rows:
        GPIO.setup(row, GPIO.IN,    pull_up_down=GPIO.PUD_DOWN)
    #Set Column Pins for Output, Default LOW
    for col in cols:
        GPIO.setup(col, GPIO.OUT)
        GPIO.output(col, GPIO.LOW)
    print "Keypad Ready"
    while True:
            try:
                #Turn on Column Pins in Sequence
                for x, col in enumerate(cols):
                    if x==0:
                            GPIO.setup(cols[3], GPIO.IN)
                    else:
                            GPIO.setup(cols[x-1], GPIO.IN)
                    GPIO.output(cols[x], GPIO.HIGH)
                    #Check row inputs for each HIGH column and
display if caught
                    for y,row in enumerate(rows):
                        if GPIO.input(row)==1:
                            print "Pressed:
",keypad[x][y]
                    time.sleep(0.2)
            except KeyboardInterrupt:
                print "Ctrl-C Detected"
                break
    if __name__=='__main__':
        main()
```

4. The column outputs are initially set to LOW and then sent through a loop which cycles a value of HIGH through each of the columns. If a button is pressed, an input row will switch to HIGH, and by knowing which column was on in the cycle, we can translate that to the list that contains our keypad configuration. For any keypad like this, as long as you know which pins are columns and which are rows, all you need to change are the rows, `cols`, and `keypad` values to match the keypad and pin configuration of the one you are using.

5. If everything is connected correctly, running `sudo python keypad.py` should prompt you to try out your keypad, giving you something like the following output:

```
pi@rpz14101:~/share/ch8 $ sudo python keypad.py
Keypad Ready
Pressed:  1
Pressed:  2
Pressed:  3
Pressed:  A
^CCrtl-C Detected
```

Interfacing RTC to get accurate time

The real-time clock (RTC) is a way to keep the right time even if you've lost power. The low-power requirements of a clock make it easy to accurately keep time, and it can run for years on just a small battery. If your Raspberry Pi Zero is going to live somewhere it will be off and unable to access an NTP server over a network, an RTC board will help when keeping accurate time is important.

Getting ready

You'll need an RTC board. I used the board included in the Elego Super Complete Starter Kit, which uses the DS3231 chip. There are a few different RTC boards available, most of which will work with your Raspberry Pi Zero.

You'll also need to ensure that I2C is enabled on your RPZ. The recipe on I2C basics in Chapter 5, *Getting Your Hands Dirty Using the GPIO Header* can step you through getting I2C and its tools set up if you haven't already.

How to do it…

1. Configure the RTC clock pins to the Raspberry Pi as follows:

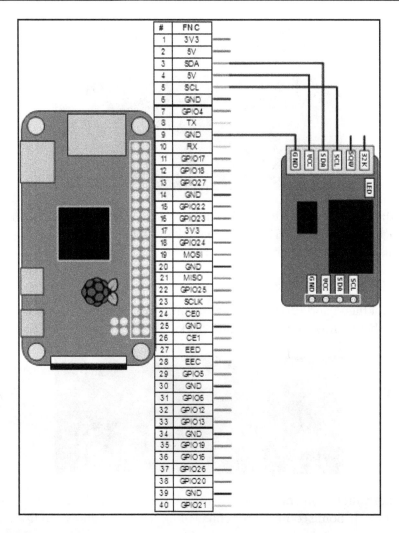

#	FNC
1	3V3
2	5V
3	SDA
4	5V
5	SCL
6	GND
7	GPIO4
8	TX
9	GND
10	RX
11	GPIO17
12	GPIO18
13	GPIO27
14	GND
15	GPIO22
16	GPIO23
17	3V3
18	GPIO24
19	MOSI
20	GND
21	MISO
22	GPIO25
23	SCLK
24	CE0
25	GND
26	CE1
27	EED
28	EEC
29	GPIO5
30	GND
31	GPIO6
32	GPIO12
33	GPIO13
34	GND
35	GPIO19
36	GPIO16
37	GPIO26
38	GPIO20
39	GND
40	GPIO21

 If you are connecting the RTC board while the RPZ is powered on, they should connect the GND pin first, then the 5V pin (at which point the red LED lights up) and finally the SDA & SCL pins. This ensures voltage doesn't accidentally leak through the GPIO pins to the RTC board.

2. You can use the pins on either side of the board to connect. Elego's DS3231 had the left side of the board already soldered with pins, so it was easy to drop onto a breadboard.

3. Once your board is connected, you should see a red LED, indicating the power is on. We can see whether the board is found in I2C using the `i2cdetect` utility:

```
pi@raspberrypi:~ $ sudo i2cdetect -y 1
     0  1  2  3  4  5  6  7  8  9  a  b  c  d  e  f
00:          -- -- -- -- -- -- -- -- -- -- -- --
10: -- -- -- -- -- -- -- -- -- -- -- -- -- -- -- --
20: -- -- -- -- -- -- -- -- -- -- -- -- -- -- -- --
30: -- -- -- -- -- -- -- -- -- -- -- -- -- -- -- --
40: -- -- -- -- -- -- -- -- -- -- -- -- -- -- -- --
50: -- -- -- -- -- -- -- 57 -- -- -- -- -- -- -- --
60: -- -- -- -- -- -- -- -- 68 -- -- -- -- -- -- --
70: -- -- -- -- -- -- -- --
```

4. Address `68` is the one we are looking for. We want this to change to the `UU` state, which will mean the drivers are loaded and the board is ready to go. To do this, we'll add a line to `/boot/config.txt`:

```
dtoverlay=i2c-rtc,ds3231
```

5. Reboot the Pi and run `i2cdetect` again. Your device should have changed state, now that it knows it is a real-time clock:

```
pi@rpz14103:~ $ sudo i2cdetect -y 1
     0  1  2  3  4  5  6  7  8  9  a  b  c  d  e  f
00:          -- -- -- -- -- -- -- -- -- -- -- --
10: -- -- -- -- -- -- -- -- -- -- -- -- -- -- -- --
20: -- -- -- -- -- -- -- -- -- -- -- -- -- -- -- --
30: -- -- -- -- -- -- -- -- -- -- -- -- -- -- -- --
40: -- -- -- -- -- -- -- -- -- -- -- -- -- -- -- --
50: -- -- -- -- -- -- -- 57 -- -- -- -- -- -- -- --
60: -- -- -- -- -- -- -- -- UU -- -- -- -- -- -- --
70: -- -- -- -- -- -- -- --
```

6. You are almost finished! The `hwclock` command will help you check and set up your clock. Some common functions of `hwclock` are shown in this screenshot:

```
pi@rpz14103:~ $ sudo hwclock -r
Fri 11 Nov 2016 07:00:07 UTC  -0.813147 seconds
pi@rpz14103:~ $ sudo hwclock -c
hw-time      system-time              freq-offset-ppm    tick
1478847621   1481479491.345908
1478847633   1481479503.346748                     70       1
1478847644   1481479514.346758                     37       0
^Cpi@rpz14103:~ $ sudo hwclock -w
pi@rpz14103:~ $ sudo hwclock -r
Sun 11 Dec 2016 18:05:24 UTC  -0.079080 seconds
```

7. The `hwclock -r` command reads the time currently running on the RTC board. To compare the system time with the RTC clock, the `hwclock -c` command is used. Depending on which time is the accurate time (the RTC clock must be set first), we can use `hwclock -s` to write the RTC clock time to the system or the `hwclock -w` command to set the RTC clock with the current system time.

There's more...

1. Adafruit's tutorial on Raspberry Pis and RTC boards is one of their many awesome online instructions. Their recommendation, which makes a lot of sense, is to remove the `fake-hwclock` utility, as it can contend with your new real-hardware clock. First, you remove the application:

   ```
   sudo apt-get remove fake-hwclock
   ```

2. Next, you eliminate the initialization of the service:

   ```
   sudo update-rc.d -f fake-hwclock remove
   ```

3. Finally, comment out the additions to the `/lib/udev/hwclock-set` script:

   ```
   #!/bin/sh
   # Reset the System Clock to UTC if the hardware clock from which it
   # was copied by the kernel was in localtime.

   dev=$1

   #if [ -e /run/systemd/system ] ; then
   #    exit 0
   #fi
   ```

4. Now your hardware clock should function normally, without any potential conflict from the default installation of `fake-hwclock`.

Setting up Interrupts on a toggle switch through GPIO

An interrupt is a notification that a monitored event has occurred. In a program, it will be an event that is being listened for but isn't holding up the entire program's operation waiting for the event to happen. When the even does happen, this triggers an interruption to let the program know that the event has occurred. Using interrupts with the RPi.GPIO library is a powerful tool for receiving new information as it happens, rather than checking periodically to see whether new information exists or sitting and waiting on an event to occur.

A real-world analogy would be baking a cake. You put the cake in the oven, set a timer, and then go on to doing other things. You don't have to wait there by the oven for the cake to bake, because at some point, the timer will interrupt you to let you know you need to check on it. A program may log data to a file during normal operation but, if sent an interrupt, will know it has to do something different (for example, write to the same log that a key was pressed).

In many cases, it is not the state of something that is important; it is the event where the state changes that you want to trigger something to happen. Python and the RPi.GPIO library make it easy to work with interrupts.

Getting ready

Here's what we will need for our test circuit:

- Three 330-Ohm resistors
- One piezo buzzer
- One four-leg pushbutton
- One toggle switch
- One RGB LED

How to do it...

1. Here is the diagram to put together:

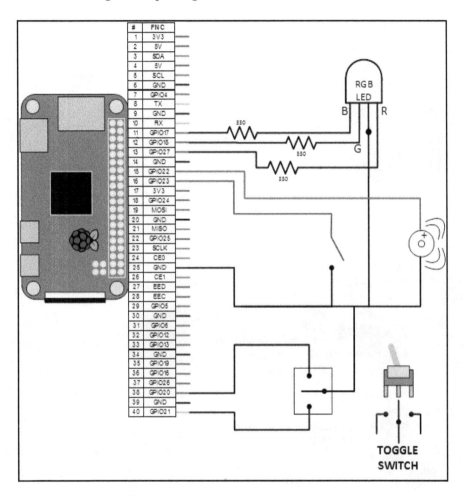

2. We'll use the versatile RPi.GPIO library again to control the interrupt. Create the int.py file in the ch8 directory with the following code:

```
# Raspberry Pi Zero Cookbook
# Chapter 8
# Handing input interrupts
import time
import os
import RPi.GPIO as GPIO
```

```
GPIO.setmode(GPIO.BCM)
#LED output pins
redpin=17
greenpin=18
bluepin=27
#Pushbutton input pin
buttonpin=23
togglea=20
toggleb=21
#Buzzer output pin
buzzerpin=22
#Configure inputs and outputs
GPIO.setup(redpin, GPIO.OUT)
GPIO.setup(greenpin, GPIO.OUT)
GPIO.setup(bluepin, GPIO.OUT)
GPIO.setup(buttonpin, GPIO.IN, pull_up_down=GPIO.PUD_UP)
GPIO.setup(togglea, GPIO.IN, pull_up_down=GPIO.PUD_UP)
GPIO.setup(toggleb, GPIO.IN, pull_up_down=GPIO.PUD_UP)
GPIO.setup(buzzerpin, GPIO.OUT)
buzzer = GPIO.PWM(buzzerpin, 0.5)
def main():
    alloff()
    print "Toggle Switch and press button"
    GPIO.add_event_detect(buttonpin,GPIO.FALLING,callback=
 buttonpress,bouncetime=200)
    try:
            while True:
                    time.sleep(0.5)
    except KeyboardInterrupt:
            print "Finished"
    finally:
            GPIO.cleanup()
def buttonpress(buttonpin):
    if GPIO.input(togglea)==False:
            print "Lights!"
            playlights()
    elif GPIO.input(toggleb)==False:
            print "Sounds!"
            playsounds()
    else:
            print "System!"
            print "Logged ",os.popen('vcgencmd
            measure_temp').readline()," at ",time.time()
def playsounds():
    e7=2637
    c7=2093
    g6=1568
    g7=3136
```

```
        e6=1319
        a6=1760
        b6=1976
        as6=1865
        seq=[g6,c7,g6,e6,a6,b6,as6,a6]
        buzzer.start(50)
        for note in seq:
                buzzer.ChangeFrequency(note)
                time.sleep(0.15)
        alloff()
def alloff():
        rgblight(0,0,0)
        buzzer.stop()
def playlights():
        for loop in range(0,3):
                for x in range(1,8):
                        colorcycle(x)
                        time.sleep(0.2)
        alloff()
def colorcycle(bincolor):
        rgb=list(bin(bincolor).replace("0b",""))
        if (len(rgb)==1):
                rgblight(0,0,1)
        if (len(rgb)==2):
                rgblight(0,int(rgb[0]),int(rgb[1]))
        if (len(rgb)==3):
                rgblight(int(rgb[0]),int(rgb[1]),int(rgb[2]))
def rgblight(r,g,b):
        #print r,g,b
        GPIO.output(redpin,r)
        GPIO.output(greenpin,g)
        GPIO.output(bluepin,b)
if __name__=="__main__":
        main()
```

3. Here, we tie the interrupt event to the tactile button. We can set this interrupt up with just one line:

```
GPIO.add_event_detect(buttonpin,GPIO.FALLING,callback=buttonpress
,bouncetime=200)
```

4. This will look for the button to be pressed (True->False is FALLING, False->True is RISING) and set a debounce of 200 milliseconds. When the interrupt event occurs (which is pressing the button), it will call the `buttonpress` function and execute the code in there, in a different thread. The main program will continue running, which in this case is only waiting half a second and looping until *Ctrl+C* is hit. When the button is pressed, it first looks at the state of the toggle switch and decides what to do from there. If toggled one way, you get a brief light show. The other way will play a sequence of notes through the piezo buzzer. Finally, the center toggle will return the Raspberry Pi Zero temperature to the console.

Interfacing RFID tags with the RPZ

Radio frequency identification, or RFID, is a common method of near-field communication. You can teach your Raspberry Pi to understand an RFID board's communication with RFID cards and keyfobs.

Getting ready

There are a few different RFID kits available. I used the Elegoo RC522 included in their kit, which is a fairly typical RFID board. Adafruit also has kits that detect both RFID cards and NFC signals typically used on smartphones, and they always include great instructions. You'll also need a red-and-green LED and a couple of 330-Ohm resistors. Finally, you will need SPI enabled on your Raspberry Pi Zero; if you haven't done that already, refer to *Basics of SPI and Setting up the SPI Module* in `Chapter 5`, Getting Your Hands Dirty Using the GPIO Header.

How to do it...

If you completed the previous recipe and have an RTC board connected, you don't have to remove it! The RFID board communicates over SPI, whereas the RTC talks on I2C.

1. Configure the RFID board with the Raspberry Pi Zero as follows:

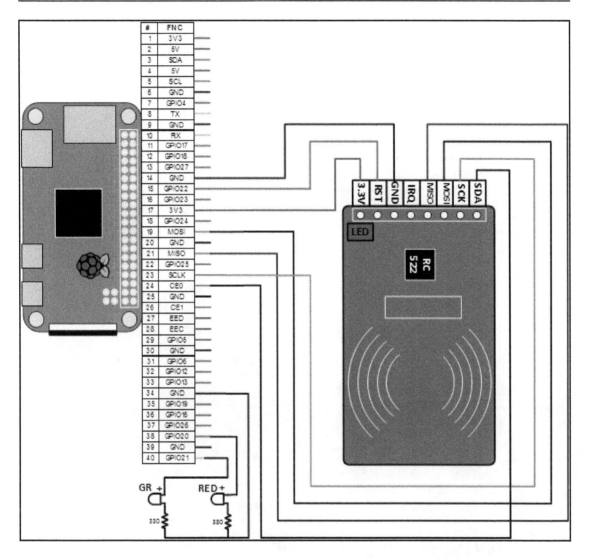

2. With SPI enabled on your RPZ, you can create a simple RFID access card program with the following code. In your `ch8` directory, first make two empty files, `rfid_allow.txt` and `rfid_deny.txt`. Then, create the `rfidpass.py` file and enter the following code:

```
#!/usr/bin/env python
# Raspberry Pi Zero Cookbook
# Chapter 8 - RFID Card Reader Control
import time
import RPi.GPIO as GPIO
```

```
from pirc522 import RFID
#Use Board Mode to stay consistent with RFID and SPI      Libraries
GPIO.setmode(GPIO.BOARD)
#Set allow and deny files
allowfile="./rfid_allow.txt"
denyfile="./rfid_deny.txt"
#led output pins
redpin=38
greenpin=40
GPIO.setwarnings(False)
GPIO.setup(redpin,GPIO.OUT)
GPIO.setup(greenpin,GPIO.OUT)
GPIO.output(redpin,1)
GPIO.output(greenpin,0)
scanner = RFID()
def main():
    print "Scanner Ready"
    try:
            while True:
                    (error,resp) = scanner.request()
                    if not error:
                            (error,uid)=scanner.anticoll()
                            if not error:
                                    print "Detected ",uid
                                    checkpass(uid)
    except KeyboardInterrupt:
            print "Scanner Stopped"
    finally:
            GPIO.output(redpin,0)
            GPIO.output(greenpin,0)
def checkpass(uid):
    nolist=open(denyfile,'a+')
    for baduid in nolist:
            idsplit=baduid.split(",")
            if int(idsplit[0])==uid[0] and int(idsplit[1])==uid[1] and
int(idsplit[2])==uid[2] and int(idsplit[3])==uid[3] and
int(idsplit[4])==uid[4]:
                    print "Detected UID on blocked list"
                    for x in range(0,20):
                            GPIO.output(redpin,0)
                            time.sleep(0.1)
                            GPIO.output(redpin,1)
                            time.sleep(0.1)
                    return
    yeslist=open(allowfile,'a+')
    for gooduid in yeslist.readlines():
            idsplit=gooduid.split(",")
            if int(idsplit[0])==uid[0] and int(idsplit[1])==uid[1] and
```

```
int(idsplit[2])==uid[2] and int(idsplit[3])==uid[3] and
int(idsplit[4])==uid[4]:
                              print "Detected UID on allow list"
                              GPIO.output(redpin,0)
                              for x in range(0,20):
                                      GPIO.output(greenpin,1)
                                      time.sleep(0.1)
                                      GPIO.output(greenpin,0)
                                      time.sleep(0.1)
                              GPIO.output(redpin,1)
                              return
            newrfid = raw_input('New ID Detected.  (A)dd\(B)lock\(I)gnore?')
            print newrfid
            if newrfid=="A":
addrfid=str(uid[0])+","+str(uid[1])+","+str(uid[2])+","+str(uid[3])+","+str
(uid[4])+"\n"
                  yeslist.write(addrfid)
                  print "Added to Allow List"
            elif newrfid=="B":
addrfid=str(uid[0])+","+str(uid[1])+","+str(uid[2])+","+str(uid[3])+","+str
(uid[4])+"\n"
                  nolist.write(addrfid)
                  print "Added to blocked list"
            else:
                  print "No action taken"

    if __name__=='__main__':
        main()
```

3. Running this script with `sudo python rfidpass.py` should have it start with a simple output that the scanner is ready. Take one of the RFID cards or keyfobs (the Elegoo kit includes one of each, and every other board I've seen includes at least one test card). With no cards in either the allow or deny file, any new card introduced will be read and then prompt the user whether the UID of the card should be allowed, blocked, or ignored. If `Allowed` is selected, the UID of the RFID card will be added to the `rfid_allow.txt` file. If `Blocked` is selected, the card UID will be stored in `rfid_deny.txt`. If any card that has a UID stored is run against the reader, it will either send a blinking signal to the green LED (indicating allowed) or to the red LED (indicating denied). After that, the program returns to a steady red LED. Here is the output returned from adding one UID to the allow list, another to the deny list, and then attempting to scan either:

```
pi@rpz14103:~ $ sudo python rfidpass.py
Scanner Ready
Detected  [241, 254, 62, 213, 228]
New ID Detected. (A)dd\(B)lock\(I)gnore?A
Added to Allow List
Detected  [102, 207, 238, 116, 51]
New ID Detected. (A)dd\(B)lock\(I)gnore?B
Added to blocked list
Detected  [241, 254, 62, 213, 228]
Detected UID on allow list
Detected  [102, 207, 238, 116, 51]
Detected UID on blocked list
```

With just a few lines of code, you have a system that scans and stores RFID cards for future use. Lighting an LED green or red is just the beginning–you can just as easily replace the LED with a mechanical relay or motor to unlock a door, turn on lights, or open curtains.

 If you are considering a solution that requires a high degree of security, use relational databases or other secure data stores to hold you UID data. With that, you can restrict access to the database, and even encrypt the UIDs, to reduce the risk of your system being compromised or data being stolen. It is good to consider security first–more secure is always better, but if you just want a keyfob to turn on a light, a simpler solution such as the previous one will be easier to implement and troubleshoot.

Interfacing a GPS module with the RPZ

If your Raspberry Pi Zero is on the go, maybe you want to know where it is. Using the global positioning system (GPS), your Raspberry Pi Zero can record or report its location as long as it can see the sky.

Getting ready

I used Adafruit's Ultimate GPS Breakout board (v3) for this recipe along with a tactile pushbutton switch, the same one in the first recipe in this chapter. You can do it the "easy way" and connect with a USB-to-serial adapter, but in this recipe, we will wire it directly to the UART and save our USB port. Either way, you will be communicating with the GPS receiver on your serial connection. If you go with the direct serial connection, make sure you have UART enabled and that you aren't using your serial connection for incoming console sessions.

You may need to edit/boot or use `cmdline.txt` to do this. Remove any references to your serial port (`ttyAMA0`). After rebooting, make sure the console service is stopped and disabled with these commands:

```
sudo systemctl stop serial-getty@ttyAMA0.serivce
sudo systemctl disable serial-getty@ttyAMA0.serivce
```

You'll also need the GPS daemon and a few Python libraries to control your GPS:

```
sudo apt-get install gpsd gpsd-clients python-gps python-serial
```

Enabling the Google Geocoding API

1. If you don't have a Google account yet, you'll need one to access the Google APIs. The *Google Spreadsheets* recipe in `Chapter 4`, *Programming with Python*, steps you through it. Once you have an API key, go to the Console Dashboard at `https://console.developers.google.com/apis/dashboard`.

2. The front page of the dashboard looks like this:

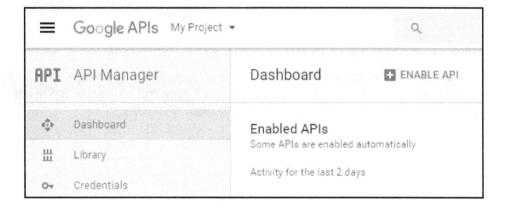

3. Select **ENABLE API** and go to the next page:

4. There are a lot of different APIs that can be enabled! For this recipe, you'll just need the Google Maps Geocoding API, a little over halfway down the list of available Maps APIs. Click on the link for the next screen:

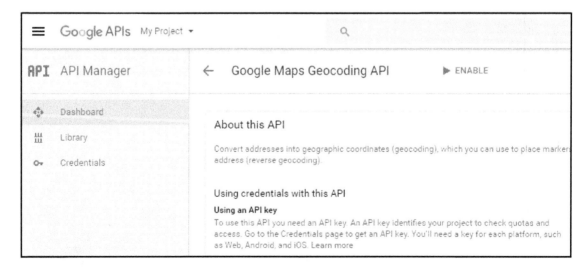

5. Click on the **ENABLE** link, and you are ready to go. The page will change to a list of metrics on API usage, errors, and latency.

6. Now, if you use your API key in this recipe (available in the **Credentials** link in the left-hand side of the API Manager), Google will provide responses to your API requests.

 Google APIs each have usage limits or require paid or premium accounts to increase the number of API requests you can make per second or day. If you don't have a billing account and use up your API calls, new API requests will be rejected. Each API has different usage limits, documented in that API's documentation.

How to do it...

1. Wire up the GPS receiver to the Raspberry Pi Zero's UART pins as follows:

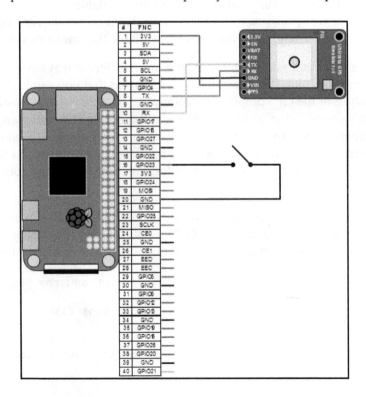

2. Once it is wired up, we can quickly verify whether things are working with the screen utility. Connect to your serial terminal:

    sudo screen /dev/ttyAMA0

3. You should start seeing a lot of data coming in, like this:

```
$GPGSV,3,1,11,1832,21,77,061,21,15,42,076,23,10,41,234,18*71
$GPGSV,3,2,11,20,36,059,20,27,33,311,26,16,27,268,26,13,22,046,21*7A
$GPGSV,3,3,11,29,20,152,18,26,18,240,17,47,,,*71
$GPRMC,160604.000,A,4321.7654,N,12350.3321,W,0.34,160.35,241216,,,A*79
$GPZDA,160604.000,24,12,2016,,*53
$GPGGA,160605.000,4321.7654,N,12350.3321,W,1,10,0.91,67.7,M,-19.6,M,,*66
$GPGSA,A,3,15,21,13,26,10,29,16,20,18,27,,,1.22,0.91,0.82*03
```

What you are seeing here is the data your GPS board is transmitting over the serial port. These are called NMEA sentences and represent data that the GPS is picking up from the satellite signals it can detect. There is some great documentation available at http://freenmea.net/docs to understand what every value means; fortunately, there are utilities available that make this unnecessary

 The more you play with Linux, the more different ways you learn to do the same thing. While writing this, I learned that you can look at the output of the GPS device with a simple cat /dev/ttyAMA0–there really isn't a need to log on to screen because you aren't sending any information to the GPS; you just want to see what the GPS board is sending to you. If you just want to see a device's output (and the device is outputting data without the need for any inputs), the cat command is perfect.

4. It was my experience, and of many on the Internet, that Raspbian has some problems with the binding of the GPS ports to the service. Using your favorite text editor, as root, edit the /etc/default/gpsd file to match this text:

```
# Default settings for the gpsd init script and the hotplug wrapper.

# Start the gpsd daemon automatically at boot time
START_DAEMON="true"

# Use USB hotplugging to add new USB devices automatically to the
daemon
USBAUTO="true"

# Devices gpsd should collect to at boot time.
```

```
# They need to be read/writeable, either by user gpsd or the group dialout.
DEVICES=""

        # Other options you want to pass to gpsd
GPSD_OPTIONS="-n /dev/ttyAMA0"
GPSD_SOCKET="/var/run/gpsd.sock"
```

5. Next, make sure your service is enabled and ready to go:

    ```
    sudo systemctl restart gpsd
    sudo systemctl enable gpsd
    ```

6. You shouldn't have to reboot (though it never hurts to). If everything starts OK, you can test out the service with `sudo cgps`. If something isn't configured correctly, this utility won't output any data and time out. When it does work, you will get a bit more human-friendly output:

```
Time:          2016-12-24T16:00:05.000Z     PRN:   Elev:   Azim:   SNR:   Used:
Latitude:       45.372493 N                   21     78      052     24      Y
Longitude:     121.698604 W                   18     75      228     34      Y
Altitude:      169.4 m                        15     42      080     14      Y
Speed:         0.7 kph                        10     39      233     20      Y
Heading:       293.7 deg (true)               20     38      059     00      Y
Climb:         0.0 m/min                      27     31      312     25      Y
Status:        3D FIX (14 secs)               16     28      271     21      Y
Longitude Err: +/- 28 m                       29     23      151     00      Y
Latitude Err:  +/- 39 m                       13     23      049     17      N
Altitude Err:  +/- 19 m                       26     20      242     20      N
Course Err:    n/a                           122     00      000     00      N
Speed Err:     +/- 286 kph
Time offset:   0.528
Grid Square:   CN95ej
```

```
{"class":"TPV","tag":"RMC","device":"/dev/ttyAMA0","mode":3,"time":"2016-12-24T1
lt":69.500,"epx":28.384,"epy":39.862,"epv":19.090,"track":307.9600,"speed":0.273
{"class":"TPV","tag":"RMC","device":"/dev/ttyAMA0","mode":3,"time":"2016-12-24T16
lt":69.500,"epx":28.384,"epy":39.862,"epv":34.270,"track":313.8600,"speed":0.252
{"class":"TPV","tag":"RMC","device":"/dev/ttyAMA0","mode":3,"time":"2016-12-24T16
lt":69.500,"epx":28.384,"epy":39.862,"epv":19.090,"track":344.8400,"speed":0.365
{"class":"TPV","tag":"RMC","device":"/dev/ttyAMA0","mode":3,"time":"2016-12-24T16
lt":69.400,"epx":28.384,"epy":39.862,"epv":19.780,"track":332.3000,"speed":0.360
{"class":"TPV","tag":"RMC","device":"/dev/ttyAMA0","mode":3,"time":"2016-12-24T16
lt":69.400,"epx":28.384,"epy":39.862,"epv":19.780,"track":316.1500,"speed":0.159
{"class":"SKY","tag":"GSV","device":"/dev/ttyAMA0","xdop":1.89,"ydop":2.66,"vdop
:[{"PRN":21,"el":78,"az":52,"ss":24,"used":true},{"PRN":18,"el":75,"az":228,"ss"
N":10,"el":39,"az":233,"ss":20,"used":true},{"PRN":20,"el":38,"az":59,"ss":0,"use
,"el":28,"az":271,"ss":21,"used":true},{"PRN":29,"el":23,"az":151,"ss":0,"used":
```

Typical cgps output

What this utility does is translate the incoming NMEA sentences into something more readable. At the bottom, you'll see incoming NMEA sentences converted to JSON (JavaScript Object Notation) format. On top, you can see your latitude, longitude, altitude, and which satellites are being used to identify your location. `Grid Square` is a notation familiar to amateur radio operators, and represents the approximate location per the Maidenhead Locator System.

7. Now that things look to be working, let's put together something in Python. This program will wait for the button to be pressed and then query the GPS for its current location. Once it acquires that, it will ask the Google Maps API for the approximate location based on the latitude and longitude coordinates. It will log the time, latitude, longitude, and altitude to a log file named `whereami.log`, but it will also report back to the terminal approximately where you are. Create a blank file named `whereami.log` as well as a file named `whereami.py`, and enter the following script:

```python
#/usr/bin/env python
#Raspberry Pi Zero Cookbook
#Chapter 8 - Using a GPS Board
import time
import requests
import RPi.GPIO as GPIO
from gps import *
import json
apikey = "<<YOUR GOOGLE API KEY HERE>>"
logfile = "whereami.log"
GPIO.setwarnings(False)
GPIO.setmode(GPIO.BCM)
buttonpin = 23
#Google geocode API exmaple
#https://maps.googleapis.com/maps/api/geocode/json?    latlng=40.714224
,-73.961452&key=YOUR_API_KEY
mapurl = "https://maps.googleapis.com/maps/api/geocode/json"
GPIO.setup(buttonpin,GPIO.IN,pull_up_down=GPIO.PUD_UP)
def main():
        print "Press the button to log your location"
        try:
                while True:
                        if GPIO.input(buttonpin)==False:
                                time.sleep(0.2)
                                getfix()
        except KeyboardInterrupt:
                print "Finished!"
        finally:
```

```
            GPIO.cleanup()
    def getfix():
        global ts
        whereami = gps(mode=WATCH_ENABLE)
        whereami.next()
        while whereami.data['class'] != 'TPV':
                whereami.next()
        lat = whereami.fix.latitude
        lng = whereami.fix.longitude
        alt = whereami.fix.altitude
        ts = whereami.data['time']
        latlng=str(lat)+","+str(lng)
        whereami.close()
        apiparams =
{"latlng":latlng,"location_type":"APPROXIMATE","key":apikey}
        response = requests.get(mapurl,params=apiparams)
        #If you run into problems you can test the URL output by
uncommenting the line below
        #print response.url
        y = json.loads(response.text,object_hook=findloc)
        logout = open(logfile,'a+')
        logout.write(ts+"\t"+str(lat)+"\t"+str(lng)+"\t"+str(alt)+"\n")
        logout.close()
    def findloc(dct):
        global ts
        detail_level=["locality","political"]
        if "formatted_address" in dct:
                if dct["types"]==detail_level:
                        print "GPS fix in",dct["formatted_address"],"at",ts
                        #return dct["formatted_address"];
    if __name__=="__main__":
        main()
```

8. With a good Google API key and enabled API, each press of the button does two things. First, it captures the current GPS data and log the timestamp, latitude, longitude, and altitude to `whereami.log`. Next, it uses the `requests` library to build and retrieve a request for the Geocoding API, and it uses the `json` library to retrieve our location from the API response. The `location_type=APPROXIMATE` parameter is used in this recipe to demonstrate parameter use, but you can increase the precision down to the street address level. A sample of the console output and tab-delimited log file is shown here:

```
pi@rpz14103:~ $ python whereami.py
Press the button to log your location
GPS fix in Beaverton, OR, USA at 2017-01-01T00:23:31.000Z
GPS fix in Beaverton, OR, USA at 2017-01-01T00:23:35.000Z
GPS fix in Beaverton, OR, USA at 2017-01-01T00:23:39.000Z
GPS fix in Beaverton, OR, USA at 2017-01-01T00:23:43.000Z
GPS fix in Beaverton, OR, USA at 2017-01-01T00:23:47.000Z
^CFinished!
pi@rpz14103:~ $ cat whereami.log
2017-01-01T00:19:02.000Z          45.                              67.9
2017-01-01T00:23:31.000Z          45.                              66.9
2017-01-01T00:23:35.000Z          45.              -12             67.7
2017-01-01T00:23:39.000Z          45.                      67.9
2017-01-01T00:23:43.000Z          45.              -12             68.0
2017-01-01T00:23:47.000Z          45.              -12             68.8
```

9. Changing the API is easy; uncomment this line:

```
print response.url
```

The console will display the request being sent to Google. If you paste this into your browser, you can get the entire pre-parsed JSON output. With adjustments to `location_type` in the API and the `detail_level` key in the JSON response, you can log and report any level of detail your GPS is able to get a fix on.

9
Interfacing Sensors with the Raspberry Pi Zero

In this chapter, we will cover the following recipes:

- Interfacing any resistive sensor on GPIO
- Interfacing an LDO with the RPZ
- Interfacing an ultrasonic sensor with the RPZ
- Interfacing an analog-to-digital convertor to interface any analog sensor with the RPZ
- Interfacing an infrared receiver to read remote controls and control a TV with the RPZ
- Interfacing a motion sensor
- Interfacing a temperature humidity sensor using bit-banging
- Interfacing a gyroscope and accelerometer with the RPZ
- Pulling it all together with the Pi Sense Hat

Interfacing any resistive sensor on GPIO

Resistive sensors are devices whose resistance changes when the sensor's input is altered. A photoresistor will change based on the amount of light, and a thermistor's resistance changes with temperature. With a simple circuit, you can configure your GPIO to read changes in a resistive sensor's values.

Getting ready

For this recipe, I used a photoresistor as they are the easiest ones to change values on. Any two-lead resistive sensor will work for this recipe. You'll also need a 1uF electrolytic capacitor.

How to do it...

1. Configure the following circuit and wire it to the Raspberry Pi:

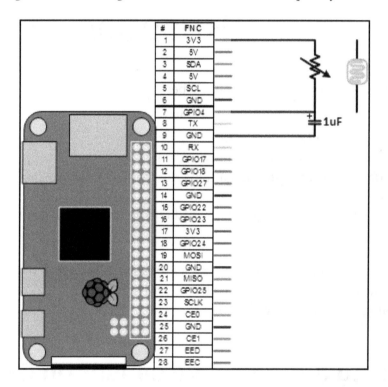

2. Using RPi.GPIO again, we can put together a simple program that tracks our sensor. Create photoresitor.py in the ch9 directory with the following code:

```
#!/usr/bin/env python
# Raspberry Pi Zero Cookbook
# Chapter 9 - Analog Sensors
import RPi.GPIO as GPIO
import sys
import time
```

```
import os
#GPIO.setwarnings(False)
GPIO.setmode(GPIO.BCM)
sensorpin = 4
def main():
    try:
            while True:
                    sensor=0
                    GPIO.setup(sensorpin, GPIO.OUT, initial=GPIO.LOW)
                    time.sleep(0.1)
                    GPIO.setup(sensorpin, GPIO.IN,
pull_up_down=GPIO.PUD_DOWN)
                        while (GPIO.input(sensorpin) == GPIO.LOW):
                                sensor +=1
                    if sensor>0:
                                sys.stdout.write("Sensor Reading: %d   \r"
% (sensor))
                                    sys.stdout.flush()
        except KeyboardInterrupt:
                print "\nFinished!"
        finally:
                GPIO.cleanup()
    if __name__== "__main__":
        main()
```

3. Running the program with `sudo python photoresitor.py` will return the relative brightness.

Interfacing an LDO with the RPZ

Analog resistance isn't the only thing you can calculate with the Raspberry Pi Zero GPIO. You can also capture the voltage levels from something like a low dropout voltage regulator. These regulators will work even when the input voltage is very close to the output voltage. By reading the sensor, we can read values of things such as rechargeable battery packs.

Getting ready

We can demonstrate this concept with only a variable resistor and a 1 uF capacitor. I used the 10K variable resistor included in the Elego kit.

How to do it...

1. With the following circuit, we can control the voltage divider from the 3.3 volt Raspberry Pi Zero output and read its value. As you can see, it is just like the previous recipe on resistive sensors. This time, we will track the voltage instead.

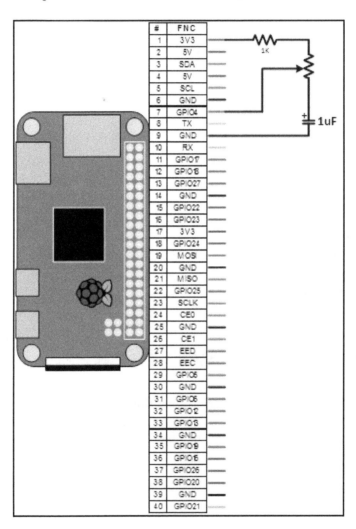

2. If you were measuring higher voltages, you would use a higher capacitor value to be able to more accurately track the discharge time. It's how we determine the voltage value this time, but timing capacitor discharge on a digital input isn't always going to be as reliable as an analog input. The MCP3008 used in the analog-to-digital sensor recipes later on is a much straightforward way to track analog voltage readings.

3. Create the `ldo.py` file and enter the following code:

```python
#!/usr/bin/env python
# Raspberry Pi Zero Cookbook
# Chapter 9 - Analog Voltage Reads
import RPi.GPIO as GPIO
import sys
import time
import os
#GPIO.setwarnings(False)
GPIO.setmode(GPIO.BCM)
sensorpin = 4
def main():
    try:
        while True:
            sensor=0
            GPIO.setup(sensorpin, GPIO.OUT, initial=GPIO.LOW)
            time.sleep(0.1)
            GPIO.setup(sensorpin, GPIO.IN,
pull_up_down=GPIO.PUD_DOWN)
            while (GPIO.input(sensorpin) == GPIO.LOW):
                sensor +=1
            if sensor>0:
                sys.stdout.write("Sensor Reading: %d    \r"
% (sensor))
                sys.stdout.flush()
    except KeyboardInterrupt:
        print "\nFinished!"
    finally:
        GPIO.cleanup()
if __name__== "__main__":
    main()
```

4. You'll notice this code is almost exactly like the photoresistor code, but we have control over the variable resistor we are using. As the resistor is adjusted, the capacitor will charge more or less, which becomes our relative reading of the maximum voltage. Using a multimeter and determining voltages will make it possible to convert the times to voltages being output from your LDO.

Interfacing an ultrasonic sensor with the RPZ

Ultrasonic sensors can give you an accurate distance measurement. The transmitting side of the sensor sends out an ultrasonic pulse, which will bounce back off the target, to be caught by the receiving side of the transmitter. Knowing that the pulse travels at the speed of sound, we can determine how far away an object is by capturing the time between sending and receiving.

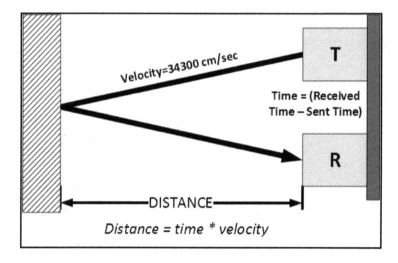

You can use your Raspberry Pi Zero to understand the ultrasonic sensor's data and report to you how far away an object is. Let's take a look!

Getting ready

For this recipe, we will use the following components

- One 1 KOhm resistor
- One 2 KOhm resistor
- One tactile pushbutton switch
- The Elego HC-SR04 Ultrasonic sensor (though any four-pin ultrasonic sensor should work)

How to do it…

1. The following diagram shows how to connect the switch, resistors, and sensor to the Raspberry Pi Zero:

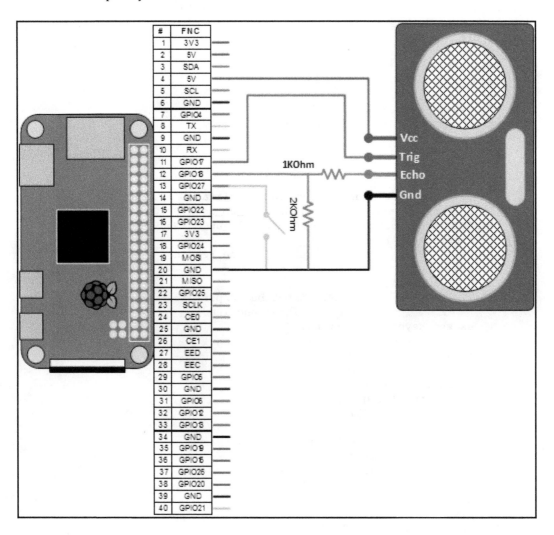

2. The Python code for setting up this recipe is quite simple. Enter the following code as `ultrasonic.py` in the `ch9` directory:

```python
#!/usr/bin/env python
# Raspberry Pi Zero Cookbook
# Chapter 9 - Getting distance with ultrasonic
# Transmitter\Receiver
import RPi.GPIO as GPIO
import sys
import time
import os
#GPIO.setwarnings(False)
GPIO.setmode(GPIO.BCM)
mach1 = 34320    #speed of sound cm/s
triggerpin = 17
echopin = 18
buttonpin = 27
def main():
    GPIO.setup(triggerpin, GPIO.OUT, initial=GPIO.LOW)
    GPIO.setup(echopin, GPIO.IN, pull_up_down=GPIO.PUD_DOWN)
    GPIO.setup(buttonpin, GPIO.IN, pull_up_down=GPIO.PUD_UP)
    time.sleep(1)
    print "Press button to take distance reading"
    try:
            while True:
                    if GPIO.input(buttonpin) == False:
                            ultrasoundping()
    except KeyboardInterrupt:
            print "\nFinished!"
    finally:
            GPIO.cleanup()
def ultrasoundping():
    GPIO.output(triggerpin, True)
    time.sleep(0.00001)
    GPIO.output(triggerpin, False)
    while GPIO.input(echopin)==0:
            snd = time.time()
    while GPIO.input(echopin)==1:
            rec = time.time()
    hittime = (rec-snd)/2.000
    distcm = mach1*hittime
    distus = distcm * 0.394
    print "DISTANCE -- Metric: %0.2f centimeters" % distcm, "US: %0.2f
inches" %distus
    time.sleep(0.2)
    GPIO.output(triggerpin, False)
if __name__== "__main__":
    main()
```

3. Running the program using sudo python `ultrasonic.py` will give you a prompt to push the button. Put an object in front of the sensor and press the button. Then, move it closer or farther away and try it again. You should see a response similar to this:

```
pi@rpz14101:~/share/ch9 $ sudo python ultrasonic.py
Press button to take distance reading
DISTANCE -- Metric: 5.94 centimeters US: 2.34 inches
DISTANCE -- Metric: 16.05 centimeters US: 6.32 inches
DISTANCE -- Metric: 28.79 centimeters US: 11.34 inches
DISTANCE -- Metric: 4.22 centimeters US: 1.66 inches
^C
Finished!
```

Interfacing an analog-to-digital convertor to interface any analog sensor with the RPZ

The Raspberry Pi Zero GPIO is a great interface, but it does lack the analog ports you would find on something like an Arduino. We can use PWM to utilize analog devices over the digital ports, like we did with the first photoresistor recipe, or we can add an analog-to-digital convertor (ADC) to our circuit. As you can probably guess, the ADC will read the voltage and convert it into a digital signal that the Raspberry Pi understands natively. The MCP3008 analog-to-digital convertor will handle up to eight analog signals and report back over the SPI interface. Let's get started!

Getting ready

We will use the MCP3008 ADC. Along with that, you'll need the following:

- One photoresistor (the one used in the earlier recipe is fine)
- One thermistor
- Two 10K resistors

You can add more analog sensors to this recipe as you'd like, up to eight of them! I used two different sensors to give you an idea. The MCP3008 is a very easy-to-find and inexpensive ADC ($3-$5 US) and works great with the Raspberry Pi Zero, but there are lots of different ADCs available.

The Python mcp3008 library works great for this recipe, and can be installed with this command:

```
sudo pip install mcp3008
```

How to do it...

1. There are quite a few pins on the ADC. One side of the chip is all for analog input (marked CH0-CH7 in the next diagram). The other side of the chip is the digital interface that will talk to the Raspberry Pi Zero, power, and ground. Let's go over the pins and what they do.

Label	Function	Connect to
VDD	Power	3.3V
VREF	Analog Reference Voltage	3.3V
AGND	Analog Ground (for VREF)	Ground
CLK	Clock	GPIO SCLK
DOUT	Digital Out	GPIO MOSI
DIN	Digital In	GPIO MISO
CS	Channel Select	GRPIO CE0
DGND	Digital Ground (for VDD)	Ground
CH0-CH7	Analog Inputs	Sensors

2. The following circuit shows the MCP3008 wired up with a photoresistor and thermistor:

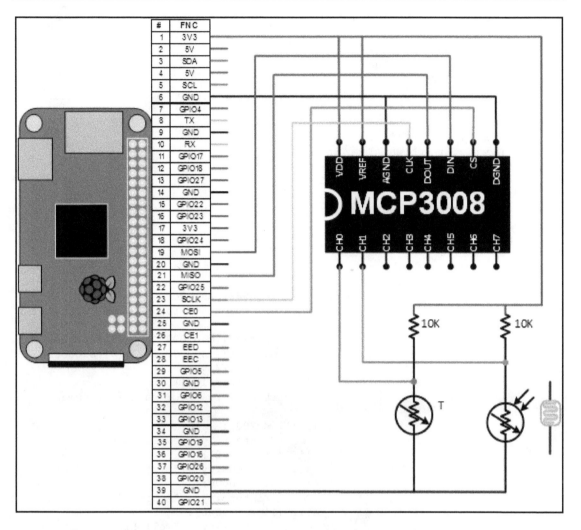

3. The code to handle the two channels used for the MCP3008 is as follows. You can add another six analog devices to your microcontroller; simply add them and read those channels. Enter this code for the two-channel version in the adc_mcp.py file:

```
#!/usr/bin/env python
# Raspberry Pi Zero Cookbook
# Chapter 9
# Using the MCP3008 ADC
import math
import time
import sys
```

```
import mcp3008
#Reference Voltage
vref = 3.30
#Fixed Resistor Value
r1 = 10000.00
#Celius to Kelvin Conversion
kelvin=273.15
#ADC Sampling Rate
bitcoeff = 3.30/1024.00
#Thermistor Ambient Temp in K
t0 = 25.00 + kelvin
#Themistor Resistance at 25C
r0 = 20000.00
#Thermistor Coefficient (varies by manufacuturer - check your
datasheet)
b = 10000.00
def main():
    try:
        while True:
            with mcp3008.MCP3008() as adc:
                #Read values of ADC for Thermistor and
Photoresistor
                t1 = adc.read([mcp3008.CH0])[0]*bitcoeff
                l1 = adc.read([mcp3008.CH1])[0]*bitcoeff
                tr = (vref*r1)/(vref-t1)
                li = r1*((vref/l1)-1)
                #Convert photoresistor values to human
friendly
                if (li < 200):
                    intensity = "Very Dark"
                elif (li < 1000):
                    intensity = "Dim"
                elif (li < 50000):
                    intensity = "Ambient"
                elif (li < 150000):
                    intensity = "Well Lit"
                elif (li < 1000000):
                    intensity = "Bright"
                elif (li >= 1000000):
                    intensity = "Very Bright"
                invtmpk = (1/t0) + (1/b)*math.log1p(tr/r0)
                tempc = (1/invtmpk) - kelvin
                sys.stdout.write("Temp C: %f " % tempc)
                sys.stdout.write("Light Intensity: %f " %
li)
                sys.stdout.write("( %s )        \r" %
intensity)
                sys.stdout.flush()
```

```
                        time.sleep(0.5)
        except KeyboardInterrupt:
                print "Finished!"
        finally:
                adc.close()
if __name__=="__main__":
        main()
```

4. The ADC reading follows a simple pattern, which you can reproduce for any resistive sensor:

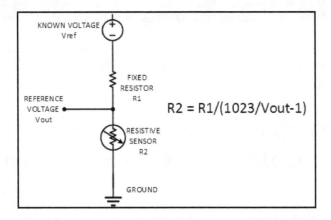

5. Once the resistive sensor value is known, we can use its datasheet to determine the reading it represents. For thermistors, as the temperature goes up, the resistance goes down. For photoresistors, as light intensity increases, the resistance also goes down. The following graph shows the relative change of resistance to light or temperature:

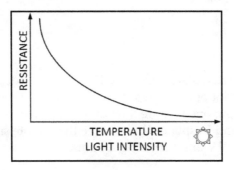

6. To determine a thermistor's temperature, the datasheet will typically indicate the values needed for the Steinhart-Hart equation, of which we use a simplified variant in the previous Python program. The light intensity too can be converted to lux using the datasheet, though a few tests make it easy to tell a human how bright the light is. If you are doing something scientific, you can capture the relative intensity instead. If everything is ready to go, running the program will give you the real-time temperature and light intensity:

```
pi@rpz14101:~/share/ch9 $ sudo python adc_mcp.py
Temp C: 18.484971 Light Intensity: 528947.368421 ( Bright )
```

7. If you keep your MCP3008 connected, you can use the same circuit for the gyroscope/accelerometer recipe later in this chapter.

Interfacing an infrared receiver to read remote controls and control a TV with the RPZ

Infrared sensors are used everywhere for remote operation. We can add an IR sensor to our Raspberry Pi to be able to control it remotely.

 The latest Raspbian version supports infrared receivers, though it was a little tricky to get working perfectly. I'll cover all of the steps it took, though it is possible future versions of Raspbian will make it a little easier to get going quickly.

Getting ready

I used the infrared sensor available in the Elego Kit. This includes both the sensor and a remote control. There are a lot of infrared sensors available online, and you can really use any remote control, including one you are already using, such as your TV remote. That can be a lot of fun: if your TV and Raspberry Pi both see the remote signal, your TV's power button can both turn on the TV and turn off the lights!

You'll also want to make sure that the infrared service is installed and up to date:

```
sudo apt-get install lirc
```

How to do it...

1. The IR sensor uses I2C like many other devices, so the wiring is very simple. Wire the sensor to the Raspberry Pi Zero as shown here:

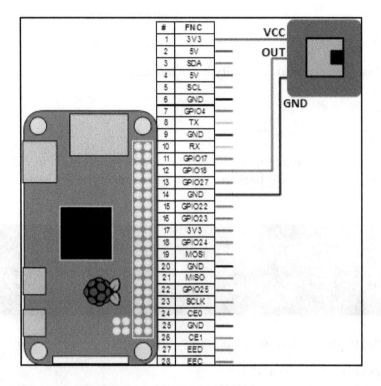

2. To get the receiver working with Raspbian, there are a few configuration changes you'll need to make. First, open `/boot/config.txt` and uncomment the `dtoverlay` setting within:

```
# Uncomment this to enable the lirc-rpi module
dtoverlay=lirc-rpi
```

3. Next, open the lirc configuration file with `sudo vim /etc/lirc/hardware.conf` and make sure that the configuration matches this:

```
#Try to load appropriate kernel modules
LOAD_MODULES=true
```

```
# Run "lircd --driver=help" for a list of supported    drivers.
DRIVER="default"
# usually /dev/lirc0 is the correct setting for    systems using udev
DEVICE="/dev/lirc0"
MODULES="lirc_rpi"

# Default configuration files for your hardware if any
LIRCD_CONF=""
LIRCMD_CONF=""
```

4. The last file you need to modify is `/etc/modules`. Open it and add the following lines:

```
lirc_dev
lirc_rpi gpio_in_pin=18
```

5. You can use any available GPIO pin, just make sure it is set in `/etc/modules`. Reboot your Pi and log back in. Check the status of the lirc service and make sure it is running:

```
pi@rpz14101:~/share/ch9 $ sudo /etc/init.d/lirc status
● lirc.service - LSB: Starts LIRC daemon.
   Loaded: loaded (/etc/init.d/lirc)
   Active: active (running) since Sat 2017-02-04 19:17:41 PST; 17h ago
  Process: 389 ExecStart=/etc/init.d/lirc start (code=exited, status=0/SUCCESS)
   CGroup: /system.slice/lirc.service
           └─447 /usr/sbin/lircd --driver=default --device=/dev/lirc0
```

6. If not, you can start it with this command:

```
sudo /etc/init.d/lirc start
```

7. If everything is configured correctly, your receiver should now be ready for incoming signals. The device path as seen in the last line of the service status is where you can access the device. If you run `cat /dev/lirc0` and hit some of the remote buttons, you should see some garbage displayed.

8. Now that your receiver is ready, you can program your remote! The lirc service is made to handle dozens of different IR signals. You can look at the full list of programmable keys by running `irrecord -list-namespace`. To program your remote so that the service understands it anytime you start, irrecord is also the tool. Use `sudo irrecord -d /dev/lirc0 /etc/lirc/lircd.conf`.

9. The irrecord program is rather user friendly and will prompt you through the steps to setting up your remote. First, it will perform some remote signal testing to see what kind of infrared signal is being sent. Once it understands that, it will prompt you to identify each key on your remote. Once complete, it will write the `lircd.conf` file to the `/etc/lirc/` directory so that it can be read by the licd service on startup. Shown here is a sample of setting up a remote's power and volume buttons:

```
Press RETURN now to start recording.
.................................................................
Found const length: 108118
Please keep on pressing buttons like described above.
.................................................................
Space/pulse encoded remote control found.
Signal length is 67.
Found possible header: 9043 4479
Found trail pulse: 575
Found repeat code: 9046 2228
Signals are space encoded.
Signal length is 32
Now enter the names for the buttons.

Please enter the name for the next button (press <ENTER> to finish recording)
KEY_POWER

Now hold down button "KEY_POWER".

Please enter the name for the next button (press <ENTER> to finish recording)
KEY_VOLUMEUP

Now hold down button "KEY_VOLUMEUP".

Please enter the name for the next button (press <ENTER> to finish recording)
KEY_VOLUMEDOWN

Now hold down button "KEY_VOLUMEDOWN".

Please enter the name for the next button (press <ENTER> to finish recording)

Checking for toggle bit mask.
Please press an arbitrary button repeatedly as fast as possible.
Make sure you keep pressing the SAME button and that you DON'T HOLD
the button down!.
If you can't see any dots appear, then wait a bit between button presses.

Press RETURN to continue.
.............................
No toggle bit mask found.
Successfully written config file.
```

10. From here, you can use lircmd to configure buttons to work with the desktop or install python-pylirc to handle signals from your Python programs. We will revisit the remote control in Chapter 10, where we will use it to control Kodi (formerly known as XBMC).

Interfacing a motion sensor

A motion sensor will report a signal when it detects any kind of motion within its range. We can incorporate this into the Raspberry Pi Zero to trigger any kind of event, take a picture, send an e-mail, or turn on a light or motor. Here, we will have our Raspberry Pi Zero understand the incoming signals from a motion sensor.

Getting ready

All you'll need for this recipe besides your Raspberry Pi Zero is an infrared sensor board. The Elego Kit includes one and they are available at many Internet of Things online suppliers.

How to do it...

1. Configure the sensor using the following circuit:

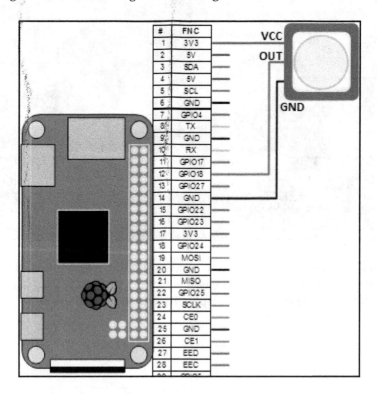

2. The code is just as easy as the circuit. Create the `motionsensor.py` file with the following code:

```python
#!/usr/bin/env python
# Raspberry Pi Zero Cookbook
# Chapter 9
# Motion Detection
import time
import RPi.GPIO as GPIO
GPIO.setmode(GPIO.BCM)
GPIO.setwarnings(False)

motionpin=17
GPIO.setup(motionpin,GPIO.IN,pull_up_down=GPIO.PUD_DOWN)
try:
    while True:
            if GPIO.input(motionpin)==True:
                    print "Motion Detected!"
            else:
                    print "Quiet"
            time.sleep(1)
except KeyboardInterrupt:
    print "Finished!"
finally:
    GPIO.cleanup()
```

3. Running this simple program does exactly what you'd expect. When the sensor detects motion, it will let you know. Otherwise, it will tell you things are OK. If you tried the Python e-mail recipe from Chapter 4, *Programming with Python*, you know it will be a piece of cake to trigger an e-mail to be sent when motion is detected.

Interfacing a temperature humidity sensor using bit-banging

Digital temperature and humidity sensors are quite common in the Internet of Things world. They are rather inexpensive and provide an easy way to record accurate temperature and humidity readings. Using a technique called "bit-banging," we can retrieve a digital signal that will tell our Raspberry Pi Zero both the temperature and relative humidity.

Getting ready

All you'll need is a digital temperature and humidity sensor and a 10 KOhm resistor. There is one included in the Elego kit, and most of the ones you'll find online operate the same way.

To test the device, I used the pydht2 tool in the Python library, installed using `sudo pip install pydht2`.

How to do it...

1. Connect your sensor to the Raspberry Pi Zero, as shown here:

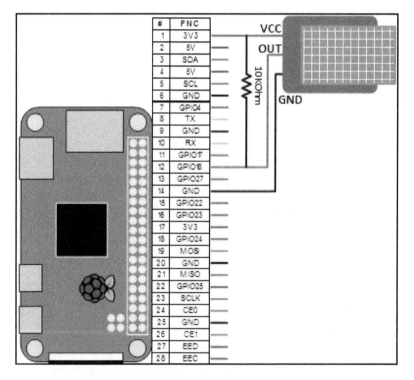

 A lot of Digital Sensors expect and provide 5 Volts for input and output, respectively. Check your sensor's data sheet to find out what voltages are supported. If you have a 5V sensor, you can easily integrate it with your Raspberry Pi Zero and a Bi-Directional Voltage converter, introduced in `Chapter 7`, *Integrating Voltage translators with RPZ*.

2. With the `pydht2` library installed, it is easy to get a reading from the sensor. What the library does is make a request to the DHT for the bit response of the sensor.

3. Next, it listens to the response and takes in the set of bits sent over a specific time period. The sequence of bytes sent is converted to the temperature and humidity by the library. There are some great references that go into detail about how bit-banging works, but we can make it easy on ourselves with Python. It is as simple as importing the library and requesting a signal from the sensor:

```
pi@rpz14101:~/share/ch9 $ python
Python 2.7.9 (default, Sep 17 2016, 20:26:04)
[GCC 4.9.2] on linux2
Type "help", "copyright", "credits" or "license" for more information.
>>> import pydht
>>> pydht.get(board_mode='BCM',pin=18)
{'humidity': 30, 'temperature': 23}
```

Interfacing a gyroscope and accelerometer with the RPZ

Gyroscopes and accelerometers are chips that detect their relative position and movement. They are the core component of things such as quadcopters that need to make fast motor adjustments for the drone to hold a position or move in a particular direction. Let's take a look at how easy it is to integrate a gyroscope with your Raspberry Pi Zero. Could you make your own quadcopter? Here's how you might start!

Getting ready

The Elego kit includes an analog gyroscope/accelerometer, which is easy to use with an ADC such as the MCP3008 used earlier in this chapter. The Raspberry Pi Zero, MCP3008, and gyroscope are all you'll need.

How to do it...

1. If you've kept your MCP3008 connected from the earlier recipe with resistive sensors, you are almost done. Here is the circuit you'll need to read your gyroscope:

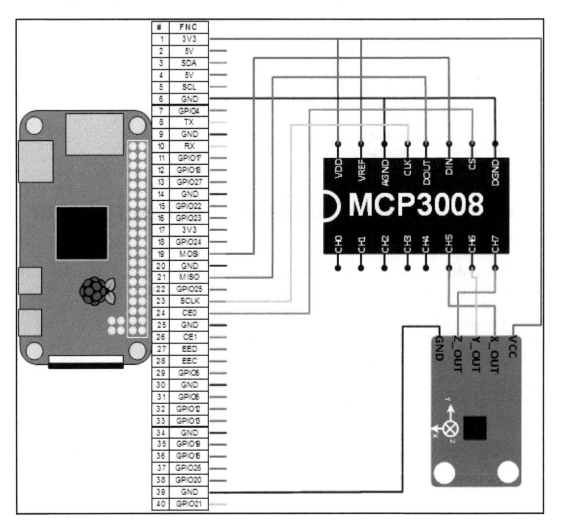

2. Using the ADC, the gyroscope is easy to read. Create the `gyro.py` file in the `ch9` folder:

```python
#!/usr/bin/env python
# Raspberry Pi Zero Cookbook
# Chapter 9
# Controlling a gyro\acelerometer
import math
import time
import sys
import mcp3008
bitcoeff = 3.30/1024.00
def main():
    while True:
            with mcp3008.MCP3008() as adc:
                    x = adc.read([mcp3008.CH5])[0]
                    y = adc.read([mcp3008.CH6])[0]
                    z = adc.read([mcp3008.CH7])[0]

                    sys.stdout.write("X: {} Y: {} Z:     {}
\r".format(x,y,z))
                    sys.stdout.flush()
                    time.sleep(0.5)
    if __name__=="__main__":
        main()
```

3. Using this base code, you can determine the relative position of your board as well as its movement and velocity. You aren't limited to the sleep time set in the previous program; if you were using this to control motors to keep a copter balanced, you would have your MCP3008 read continuously. You can see how fast it reads if you comment out the line. Give it a try!

Pulling it all together with the Pi Sense Hat

I don't go over many shields in the book, but there are a few that combine a lot of useful features for a low cost and are readily available on the Internet. One of those shields is the Sense Hat: for only $30 US, it combines eight sensors with a joystick and 8×8 RGB LED matrix. This is a quick and easy way to track several sensors with just a little hardware.

Getting ready

The Raspberry Pi Sense

Hat is available through most retailers that sell the Raspberry Pi. The Raspberry Pi Foundation website (`www.raspberrypi.org`) has links to the retailers for its products.

Make sure you have the latest version of the Python libraries installed with `sudo apt-get install sense-hat python-sense-hat`.

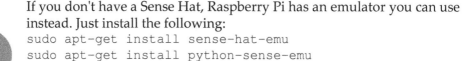 If you don't have a Sense Hat, Raspberry Pi has an emulator you can use instead. Just install the following:

```
sudo apt-get install sense-hat-emu
sudo apt-get install python-sense-emu
```

For the following code, instead of importing sense_hat, you will import sense_emu. The emulator on the Raspberry Pi Zero will execute just like the real thing.

How to do it...

1. Simply attach your Raspberry Pi Zero to the Sense Hat board GPIO. The Raspberry Pi Zero will hide beneath it as shown here:

2. Raspberry Pi has an easy-to-use Python library to control your Sense Hat. You can test it out with some simple Python:

```
>>> from sense_hat import Sense Hat
>>> sensor = SenseHat()
>>> sense.show_message("Raspberry Pi Cookbook!")
>>> sensor.get_humidity()
43.1
>>> sensor.get_temperature()
22.2
>>> sensor.get_pressure()
1013.0
>>> sensor.get_orientation()
{u'yaw': 10.0, u'roll': 0.0, u'pitch': 0.0}
>>> sensor.get_compass()
45.5
```

3. The documentation for the Python API and more advanced sensor and LED control are available online. With this board, the sensors and displays make for a fun experience where you can sense and report on the physical world.

10
Cooking up Projects to Amaze the World!

In this chapter, we will explore the following recipes:

- Setting up hardware for home automation with the RPZ
- Setting up software for home automation with the RPZ
- Making the RPZ an IoT sensor node
- Making the RPZ a media center
- Controlling the RPZ media center using an IR remote
- Heartrate monitoring wearable device

Introduction

For the final chapter, we will look at home automation systems, media centers, and other ways to integrate your Raspberry Pi Zero with your home and life. We've covered many ways to get your RPZ to interact with the physical world, and here you can pick and choose what you want to do with your favorite prototypes. Hopefully, at this point, you are full of your own great ideas and have a good idea of all the things that are possible.

Setting up hardware for home automation with the RPZ

Home automation has become more popular as Internet of Things devices become more affordable and available. The Raspberry Pi Zero certainly fits the bill: for what would have cost thousands of dollars a few years ago, a handful of sensors and a few Raspberry Pis can turn your home into a "smart home," where you can not only sense what is going on (temperature, lighting, motion, and so on), but you can control things too. With a few Raspberry Pi Zeros and these recipes, you have the potential to do things such as:

- Turning lights on and off using a relay controlled by the GPIO
- Opening and closing shades with a stepper motor
- Checking the temperature in any room of your house
- Getting an alert when motion is detected

The possibilities are truly limited; in this recipe, we will look at setting up the hardware for a simple, single-node home automation system.

Getting ready

For this recipe, you will use your Raspberry Pi Zero as your "command center." You don't need any other Raspberry Pis right now, though you might want another to work as a sensor node in a later recipe. You'll also need a USB-OTG adapter and Wi-Fi adapter.

In early 2017, The Raspberry Pi Foundation released the RPZ-W. For just a slightly higher cost (certainly less than the cost of a separate adapter), you get the same power and size of the original Raspberry Pi Zero, but with on-board Wi-Fi. This eliminates the need for a Wi-Fi adapter; you can perform network installs, and you free up the USB port for other devices. While they will be hard to find for a little bit, they will certainly add a level of ease to any project you have planned for your Raspberry Pi Zero.

How to do it...

1. Generally speaking, you would put your command center in a place such as the living room or perhaps your office or computer room. Whatever things you'd like to sense in that area, you can connect, whether it is a temperature sensor, photoresistor, or motion detector. Things such as RFID readers you'd probably want to consider for an IoT node–covered in the next recipe–as that would be something more in your home's perimeter. Having it close to your Wi-Fi network will ensure a strong signal. Your initial setup might look something like this:

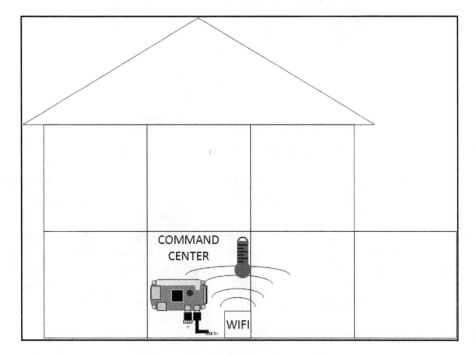

Central command located near Wi-Fi

2. The Raspberry Pi only needs Wi-Fi, power and sensors, so the diagram for this is quite simple:

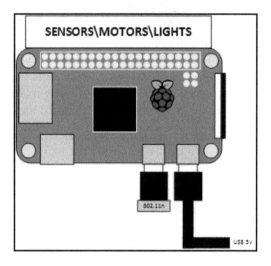

Typical sensor node or central command setup

3. You can attach whatever you like; for my command center, I used the Raspberry Pi Sense HAT that I introduced in `Chapter 9`, *Interfacing Sensors with the Raspberry Pi Zero*.

4. The home automation software we are using works great with the Raspbian operating system. You can use the Raspbian version you've been using all along for the recipes. If you want to start fresh, you can follow the Wiring a Raspbian SD Card by yourself recipe from Chapter 1 and the SSHing your RPZ in Chapter 2 to get ready. Make sure your operating system is up to date with:

```
sudo apt-get update
```

5. If this is a brand new build, you'll also need Git to download the home automation system. You can do that with:

```
sudo apt-get install git
```

6. Next, we will pull down the source for OpenHAB, the home automation software we'll be using. This is available on GitHub and can be downloaded with this command:

```
sudo git clone https://github.com/openhab/openhabian.git
/opt/openhabian
```

7. The last thing we'll do is symlink the OpenHAB setup script to /usr/local/bin. We do this with:

```
sudo ln -s /opt/openhabian/openhabian-setup.sh
/usr/local/bin/openhabian-config
```

Now our hardware is set up and ready to go. Let's move to the next recipe and make our home smarter!

Setting up software for home automation with the RPZ

In this recipe, we continue from the previous one and start setting up OpenHAB, a popular open source project for home automation. This recipe will take a while to complete, as the project is rather large and requires a lot of updates. Once it is finished, however, you will have your command center ready to go and ready to accept information from a variety of smart devices as well as sensor nodes, which we will look at in the next recipe.

Getting ready

It is quite easy to turn your Raspbian system into an OpenHABian one. If you followed the steps in the previous recipe, you are ready to go!

How to do it...

1. If your Raspberry Pi Zero isn't connected to a monitor and keyboard, that's fine if you set up Raspbian to allow SSH connections. Log on to your Raspberry Pi Zero (however you prefer), and run the following command:

```
sudo openhabian-config
```

2. You'll get a configuration screen that should look familiar to your Raspberry Pi configuration, but with a lot of different options:

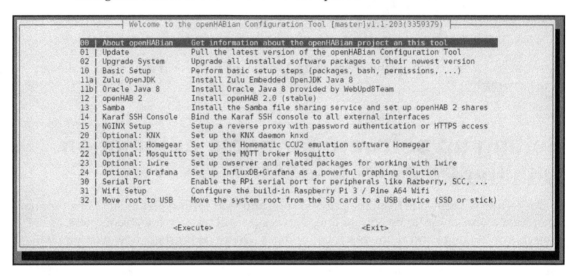

The OpenHABian configuration screen

3. You can iterate through the options one at a time. Option 01 will download the latest version of OpenHAB and default libraries. The second option upgrades the operating system. Once you have updated, upgraded, and rebooted, go back to the configuration tool and select option 10, Basic Setup. This will get OpenHAB configured on the system. You'll need to follow steps like shown here:

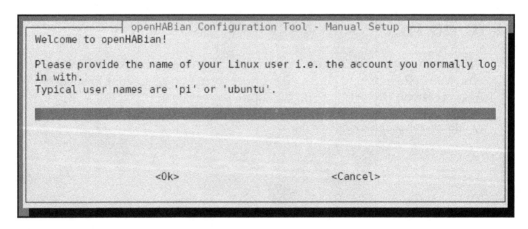

OpenHABian setup

4. In our case, unless we have created another user to work with our RPZ, pi will be the user we'd select. You'll continue through the setup and then need to reboot again. This can be another time-consuming step. Once you have rebooted, your efforts should be evident with the new welcome screen you see when you log in:

openHABian creates an informational bootup welcome page

5. Make a note of your IP address. Now let's check the status of the openHAB service with the `systemctl` command:

```
[06:20:10] pi@rpz14103:~$ sudo service openhab2 status
● openhab2.service - openHAB 2 - empowering the smart home
   Loaded: loaded (/usr/lib/systemd/system/openhab2.service; enabled)
   Active: active (running) since Thu 1970-01-01 01:00:15 CET; 47 years 1 months ago
     Docs: http://docs.openhab.org
           https://community.openhab.org
 Main PID: 473 (karaf)
   CGroup: /system.slice/openhab2.service
           ├─ 473 /bin/bash /usr/share/openhab2/runtime/bin/karaf server
           └─1152 /usr/bin/java -Dopenhab.home=/usr/share/openhab2 -Dopenhab.conf=/etc/openhab2

Jan 01 01:00:15 rpz14103 systemd[1]: Started openHAB 2 - empowering the smart home.
Jan 01 01:00:16 rpz14103 start.sh[473]: Launching the openHAB runtime...
```

openHAB service status

6. Looking good here! The system should start automatically, but if it doesn't, you can fire it up with the following command:

```
sudo systemctl openhab start
```

7. After this, checking the status again should show a running service. If not, look at the log files in the /var/log/openhab2/ directory. If everything is running properly, open a browser window. If you are using VNC Server or connected directly to HDMI, open a browser and open http://localhost:8080. If you are logging on remotely, go to http://<ipaddress>:8080, where <ipaddress> is the network address shown in the OpenHAB startup. You'll be taken to a setup screen:

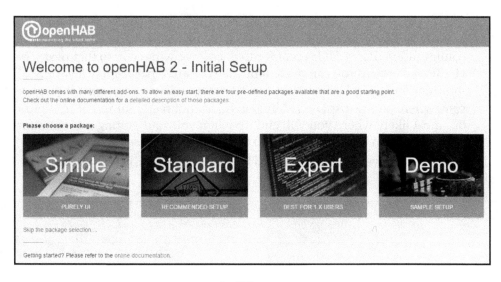

OpenHAB setup page

8. Click on **Standard**; this will load the most common add-ons available to start using your control center. You may have to refresh, but openHAB should take you to a page of choices of interfaces:

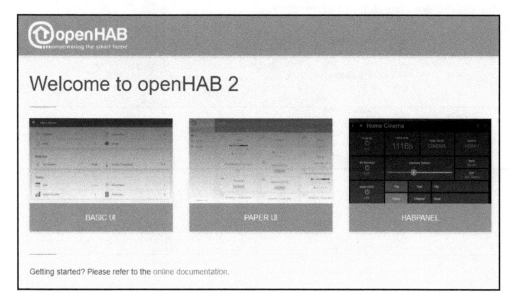

OpenHAB home

9. This is a choice of interfaces of varying degrees of difficulty. The Basic UI is truly as basic as it gets, so much so that you will need a less basic UI to start the configuration. Paper UI is great for that, and we will move to that next. The HABPanel is how you can make fancy dashboards that display a variety of information–if you know where the information is, you can have it displayed somewhere on the display. HABPanel is also not really for initial configuration but most likely where you will end up when you start getting more comfortable with the system. To start, let's jump into Paper UI and set up a few things.

10. When you arrive at the page, it will be mostly empty. Click on **Add-ons** and you will see a lot:

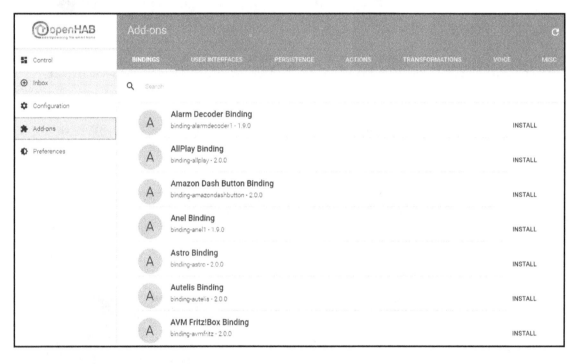

The Add-ons installation page

11. These are all the preconfigured add-ons already created by members of the OpenHAB community and available in their repository. If you are connected to the Internet, you should see more and more of these add-ons available, of which there are already dozens, and you can even make your own. It is quite surprising to see all the different integration points available:

    - Do you want to integrate a smart thermostat such as a Nest? Install the Nest add-on!
    - Have a Chromecast or smart TV? There are add-ons for many different TVs and manufacturers.
    - Have you built a Kodi? We will in a later recipe, and you can integrate that too!
    - Want to talk to your Tesla? There is an integration point for the Tesla S. Also, if you let me borrow it (hint hint), I promise to include detailed integration instructions in a later edition.

12. This list continues to grow, and integrating any smart device with a central home system is possible with OpenHAB2. For now, let's install just a few bindings to make a basic dashboard:

    - Network binding: This will let us discover other devices on our local network
    - GPIO binding: With this binding, we can communicate with our GPIO interface
    - Weather binding: This will let us pull weather information to include on our dashboard

13. If you plan to build an XBMC/Kodi system or already have, you can also install that binding to control your media center through OpenHAB. Once we have the bindings we like, let's look at the other add-ons available, starting with user interfaces:

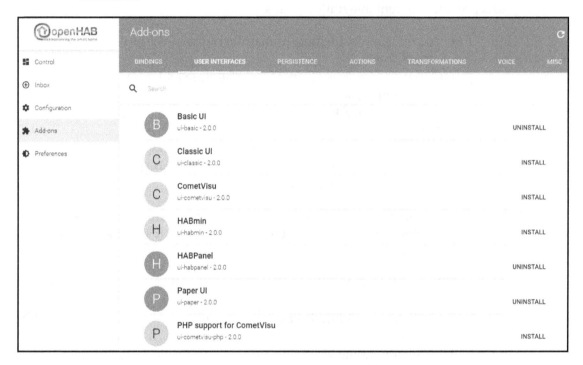

User interface add-ons

14. As you get more comfortable and advanced with OpenHAB, you may find the HABmin to be more to your liking. CometVisu is a lot like HABPanel, with a different (but still glossy) look and feel. As you install new ones, they will become available with the ones provided in the standard setup on the front page. The remaining add-ons are also quite useful, and they contain a useful set of functionalities to complement OpenHAB:

- *Persistence* contains add-ons that allow you to save your incoming data to persistent data stores so that they are stored more permanently. OpenHAB uses PostgreSQL by default, which is a great choice; these add-ons give you the option to persist your data to a variety of different data stores.

- *Actions*, formerly known as rules, are add-ons that do things as events are triggered. You might want to install the Mail or Twitter actions if you would like to notify yourself of an event that OpenHAB detects.
- *Transformations* are utilities for understanding output or data received from different sources. If you are looking to interpret the output of a shell script to display pertinent data on your dashboard or break down a JSON payload, these are the add-ons for you.
- *Voice* add-ons will provide text-to-speech capabilities, so you can get your house to talk to you. OpenHAB also allows speech-to-text, so you can even have conversations with your house.
- The last add-on category is *Misc*, which I'm sure you've guessed are miscellaneous add-ons. Experimental add-ons, schedulers, and larger integrations (with other smart-home systems, for example) are available here. Once you've installed the add-ons you want, you will see many of them available in the "Bindings" section under the Configuration menu, shown here:

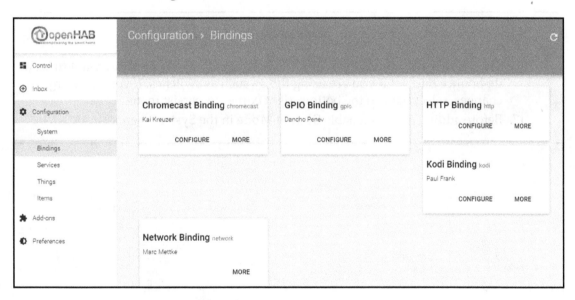

Successfully configured add-ons

 Not all bindings show up here, even in OpenHAB version 2. There are some bindings that require more manual configuration, which we will get to later.

15. The configuration is different for each binding. Let's look at the GPIO:

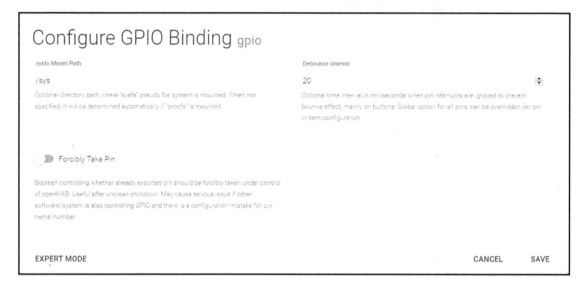

GPIO binding configuration

16. The binding path shouldn't require any changes, but you probably want to set a de-bounce interval if you are using things such as switches. If you make any changes, select **Save** in the bottom-right corner to persist them.

17. Before adding devices, enable **Simple Mode** in the System menu:

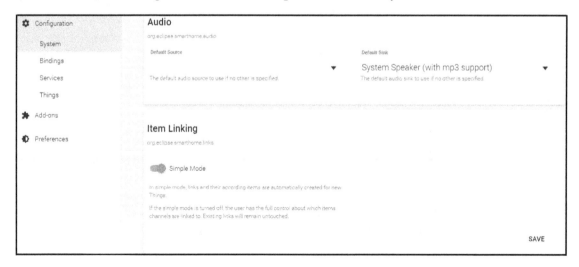

Switching Item Linking to Simple Mode

18. After switching over to Simple, save the setting. This will make turning items into Things much easier.

19. The Inbox is where you can find and add new devices to your configuration panel. The icon in the top-right corner allows you to scan for new devices that you have bindings for. If you select the Network binding (and you have other devices on your network), you should start seeing the list of used IP addresses:

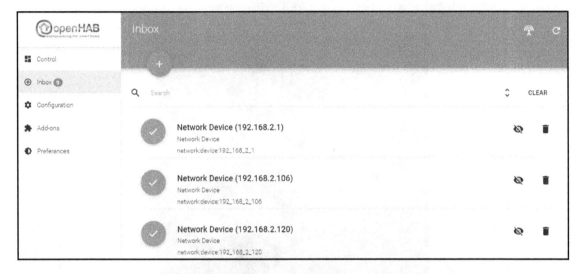

Network devices found after searching with the Network binding

20. By clicking on the checkbox next to the device, you can name it, configure it, and add it to your control panel:

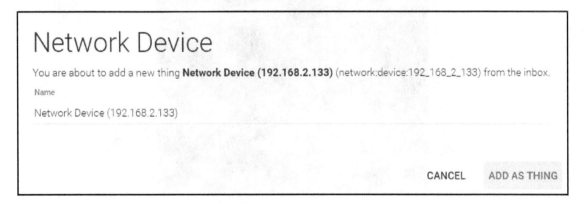

Adding a network device to OpenHAB

21. As you add these, you should see their information become available in the Control menu item at the top. Add all the devices you'd like to keep an eye on in your home network. As you get more comfortable with the system, adding different bindings will be a snap.

22. To bind things in the Basic UI, oftentimes, some manual work is required. Setting up OpenHAB 2 with the instructions here, there will be a configuration directory under /etc/openhab2. Let's take a look with the `tree` command:

```
[08:52:57] pi@rpz14103:/etc/openhab2$ tree
.
├── html
│   ├── index.html
│   └── readme.txt
├── icons
│   └── classic
│       └── readme.txt
├── items
│   ├── default.items
│   └── readme.txt
├── persistence
│   └── readme.txt
├── rules
│   └── readme.txt
├── scripts
│   └── readme.txt
├── services
│   ├── addons.cfg
│   ├── http.cfg
│   ├── mqtt.cfg
│   ├── mqtt-eventbus.cfg
│   ├── readme.txt
│   ├── runtime.cfg
│   └── weather.cfg
├── sitemaps
│   ├── default.sitemap
│   └── readme.txt
├── sounds
│   ├── barking.mp3
│   └── doorbell.mp3
├── things
│   └── readme.txt
└── transform
    ├── de.map
    ├── en.map
    └── readme.txt

12 directories, 23 files
```

The OpenHAB directory tree

23. We are going to create a default.sitemap and default.items file in their respective directories. The Basic UI reads through the items directory to understand what is available to read and how to do it. Then it reads through the sitemap directory to understand what to display. It can also leverage the icons directory for images to correspond with the items you are displaying. We will start with something simple and just get our local weather. We can see the weather configuration file (if we added the binding) in the services directory as weather.cfg. You can use a variety of different wether service APIs to call in; you'll have to create an account for the one you choose. All of the services have free tiers that provide a limited number of calls, though plenty for this recipe. Any of the following weather APIs will be great for OpenHAB's weather binding:

- Hamweather: You will get two keys, a client ID, and a client secret. You can sign up for a free account at `https://www.aerisweather.com/signup/pricing/`.
- ForecastIo: Sign up for the Dark Sky API here at `https://darksky.net/dev/register`.
- OpenWeatherMap: `https://openweathermap.org/api`.
- World Weather Online: `https://developer.worldweatheronline.com/api/default.aspx`.
- Weather Underground: `https://www.wunderground.com/weather/api`.
- MeteoBlue: `https://content.meteoblue.com/en/products/transmission/meteoblue-weather-api`.

24. Once you have your key for the provider you chose, open the `services/weather.cfg` file, put in your API key (and secret for Hamweather) and your latitude, longitude, provider, language, and update interval time (in minutes). An example file using Weather Underground is as follows:

```
# The apikey for the different weather providers, at least one must be
specified
    # Note: Hamweather requires two apikeys:      client_id=apikey,
client_secret=apikey2
    #apikey.ForecastIo=
    #apikey.OpenWeatherMap=
    #apikey.WorldWeatherOnline=
    apikey.Wunderground=ABCDEFGHIJK
    #apikey.Hamweather=
    #apikey2.Hamweather=
    #apikey.Meteoblue=
```

```
# location configuration, you can specify multiple      locations
location.home.name=home
location.home.latitude=45.5231
location.home.longitude=-122.6765
#location.<locationId1>.woeid=      (required for      Yahoo provider)
location.home.provider=Wunderground
location.home.language=en
location.home.updateInterval=15
```

25. Next, create a default.items file in the items directory. The entire list of weather items available in the binding can be found in `https://github.com/openhab/openhab1-addons/wiki/Weather-Binding`, but we can use a more minimal set of items for our dashboard.

```
Number    Humidity          "Humidity [%d %%]"
{weather="locationId=home, type=atmosphere,      property=humidity"}
Number    Temperature_F     "Temperature [%.2f °F]"
{weather="locationId=home, type=temperature,      property=current,
unit=fahrenheit"}
Number    Pressure          "Pressure [%.2f mb]"
{weather="locationId=home, type=atmosphere,      property=pressure"}
String    Pressure_Trend    "Pressuretrend [%s]"
{weather="locationId=home, type=atmosphere,
property=pressureTrend"}
String    Condition         "Condition [%s]"
{weather="locationId=home, type=condition,      property=text"}
Number    Rain              "Rain [%.2f mm/h]"
{weather="locationId=home, type=precipitation,      property=rain"}
Number    Wind_Speed          "Windspeed [%.2f km/h]"
{weather="locationId=home, type=wind, property=speed"}
String    Wind_Direction      "Wind direction [%s]"
{weather="locationId=home, type=wind,      property=direction"}
Number    Precip_Total_Inches  "Precip total [%d in]"
{weather="locationId=home, type=precipitation,      property=total,
unit=inches"}
String    Station_Name        "Station Name [%s]"
{weather="locationId=home, type=station, property=name"}
```

26. Next, create the default.sitemap file in the `sitemaps` directory, and make your first dashboard:

```
sitemap default label="RPZ Home"
{
Frame label="Portland, OR Weather"
{
  {
  Text item=Temperature_F
```

```
Text  item=Humidity
Text  item=Pressure
Text  item=Pressure_Trend
Text  item=Condition
Text  item=Rain
Text  item=Wind_Speed
Text  item=Wind_Direction
Text  item=Precip_Total_Inches
Text  item=Station_Name
    }
}}
```

27. If you got everything right and your API key is working, the Basic UI should bring up your weather with a refresh:

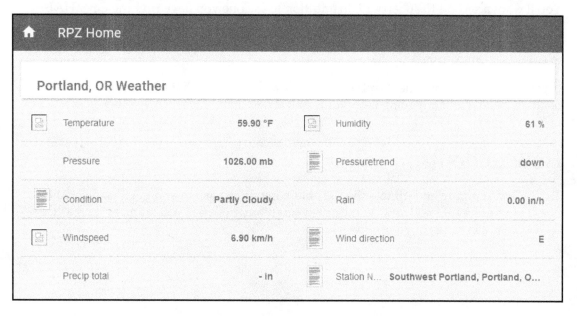

Basic UI with weather information

Once you get the hang of bindings, items, and sitemaps, you really can control anything. Whether the configuration in Paper UI is available or not, you can add anything to your OpenHAB dashboard.

Making the RPZ an IoT Sensor Node

An Internet of Things sensor node is a set of sensors (but could also be output devices) that you would generally put in a remote area and have report to a central command. This way, you can have multiple sets of sensors (in the garage, or attic, or chicken house), all sending in their environmental information to a central processor. In this recipe, we will work with our previous installation of OpenHAB to have a remote Raspberry Pi Zero communicate back and forth.

Getting ready

You'll want a second Raspberry Pi, in addition to the one you have running OpenHAB, with a Wi-Fi adapter. The Zero works great, but really any version will do. Install the Raspbian operating system on your sensor node. You'll also want any sensors you will want to collect readings from.

If you are only running one Raspberry Pi Zero, as long as you have Raspbian, the tools will be there, even if you are doing it on your central command OpenHAB system.

How to do it...

1. Configure and update the Raspbian operating system and get it connected to your Wi-Fi network. You can have as many nodes as you want, as long as they are in range of your network:

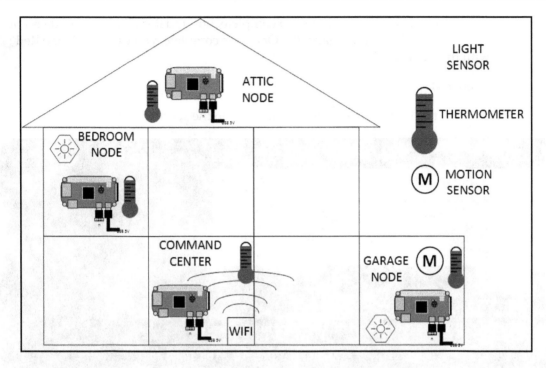

Multiple nodes and central command

As long as nodes are within Wi-Fi range, they will be able to talk to OpenHAB.

2. We are going to use a protocol called mosquito to communicate back with OpenHAB Central. On your command center Raspberry Pi Zero (the one running OpenHAB 2), install the `mosquitto` service:

```
sudo apt-get install mosquito
```

3. The service should install and start running automatically. You can also update the configuration of your OpenHAB file at this point, by adding the following line to the `mqtt.cfg` file to the `/etc/openhab2/services/` directory:

```
mosquitto.url=tcp://localhost:1883
```

4. MQTT, or Message Queue Telemetry Transport, is a lightweight protocol, great for communicating IoT device information. Mosquitto is a service known as an MQTT broker, which publishers and subscribers can connect to and retrieve recent events.

```
sudo update-nodejs-and-nodered
```

5. This step takes about 45 minutes to complete, but updates all of your node.js and Node Red packages automatically. Once it is complete, you can start Node Red with this command:

```
sudo node-red-start
```

6. You'll get a startup screen and information on the service:

```
pi@rpz14101:~/share/ch9 $ sudo node-red-start



    node.js v0.10.29 is NO LONGER supported.
    please consider upgrading to node.js 4.15.

    you can do this with the following command:
        update-nodejs-and-nodered


Start Node-RED

Once Node-RED has started, point a browser at http://192.168.2.42:1880
On Pi Node-RED works better with the Firefox browser

Use   node-red-stop                          to stop Node-RED
Use   node-red-start                         to start Node-RED again
Use   node-red-log                           to view the recent log output
Use   sudo systemctl enable nodered.service  to autostart Node-RED at every boot
Use   sudo systemctl disable nodered.service to disable autostart on boot

To find more nodes and example flows - go to http://flows.nodered.org
You may also need to install and upgrade npm
    sudo apt-get install npm
    sudo npm i -g npm@2.x

Started Node-RED graphical event wiring tool..
Welcome to Node-RED
===================
11 Mar 20:58:36 - [info] Node-RED version: v0.15.2
11 Mar 20:58:36 - [info] Node.js  version: v0.10.29
11 Mar 20:58:36 - [info] Linux 4.4.47+ arm LE
11 Mar 20:58:42 - [info] Loading palette nodes
```

Starting Node-RED

7. Open a browser using the link shown in the screenshot. You'll get to the Node start page. Node Red is an object-oriented messaging system that is capable of reading GPIO pin states, execution output, or any variety of messages. We can start our first project using the example code accessible from the top-left menu:

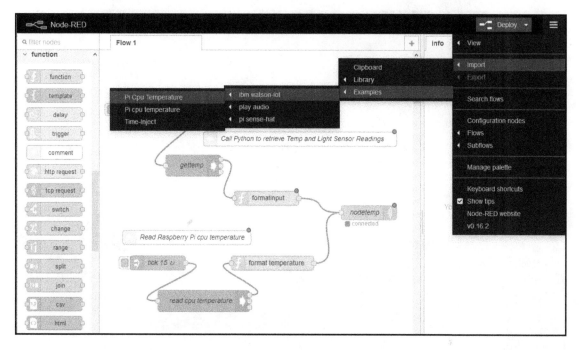

Using a Node Red example as a starter flow

8. You'll get a startup flow that checks the connected Raspberry Pi's CPU temperature. Delete the Watson IoT object at the end, and add an MQTT output node named nodetemp. Connect the endpoint of format temperature to the input of the MQTT node, as shown here:

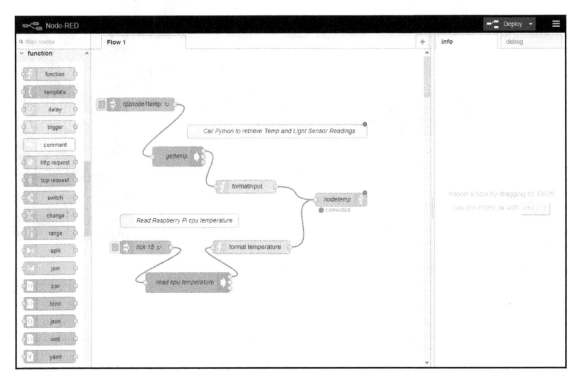

Completed flow publishes RPZ CPU temp, thermistor temp, and light intensity to the MQTT broker

9. Double-clicking on any node will bring up the configuration page for that item. If we double-click on the MQTT node, we can add the address of the Mosquitto broker we created at the beginning of this recipe:

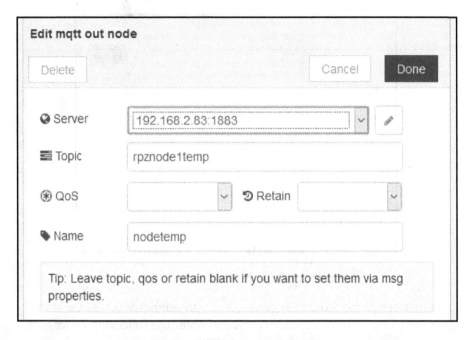

Attaching the MQTT node to the broker in OpenHAB

10. If we create and add a new execution node, we will reference a script that will retrieve the temperature and light intensity from connected to the MCP3008 analog-to-digital convertor:

Execution node runs the Python script to retrieve light intensity and temperature

11. Create a script named `light_temp_c.py` to reference this node in the `/home/pi/share/ch10/` directory, and enter the following code:

```
#!/usr/bin/env python
# Raspberry Pi Zero Cookbook
# Chapter 10
# Script for communicating temp and light to Node Red
import sys
import math
import time
import mcp3008
vref = 3.30
r1 = 10000.00
kelvin=273.15
bitcoeff = 3.3/1024.0
ca =  0.001176724715543
cb = 0.000235156521144
cc = 0.000000088030003
t0 = 25.00 + kelvin
r0 = 20000.00
b = 10000.00
def main():
    with mcp3008.MCP3008() as adc:
```

```
t1 = adc.read([mcp3008.CH0])[0]*bitcoeff
l1 = adc.read([mcp3008.CH1])[0]*bitcoeff
lr = (vref*r1)/(vref-l1)
tr = (vref*r1)/(vref-t1)
#print lr
#print l1, t1
invtmpk = (1/t0) + (1/b)*math.log1p(tr/r0)
tempc = (1/invtmpk) - kelvin
print tempc, lr
    if __name__=="__main__":
        main()
```

12. Connect the top endpoint of the new Exec node to the input of the MQTT node.
    The three nodes in an Exec output are stdout, sterr, and return output code.
    Connect to the stdout error to get the values returned by the temperature script.
    Next, you'll want to format the output before sending it to MQTT. We do this
    with a function node, and ours will look like this:

The function node lets you format the incoming payload from the Python script

13. Taking the output, which is the temperature, a space, and the light intensity, it is easy for us to put it into JSON payloads that we can send over MQTT. Finally, we will trigger an inject event before the execution node to fire it off every 15 seconds, just like the sample flow:

Inject nodes can be used to fire off an event that triggers execution

14. Hit Deploy one more time, and your Mosquitto broker should be receiving messages from your sensor node. With `sudo apt-get install mosquitto-clients`, you can use the `mosquitto-sub` utility to verify that the payload is being sent:

```
[22:00:32] pi@rpzi4103:/etc/openhab2$ mosquitto_sub -h 192.168.2.83 -t rpznode1temp
{"cpuTempC":35.2}
{"tempc":21.4359065989,"light":20277.2277228}
{"cpuTempC":35.8}
{"tempc":21.4359065989,"light":20197.2386588}
{"cpuTempC":35.8}
{"tempc":21.4387338245,"light":20117.8781925}
{"cpuTempC":35.8}
{"tempc":21.4359065989,"light":20157.480315}
{"cpuTempC":35.8}
{"tempc":21.4387338245,"light":10219.5608782}
{"cpuTempC":35.8}
{"tempc":21.4359065989,"light":111304.347826}
{"cpuTempC":37.4}
{"tempc":21.4359065989,"light":110107.526882}
```

Mosquitto client monitoring the sensor node's readings

15. If you are seeing you readings here, you can configure your MQTT utility on OpenHAB 2 to report the incoming metrics and make them available wherever you are!

Making the RPZ a media center

We've been using the Raspian operating system throughout the book, but the Raspberry Pi Zero is hardly limited to that distribution. There are several distributions of Linux available that are all great at doing different things. The Kodi project (formerly XBMC) is one such distribution, which is designed to turn your computer into a full-function media center. OpenELEC has a great distro running Kodi that will work fine on the Raspberry Pi Zero.

Even though the Raspberry Pi Zero will work fine as the most inexpensive media center ever, the newer multiple-core models of the Raspberry Pi will bring you a better overall experience, the increased memory and additional cores reducing lag and video choppiness. This recipe would be almost identical on a newer Raspberry Pi, but there is a different download that is tuned for newer models.

Getting ready

I would recommend a new SD card for this recipe, especially if you have become attached to your Raspbian build. OpenELEC has a download available for single-core Raspberry Pis at `http://openelec.tv/get-openelec/category/6-raspberry-pi-builds`. Download, unzip, and install this image on your SD card, using your favorite imaging tool. If you don't remember how to do this, see the *Writing a Raspbian SD Card* recipe in Chapter 1. You'll want to start with at least a mouse (there is a virtual keyboard), though a mouse and keyboard make the setup quite a bit faster.

If you are enjoying your OpenHAB setup, this might be better to do with a new Raspberry Pi Zero, as Kodi can be integrated and controlled by OpenHAB 2.

Kodi is intended to be connected to a video output directly, it doesn't have a VNC Server window, and the web-based controls require setup first. At a minimum, you will need to have your Raspberry Pi Zero configured like this:

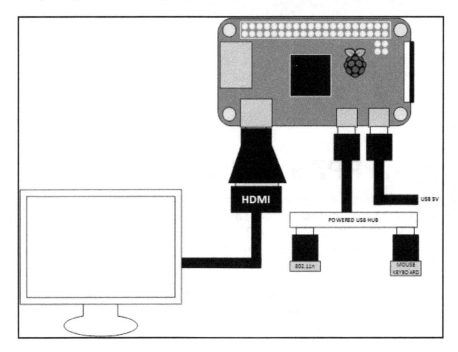

A simple Kodi connection to a TV with Wi-Fi, mouse, and keyboard

How to do it...

1. Once you install the image and start Kodi, you will first be shown a setup panel:

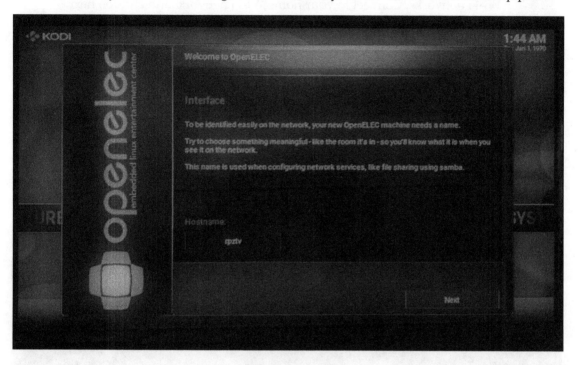

The configuration screen for Kodi

2. Step through each of the items, starting with the hostname. I went with rpztv, but you can give it any name you'd like. Next, it will take you to the Wi-Fi setup. Assuming you are using a compatible adapter, Kodi will immediately scan for Wi-Fi networks. Connect to your home Wi-Fi network, and click on next.

3. The next step is to enable services. If you'd like to access network shares that contain music and videos, enable this option. It is recommended you enable SSH access; that's what we will use in the next recipe. After going through all of the steps, Kodi will thank you and reboot:

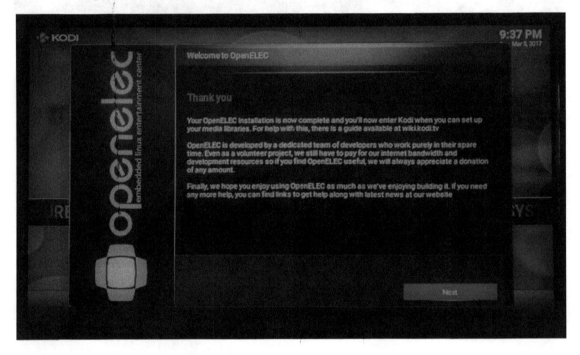

Finishing up the initial setup

4. After rebooting, the setup pages will be gone, and you'll be introduced to the home screen for your new media center:

The home screen for Kodi

5. Clicking on SYSTEM provides a myriad of options:

System settings in Kodi

6. In the **Services** section, you can configure even more. Here is where you can give your device a unique name (separate from the hostname), make the Kodi instance automatically recognized on the home network, and enable remote control from a web page or other systems (such as OpenHAB). Go through each of the options in the Services menu and configure them for your ideal environment:

Setting Up Services on Kodi

7. The Add-ons section in the Services menu is where you can really open up Kodi to the Internet and stream a variety of things to your television. It also includes utilities (such as backups) that may be useful for maintaining your system. There are far too many add-ons available to go through here, but most of them have easy setup menus so that integration is a breeze:

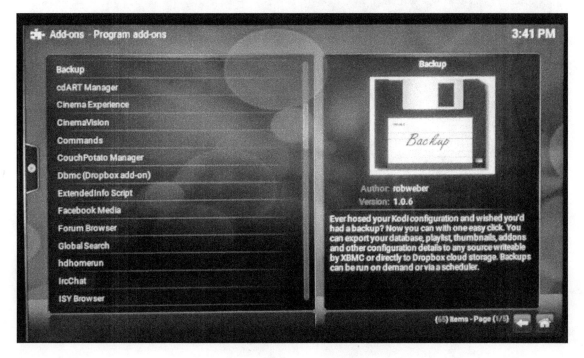

Add-ons integrate dozens of programs and utilities

8. Once you've found the add-ons you like, you can click on the Home icon in the bottom-right corner to go back to the main menu. If you roll over one of the options, such as Video, you can find even more services to connect via the XBMC/Kodi system:

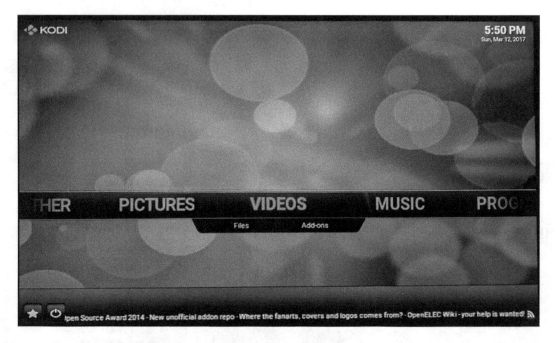

Every component has add-on libraries

9. Clicking on this Add-ons section gives you a set of choices specific to video functionality. Any streaming services that interest you can easily be added through the menu, just like the system add-ons:

The video add-ons let you stream hundreds of different online services

10. Going back to the home menu, the Weather option to the far left makes for a nice screen when you aren't watching TV:

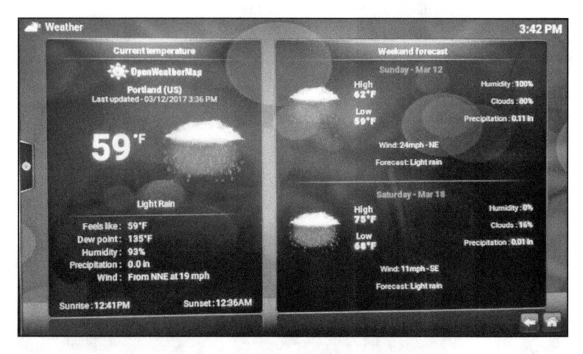

Kodi's Weather screen

11. Once you are happy with your initial setup, go have some fun! Kodi is an extremely active project, so you can expect new add-ons and updates to be applied frequently.

12. Finally, if you are running OpenHAB2 from the previous recipe, you can easily integrate its functionality for your command center. Paper UI makes it easy to add Kodi as an add-on, and then configure it as an Item. You can look at the Setting up software for Home Automation recipe for details on installing new items. Once you've added it, it is as easy to control as it is to get the temperature in your garage:

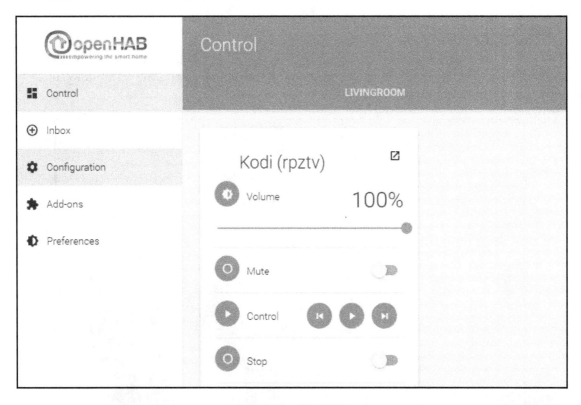

Kodi integration with OpenHAB 2

There is very little you can't do with this $5 media center!

Controlling RPZ media center using IR remote

It wouldn't be very useful to need a keyboard and mouse to watch television; we are used to having remote controls manage the functions available on a TV, stereo, or media center. Fortunately, we already know how to integrate an infrared sensor with our Raspberry Pi Zero; now let's make it work with Kodi!

Getting ready

The previous recipe went through setting up the OpenELEC distribution on the Raspberry Pi. You'll also need the parts from the previous chapter's Interfacing the Infrared Receiver recipe, with the data port located on GPIO 18, as shown here:

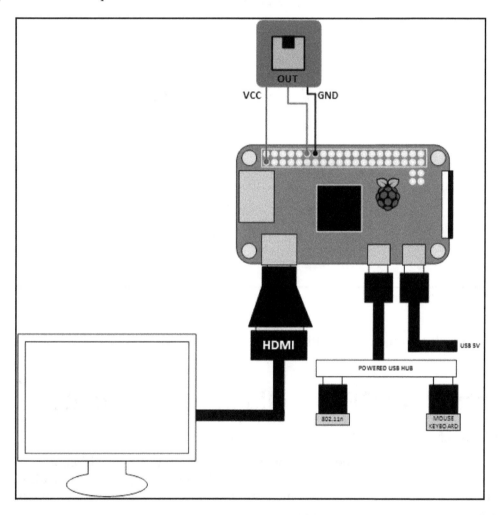

Adding the infrared receiver to your Kodi setup

How to do it...

1. The best way to configure the remote is over an SSH connection. If you followed the previous recipe, you should already have it enabled. While Kodi is a Linux server, it is configured more to work as a media center than it is a fully functional server. Utilities that come by default in Raspbian, such as apt-get and vncserver, are not available on Kodi. The reduced flexibility is an effort to improve security.

2. Log in using you favorite SSH tool. The default login for Kodi is `root`, with the password `openelec`. Be sure to change this after you log in. You'll know you are in your Kodi instance from the welcome screen:

```
###########################################################
#                    OpenELEC                            #
#              http://openelec.tv                        #
###########################################################

OpenELEC (official) Version: 6.0.3
```

The Kodi login looks different from Raspbian

3. Kodi's operating system requires a few changes that are different from Raspbian's `/boot/config.txt` file. In Kodi, this is in a different place than `/boot`.

4. To get to the `config.txt` file in Kodi, you'll need to mount it with this command:

```
mount -o remount,rw /flash
```

You don't need to use sudo with a Kodi configuration; you are already root.

5. Next, use Nano to open the `config.txt` file and add the following line to the end:

   dtoverlay=lircd-rpi

6. Save and close the file, and then remount the /flash drive:

   mount -o remount,rw /flash

7. Finally, restart your Kodi system:

   reboot

8. Log back in and verify that your device is attached:

Finding the Infrared device

9. If you see your device online as lirc0, you are ready to configure your remote. Move to the `/storage/.config` directory with the `cd` command:

   cd /storage/.config/

10. Next, run the irrecord utility and make a new configuration file for your remote and Kodi to use:

    irrecord -d /dev/lirc0 lircd.conf

 If you receive the message Device or resource busy, first run killall lircd and try irrecord again.

11. Just like in Chapter 9, configure your remote using the KEY_FUNCTION values. The more useful ones for operating Kodi are shown here:

Class	Function	Key value for irrecord
System	Power	KEY_POWER
Direction	Up/Down/Left/Right	KEY_UP\KEY_DOWN\KEY_LEFT\KEY_RIGHT
Menu	Menu/OK/Back	KEY_MENU\KEY_OK\ KEY_BACK

Media Control	Play/Stop/Fast Forward/Rewind	KEY_PLAY\KEY_STOP\KEY_FASTFORWARD\KEY_REWIND
Volume Control	Volume Up/Down/Mute	KEY_VOLUMEUP\KEY_VOLUMEDOWN\KEY_MUTE

12. Once you finish irrecord, reboot one more time. Once Kodi starts back up, your remote should be working with your media center!

Heartrate monitoring wearable device

The Raspberry Pi Zero is small enough that you could bring it with you, power it, and attach monitors without the need to be directly connected to anything. Using the MQTT protocol, we can communicate whenever the network is available, as long as we have a running broker available.

Getting ready

You'll need your Raspberry Pi Zero running Raspbian, an MCP3008 ADC, and a Pulse Sensor. A popular and inexpensive open source pulse sensor is available at `http://pulsesensor.com/`.

This is really another recipe that could use its own Raspberry Pi; with a small USB battery pack, this would be easy to incorporate into a wearable to keep track of your pulse throughout the day.

If you want to publish to your OpenHAB MQTT broker, you'll want to have an OpenHAB instance as shown in the Setting up your hardware for home Automation recipe. Finally, you'll want a Mosquitto broker running somewhere (which works fine on your OpenHAB instance), but you can install it on any available Raspberry Pi with this command:

```
sudo apt-get install mosquitto mosquitto-clients
```

How to do it…

1. The circuit for the Pulse Sensor is very easy with the MCP3008 chip in place. Connect your circuit as shown here:

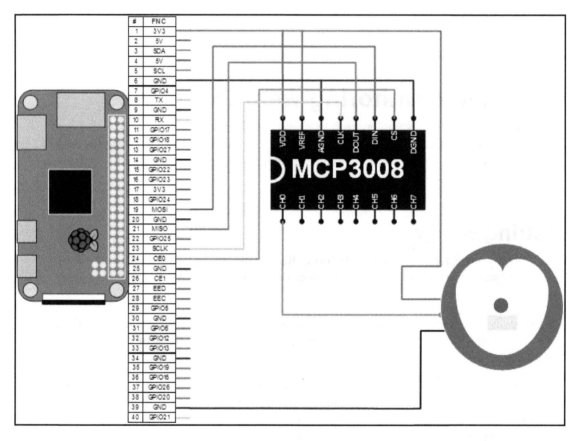

The heart sensor wiring diagram

2. We can get an idea of the pulse functionality with a simple script. Create a file named pulse.py in the /home/pi/share/ch10 directory of your pulse monitor node and enter the following:

```
#!/usr/bin/env python
# Raspberry Pi Zero Cookbook
# Chapter 10
# Pulse Sensor with Python!
import sys
```

```
import math
import time
import mcp3008
def main():
    with mcp3008.MCP3008() as adc:
            while True:
                    p1 = adc.read([mcp3008.CH2])[0]
                    print p1
                    for i in range(p1 / 100):
                            print ".",
                    time.sleep(0.1)
if __name__=="__main__":
    main()
```

3. Running this simple script with your finger on the sensor should give you an idea of how the sensor works:

Readings from the Pulse Sensor via the MCP3008

4. The pulse sensor will return a value between 0 and 1023, based on a photoresistor in the pulse sensor. When you hold the sensor to something like your index finger, it will spike as it detects a change in the photoresistance, which changes with the pulse in your finger. If we instead wanted to send this data into an MQTT broker for consumption with something like OpenHAB, we can easily do that with the Paho MQTT client, installed with this command:

```
sudo pip install paho-mqtt
```

5. Create a file named pulse_mqtt.py and enter the following:

```python
#!/usr/bin/env python
# Raspberry Pi Zero Cookbook
# Chapter 10
# Pulse Sensor to MQTT
import sys
import math
import time
import mcp3008
import paho.mqtt.publish as publish

def main():
    with mcp3008.MCP3008() as adc:
        while True:
            p1 = adc.read([mcp3008.CH2])[0]
            publish.single("humannode1/pulse",p1,
hostname="192.168.2.83")
            time.sleep(0.2)
    if __name__=="__main__":
        main()
```

6. Running this will publish your ADC readings, which we can take a look at with an MQTT client:

Pulse sensor readings published to the Moquitto broker for consumption by OpenHAB

Once you are publishing to MQTT, home integration becomes a breeze! Welcome to central command, humannode1!

Index

www.ingramcontent.com/pod-product-compliance
Lightning Source LLC
Chambersburg PA
CBHW081502050326
40690CB00015B/2897

* 9 7 8 1 7 8 6 4 6 3 8 5 2 *